SOTHEBY'S
CONCISE ENCYCLOPEDIA OF
FURNITURE

SOTHEBY'S
CONCISE ENCYCLOPEDIA OF
FURNITURE

GENERAL EDITOR
CHRISTOPHER PAYNE

CONRAN OCTOPUS

First published in 1989 by
Conran Octopus Limited
37 Shelton Street, London WC2H 9HN

British Library Cataloguing in Publication Data

Sotheby's concise encyclopedia of furniture.
1. Furniture, to 1989. Encyclopaedias
I. Payne, Christopher, 1948
749.2'003'21

ISBN 1-85029-197-7

SERIES EDITOR Polly Powell
ART EDITOR Helen Lewis

COPY EDITORS Paul Barnett
Patricia Bayer
JUNIOR EDITOR Debora Robertson
PICTURE RESEARCHERS Nadine Bazar
Kathy Lockley
ILLUSTRATOR Coral Mula
PRODUCTION Michel Blake

Typeset by Servis Filmsetting
Printed in Great Britain by
Butler & Tanner Ltd Frome and London.

The publisher would like to thank Roy L. Davids, Graham Child and
Elizabeth White for their help in the production of this book.

The publisher would also like to thank the following people:
Jonathan Bourne, Leslie Keno, John Taylor, Isobel Ozanne
and David Grollman.

The jacket photograph was styled by Claire Lloyd and the
backcloth was painted by Tabby Riley.
The following companies kindly lent items for the jacket photograph:
Mallet at Bourdon House Limited (wall sconces); Paul Jones
(cushions); Gallery of Antique Costume and Textiles (fabric).
Other companies who kindly lent items for photography included
Authentics (chairs on pages 173 and 174) and Freud (fan on page 173).

ILLUSTRATIONS ON PAGES 1–10

page 1: Detail of Dutch secretaire cabinet, late 18th century
page 2: Dining-table and chairs, Eliel Saarinen, 1930
pages 4–5: Bureau Mazarin, late 17th century
page 7: The Apartment of Mary Ellen Best, *c.*1844
page 8: Hill House, C.R. Mackintosh, 1903–4
page 10: Queen Anne-style bureau-cabinet, *c.*1710

MEGAN ALDRICH
The Baroque (Continental Europe)

Megan Aldrich has a Ph.D. from the University of Toronto and is the furniture expert on the Works of Art Course for Sotheby's Educational Studies. She has published several articles on furniture, architecture and interiors for various magazines.

PATRICIA BAYER
Craft and Design (Continental Europe)

Patricia Bayer is an art historian and writer and her books include the *Art Deco Source Book, The Art of Réné Lalique* (co-author), *The Antiques World Travel Guide to America* (co-author) and *Lalique Perfume Bottles*. Her articles have appeared in *Art and Antiques, The Connoisseur* and *Antiques World*, and she has worked at the Metropolitan Museum of Art in New York and the Virginia Museum of Fine Arts in Richmond.

GEOFFREY BEARD
The Renaissance (Continental Europe)

Geoffrey Beard is a co-founder of the Furniture History Society. He has written a number of books on interior decoration in the seventeenth and eighteenth centuries, including standard works on Georgian interior decoration and English decorative plasterwork. These include *The National Trust Book of English Furniture, Stucco and Decorative Plasterwork in Europe* and *The Work of Robert Adam*.

ROBERT BOWMAN
Modern Times

Robert Bowman has been with Sotheby's London for eleven years and is now a Departmental Director specializing in the decorative arts. He is a regular contributor to *The Antique Collector* and has compiled several price guides, including the annual revisions to the price guide in Christopher Payne's book, *Animals in Bronze*. His latest project is a book on Art Deco metal objects.

VICTOR CHINNERY
The Renaissance and The Baroque (Britain and the United States to 1675)

Victor Chinnery is a leading authority on the history of early furniture. He is a consultant for Sotheby's London and for many museums and private collections. His book, *Oak Furniture: The British Tradition*, is the definitive work on this aspect of furniture history.

PETER DORMER
The Machine Age

Peter Dormer is a writer and lecturer specializing in contemporary applied arts and is a director of Design Analysis International Ltd.. He has written several books, including *New Furniture: Trends and Traditions, New Ceramics: Trends and Traditions* and, with Ralph Turner, *New Jewellery: Trends and Traditions*. His articles have appeared in *Blueprint, Modern Painters, Art Monthly, Design* and several other journals.

MALCOLM HASLAM
Craft and Design (Britain and the United States)

Malcolm Haslam was an antiques dealer for several years before becoming a writer and lecturer specializing in the decorative arts. He is a regular contributor to magazines and the author of several books, including *English Art Pottery 1865–1915, Marks and Monograms of the Modern Movement 1875–1930, Art Deco, Art Nouveau* and *Arts and Crafts*.

LESLIE KENO
The Baroque from 1675, The Rococo Period and The Classical Revival (The United States)

Leslie Keno is a Vice President and the Director of the American Furniture and Decorative Arts department at Sotheby's North America. While at Williams College, he carried out an intensive study of early American furniture from the Charles M. Davenport Collection, which culminated in a catalogue and exhibition of the collection at the Williams College Museum of Art, Massachusetts.

CHRISTOPHER PAYNE
Eclecticism (Continental Europe)

Christopher Payne is a Director of Sotheby's London where he has worked for nearly twenty years. He is a regular contributor to fine-art magazines and his books include *19th Century European Furniture* and *Animals in Bronze: Reference and Price Guide*. He lectures to students and collectors and also makes frequent appearances on the BBC's Antiques Roadshow.

PETER PHILP
Early Furniture

Peter Philp has been an antiques dealer and writer for fifty years. His many publications include

Antiques Today, Antique Furniture for the Smaller Home and *Furniture of the World*. He also contributed to *World Furniture* and now writes for *The Antique Dealer and Collectors Guide* and *The Times*.

NOËL RILEY
The Baroque (Britain from 1675), The Rococo Period (Britain and Continental Europe)

Noël Riley is a respected authority on furniture and antiques. She was the general editor and a contributor to *World Furniture* and her other publications include *Tea Caddies* and *Visiting Card Cases*. She has written for nearly all the British antiques periodicals as well as some overseas publications. She belongs to the Furniture History Society and to the Regional Furniture Society.

WILLIAM W. STAHL JR.
The Baroque from 1675, The Rococo Period and The Classical Revival (The United States)

William Stahl is a Senior Vice President and a Director of Sotheby's North America. He has lectured extensively on the topic of collecting Americana and is the author of *Collecting Americana*, published in Grolier's *Year in Review, 1978*, and 'American Furniture, A New Era of Collecting', which was published in *Art at Auction, 1980*. He is presently writing a book on collecting American furniture.

JOHN TAYLOR
The Classical Revival (Britain and Continental Europe)

John Taylor studied Neoclassical painting and architecture at Peterhouse, Cambridge. He works for the furniture department of Sotheby's London, where he has a special interest in Continental Neoclassical furniture.

GILLIAN WALKLING
Eclecticism (Britain and the United States)

Gillian Walkling worked in the antiques trade before joining the curatorial staff of the Furniture and Woodwork Department at The Victoria and Albert Museum. Now a full-time writer, her publications include *Antique Bamboo Furniture, Tea Caddies* and *The Book of Wine Antiques*. She is a regular contributor to many magazines, including *The Antique Collector, The Connoisseur, Traditional Homes* and *Traditional Interior Decoration*.

CONTENTS

FOREWORD

It is astonishing how interest in furniture has escalated in the last few years – never before has Sotheby's been able to deal with such a quantity and variety of spectacular pieces through their many salerooms. As the fine-art market spirals beyond the reach of many of us, collectors are looking to furniture as something beautiful and useful which is also a good investment. They have awoken to the knowledge which established collectors have always had: that the cabinet-makers and designers of the past can have as much to offer us as great artists.

We want this guide to provide an essential companion to those interested in the history of furniture. The delight – and the difficulties – involved in gaining a thorough understanding of furniture are here accompanied by a clear, concise text. The book may be used as a ground for further exploration, or simply as an enjoyable way of refreshing one's memory. The photographs will delight the professional eye and help the beginner to discriminate between a vast and often confusing array of furniture styles as it unfolds historically and leads us through the exciting process of mastering craftsmanship, style and taste.

The Rt. Hon. The Earl of Gowrie

INTRODUCTION

This book weaves together the story of furniture, from the earliest hand-made pieces of the ancient Mediterranean civilizations to the technologically advanced works of today. In particular, the book underlines the essential, but often ignored, relationship between furniture and architecture. As early as the fifteenth century, for example, Italian intarsia craftsmen were using classical architectural perspectives for inspiration. By the eighteenth century, Robert Adam was designing complete interior schemes for his houses. In the twentieth century, many notable architects such as Frank Lloyd Wright and Gerrit Rietveld designed houses and furniture to match.

Another theme emphasized in this book is furniture designers' constant fascination with the past. Throughout the last millennium, furniture of the ancient classical civilizations has been admired through imitation, notably in the eighteenth century when it can be argued that some of the best furniture ever made was produced. These classical ideals, however, were often rejected as fashion inevitably reacted against this enduring theme, for example, the short-lived surge of Rococo design in the second quarter of the eighteenth century. Today, Post-modernism has reintroduced the classical vocabulary and has returned us to 'safe', traditional themes.

Many of these familiar forms were traditionally passed on through the extensive use of pattern-books. The first, with designs by DuCerceau, is recorded in use in 1550, although Sebastiano Serlio's earlier *Fourth Book of Architecture* (1537), which was available in several languages, was also a 'bible' for furniture-makers. During the nineteenth century, pattern-books of the previous centuries were reprinted extensively together with books including 'improved' versions of early furniture, and were a contributing factor behind the eclecticism of this period.

References are made throughout this book to furniture in museums and other accessible collections with the intention that those with inquiring minds, inspired by the enlightening text and photography, will further learning in a practical fashion by visiting these collections as well as the many salerooms and antiques centres where furniture is on display.

EARLY FURNITURE

It would seem to be a matter of common sense that furniture should originate and proliferate in areas where there are plenty of trees to be harvested for wood, and that in such regions primitive forms would evolve into more developed ones. It comes as something of a surprise, therefore, that our earliest evidences of sophisticated furniture-making come from Egypt and Chaldea, countries which could in no way be said to have enjoyed a glut of timber. From the latter country, for example, we have a seal found at the Royal Cemetery at Ur, dated c.3500–2800BC (roughly contemporary with Early Dynastic Egypt), which depicts a throne-stool with animalized legs joined by a carved frieze. And from Egypt, there is evidence of highly developed, sophisticated carpentry from as far back as the Old Kingdom (2686–2181BC). Not only have coffins of this period been found with butt joints, mitre joints secured with dowels and shoulder-mitres, but also with dovetails and halving joints.

Of course, for all we know there may have been many areas of the world where a plenitude of timber prompted the making of fine furniture, all traces of which have since been erased by the passage of the millennia, but this is far from certain. Even today there are forest societies in which the production of furniture is limited to, at most, a ceremonial stool to serve as a chieftain's throne. When furniture is scarce, it often takes the form of status symbols rather than purely functional items.

DETAIL OF TUTANKHAMUN'S THRONE, EGYPT, NEW KINGDOM, c.1350BC

*Silver, rock crystal, lapis lazuli and cornelian are inlaid into gold foil
to form the back of this spectacular throne.*

EGYPT

Ancient Egypt was a land in which very few large trees grew. The fact that wood was so scarce seems from the outset to have encouraged the best use of what there was. The wealth of early examples of furniture from this country which survive today is a product of the practice of burying furniture in tombs, in the belief that it would be needed in the afterlife; the dryness of the desert environment and the taboo, albeit a frequently violated one, against tampering with hallowed places combined to preserve many funerary pieces for later generations.

Even craftsmen were allowed a simple chest and a stool in their graves. However, most of the ancient Egyptian furniture which survives today has come from tombs of members of royal families and the aristocratic classes, notably the Fourth-Dynasty Queen Hetepheres and, from the Eighteenth Dynasty, Yuya and Thuyu (grandparents of Akhenaton), the overseer Kha and his wife Meryet, and the Pharaoh Tutankhamun. After the suicide of Cleopatra VII in 30BC, Egypt came under Roman rule.

Skills of a very high order were developed in the First and Second Dynasties. Construction used mortise-and-tenon, dovetail and mitre joints; copper and bronze fittings were nailed. Chests had bolt systems but no locks. Tools included mallets, copper (later bronze) saws, axes, chisels, adzes and drills; the plane had yet to be invented, and so the adze was the only available tool for levelling wood. Some experts credit Egypt with the invention of the lathe, but others believe it originated with the Assyrians. For example, a relief from Nineveh, dated to the seventh century BC and now housed in the British Museum, London, shows a couch, a chair and a table which appear to have turned feet, implying that the Assyrians either had the lathe or had worked out some means of producing the same effect.

Native woods included acacia, sidder and fig; ebony, cypress and cedar were imported from Syria and the Lebanon. For economy, small pieces were joined edge-to-edge with

IVORY LEGS, FROM THE ROYAL TOMBS AT ABYDOS, EGYPT, 1ST DYNASTY c.3200–2980BC (left)

Carved to represent the hind and fore legs of a bull, later versions had lions' paws. The holes at the top were used to lash the legs to the frame with thongs.

WOODEN FOLDING SEAT, EGYPT, NEW KINGDOM, c.1250BC (left)

The crossed legs terminate in carved ducks' heads and are inlaid with ivory. The seat would have been of woven cord, but some X-framed stools of the time had fixed frames with solid seats. Both kinds were later made in Greece, Rome and medieval Europe, with different types of terminations.

RELIEF OF KING ASHUR-BANI-PAL OF ASSYRIA, 668–631BC (below)

The King reclines on a couch with a table at his side, his Queen in an armchair. The table-legs are carved and the feet appear to have been turned.

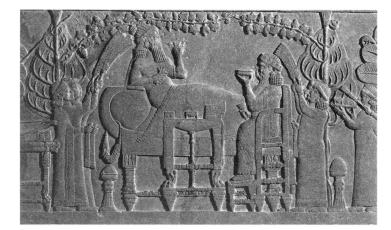

DETAIL FROM A POTTERY *KYLIX* (WINE CUP), VULCI, GREECE, c.500–470BC (opposite)

lacing, pegs, dowels or tongue-and-groove joints, and masked with veneer or painted to imitate finer items inlaid with ebony, ivory, bone, coloured earthenware or semi-precious stones; in the Eighteenth Dynasty many of the best pieces were overlaid with gold and silver. Solid ivory was sometimes used in the construction of the most expensive items. Basketwork boxes and storage chests were made of coiled fibres – palm, papyrus, reed or halfa (esparto) grass. Seats and mattresses were made resilient with interlaced cords or leather thongs.

Most people slept on floor mats, but bed frames were made. During the First Dynasty the finest had ivory legs carved in the form of bulls' feet; under the Old Kingdom, lions' paws superseded the bulls' feet. Although there was sometimes a footboard, headboards were unknown. Instead, a carved head-rest often served the dual function of headboard and pillow.

Crude, three-legged stools were common, but others had shaped seats supported on four legs, square or rounded, strengthened by vertical and diagonal struts. Folding stools with X-shaped supports, the feet carved to represent the heads of geese or ducks, appeared during the Middle Kingdom period. Footstools were made to accompany armchairs, which were used mainly as status symbols. Armless chairs of varying heights, with 'lion' legs, became numerous during the Middle Kingdom, at which time also chair-backs, which had hitherto been upright, became sloped for comfort.

Chests were made in various sizes, many having domed lids – the form was derived from the primitive practice of hollowing out logs. Whatever their style, these chests were frequently veneered with real or simulated ivory and ebony.

Egyptians did not eat at large tables. A low 'offering table' for personal use, usually made of alabaster, was supplemented by a tall stand which had a ring rather than a top so that it could support a basin or ewer. Also extant are gaming-tables, whose tops are inlaid very much like that of a chess-board; sometimes these tables have detachable 'bull' or, from later periods, 'lion' legs. There was a drawer at one end to hold the pieces.

GREECE

Our knowledge of the furniture of ancient Greece is based on those few pieces which have survived intact, the stone seats in the theatres of Athens and Epidauros which clearly were carved to resemble domestic chairs, and the many more which appear on painted pottery and in sculpture. All in all, we have sufficient evidence upon which to base our ideas of the range and character of Greek furniture. During the Mycenaean Age (c.1600–1200BC, largely contemporary with the New Kingdom in Egypt) much decorated furniture was made.

After the collapse of the Mycenaean civilization, the Hellenic Greeks adopted types and techniques from both Egypt and the Orient, and went on to develop their own style. The conquests of Alexander the Great, during the fourth century BC, resulted in the spread of Hellenization – including ideas about furniture – to Asia Minor, the Crimea, North Africa and Italy.

Greece had enough timber – oak, maple, beech, citrus, willow – to make it unnecessary to use veneering for reasons of economy, and it was not until Roman times that the notion of exploiting veneering for decorative effect had any impact. Marble and bronze were used in conjunction with or to replace wood, and inlaid ivory, ebony and precious stones were lavished on the finest wooden pieces, which sometimes had feet of silver. Carved and painted decoration was almost commonplace in this rich market.

To the range of tools which had been available to the Egyptians was added the plane, and even before the lathe was introduced after the seventh century BC, probably from the East, there appears to have been some method of wood-turning. Joints were effected with tenons, nails and glue. Seats were fitted with perfumed and brightly coloured cushions. Homer remarked that carpenters were 'welcomed the world over'.

The *kline*, or couch, with a headboard and footboard, was used for sleeping on and to recline on while eating. Some of those earlier than the eighth century BC have carved, animalized legs, but plain legs were more usual until turning became popular. Headboards were often decorated with bronze mounts and then inlaid with silver.

The simplest stools were four-legged and plain. A box-like type, painted with geometric patterns or with figures, served as either a footstool or a mounting block for climbing onto high couches. One type, the *diphros*, resembled an Egyptian form in that it has four legs joined by stretchers. The *diphros okladias*, a cross-legged stool, was likewise borrowed from Egypt, although the birds'-head terminations of the legs were replaced

by animal feet; the legs themselves were often boldly curved. The *diphros okladias* was used both indoors and out; when masters ventured abroad they would have their stool carried after them through the streets by a slave, so that it would be ready immediately whenever they might choose to rest. The grandest stools were highly decorated backless thrones.

The *thronos*, or throne-chair, was always reserved for the use of the most important person present. Often a god was depicted on a throne which was carved with rams' heads at the ends of the arms or whose back was shaped like a snake or a horse's head. According to Homer, goddesses liked the *klismos* – an armless chair which had inwardly curving legs and a comfortably shaped horizontal bar to the back. The *klismos* reached perfection in the fifth century BC and then deteriorated into a clumsier version which had a large exaggerated slab attached to the back.

A common wooden type of table was rectangular and stood on three legs; there were two legs at one end, the third being at the centre of the other end. An example of a late-Hellenistic type – small and round, on three legs which have swans' heads and hoof feet – was found in Egypt and is now at the Musée Royaux des Beaux-Arts, Brussels. A pair of massive supports for a marble serving table has been discovered at Pergamum and dated to the second century BC. Table-legs in wood and bronze are also extant.

Like Egyptian types, Greek chests had painted or inlaid panel sides, legs that ended in lion-paw feet, and hinged lids. A terracotta relief from c.460BC, now at Reggio, shows a woman raising the lid of a chest to put a garment away. A number of Hellenistic chests used as coffins – mostly with gabled lids and some painted with flowers and figures – have survived in Egypt and the Crimea. It has been argued that some Greek chests were meant to be stood on end, so that the lid became the door, but no cupboard appears in Greek art and the Greeks did not have a word for such an item of furniture. Instead they hung some of their possessions from hooks on the wall, or placed them on an open shelf.

ETRURIA

In early times, Etruria spread over most of northern Italy but after the country had been subjugated by the Romans, during the fourth century BC, its extent was much reduced. The written language has never been fully deciphered, so much of Etruscan history remains a mystery. However, the evidence and actual furniture in Etruscan tombs, which were carved out of soft rock to simulate rooms, suggest that until the seventh century BC when Corinthian influence increased, this culture's furniture crafts owed more to the Middle East than to Greece.

The Etruscans were expert craftsmen in wood, stone and textiles and tomb paintings suggest that, like the Greeks, they existed in an atmosphere of relative comfort and luxury. Their most original contribution to furniture lay in their use of bronze. Extant are a number of bronze chests, remarkable in that they are circular. They stand on paw feet and are engraved with figures. A barrel-shaped type of chair was made of sheet bronze, riveted together, with the back and arms forming a continuous curve that joined a drum-like circular base. A funerary statue dating from the fifth century BC, now in Florence, shows an elaborate armchair with carved sphinx supports.

Large bronze candlesticks and lamp-stands, dating from the seventh to the third century BC (little or nothing survives from earlier periods, before bronze came into extensive use), have tripod bases and shafts with animal figures climbing up them. A cauldron stand of the third century, engineered with strips of bronze arranged geometrically, was found in the Regolini-Galassi Tomb, Cervetri (the ancient Caere).

WALL PAINTING FROM HERCULANEUM, ROMAN, BEFORE AD79 *(left)*

Depicting a music lesson, the girl and her teacher sit on a wide seat of sophisticated design, with turned legs and winged figures as arm-supports. Chairs of this type were made in both wood and metal.

SILVER TRIPOD STAND, FROM THE HILDESHEIM HOARD, ROMAN, 1ST CENTURY AD *(below)*

Elegant, square-tapered legs are surmounted by bearded masks and terminate in feet of human form. The X-shaped stretchers allow the stand to be folded into a compact, easily portable piece of furniture.

Roman Britain the Dorset slate known as Kimmeridge shale was a popular material. For luxurious items silver was used, both in the solid form and for plating base metals.

Couches and benches were often made from bronze and had elaborately decorated headboards in the Greek style. After about AD100 they became less ornate but, fitted with backs and sometimes side-pieces, began to look like prototype settees, while carved reliefs show benches with backs that suggest an early form of settle.

The heavy version of the Greek *klismos* was in general use. Women favoured a tub-chair often made in wickerwork – a type made in Roman Britain and depicted in a relief, dating from the third century AD, found at Trier, Germany. For men, an upright, panelled chair served for daily use, but there were also stately armchairs carved with animals or caryatid figures derived from supports representing vestal virgins at the Erechtheion, Athens. The X-framed stool enjoyed both popular and official status, the straight-legged version (*sella curulis*) being used by magistrates. This type has been excavated in Belgium and Britain, while a silver-plated example was unearthed at Ostia in Italy, and an iron one with bowed legs and representations of human feet in sandals was discovered at Nijmegen, Holland.

Box-like chests, some purely functional, some elaborately decorated with inlay and bronze or silver mounts, were produced in great numbers. More important to the evolution of furniture, for the first time in the West the cupboard with both shelves and doors was developed.

Many small round tables were made of bronze or silver; they had three or four legs surmounted by lion or leopard heads. A fine example is a silver tripod from the Hildesheim hoard in Germany. In Roman Britain, tables made of Dorset slate were sometimes carved with griffins. In Italy itself winged lions appeared on the shaped end-supports of large serving tables made in marble; an example from the first century AD was found in the house of Cornelius Rufus at Pompeii. The *mensa lunata*, a half-round console table on curved legs, was a latecomer to the rich repertoire of Roman furniture.

Little is known about Etruscan couches, but a stone monument in the Tomb of the Volumnii at Perugia, dating from the second century BC, depicts a very Greek-looking couch, the foot- and headboard of which are both shaped as swans' heads and which terminate in elaborately carved legs.

ROME

From 146BC, when Greece finally came under Roman rule, the conquerors adopted even more elements of Greek design than they had before. Eventually Graeco-Roman styles were carried to the outposts of the Empire, where many actual pieces have been discovered. Pieces have also been found in Rome itself and, preserved in volcanic materials from the eruption of Vesuvius in AD79, in Herculaneum and Pompeii. Elegant interiors, with marble columns, stucco ceilings and mosaic floors, are portrayed in frescos and marble carvings.

As well as a great variety of woods – many of them, especially the imported ones, so exotic and highly prized that they were cut into veneers – extensive use was made of bronze, marble and, in the conquered territories, special local materials. For example, in

BYZANTIUM

Byzantium, the ancient Hellenic city on the Bosphorus, had exerted an influence – partly Oriental, partly classical Greek – on Roman art and architecture for about a century before AD330, when the Emperor Constantine largely rebuilt it, chose it as his new seat of government and renamed it Constantinople. It was in this city that traditions of craftsmanship were kept alive when Barbarian invasions engulfed the West. It was here, too, that Christian art first flourished. Byzantine churches came to be built in places far from Constantinople, and their architecture and decoration influenced the design of furniture.

Like Egypt, the area surrounding the Bosphorus was short of timber. Stone buildings were superbly carved with surface ornament, and this style of decoration was found also on furniture, in the making of which wood was supplemented with stone and metal. For the finest pieces ivory was used, usually in the form of thick veneers. Sometimes pieces of ivory were used in the solid, employing panelled construction to forestall shrinkage and to reduce the tendency to warp and split. This technique is still used today in the manufacture of furniture.

Chests were made in all sizes. A number of carved ivory caskets are still in existence; these were miniature versions of the full-scale wooden types which served not only for storage but also as seats and even beds.

So far as chairs are concerned, the sixth-century ivory throne of the Emperor Maximian at Ravenna is built like a box with back and arms added – a mode of construction which was to become widely used later. At a rather different level, a type of folding, X-framed chair (a depiction appears in a twelfth-century manuscript) was made in both wood and metal. Benches with turned legs and painted decoration were commonplace. A picture in a manuscript from the late twelfth century shows a sloped footstool with the base 'arcaded' – i.e., shaped as a series of rounded arches – more in the Romanesque than the Byzantine style.

Wooden tables sometimes incorporated

IVORY THRONE, BYZANTINE, 6TH CENTURY

Known as 'Maximian's throne', this chair is richly carved with animals, birds and foliage; the panels feature Christ, St John and the Apostles.

drawers, compartments with doors and, for the scholar, adjustable lecterns. Large round tables, some of them in stone and following Roman models, were used for dining.

Classical types of beds and couches, though lacking the elegant scroll ends, were the most typical. Nevertheless, mosaics in St Mark's, Venice, show a prototype of the 'four-poster', complete with column supports and hangings. The hangings were to play an increasingly important part in the decoration of beds, especially formal beds, and much of the work was extremely fine and expensive.

Byzantine 'armoires', of architectural form with arched pediments, and open bookshelves with doors below are illustrated so frequently that they must have been in fairly general use in the Empire.

PAGE FROM THE BREVIARY OF JOHN THE FEARLESS, DUKE OF BURGUNDY, EARLY 15TH CENTURY

ROMANESQUE

The spread of Christianity as a unifying culture encouraged a grafting of what was essentially pagan art from the north onto what survived of the southern classical styles. This amalgam, which originated in Italy, drew on the vestiges of Roman skills and coupled them with those of migrant Byzantine craftsmen. It took root in France, and from there it was carried into the Netherlands, eventually reaching Scandinavia and, by courtesy of the Norman invasion in 1066, Britain.

The fortresses of the feudal lords were sparsely furnished; there were tapestries and a few pieces of carved or painted furniture, some fixed but most of it portable – a mobility that is still commemorated in such words as *mobili, meubles* and *Möbel*. Much of the Romanesque furniture that has survived is ecclesiastical, but in fact there was little difference between ecclesiastical and domestic pieces. Neither, at a time when frontiers were constantly changing, was there necessarily much by way of a readily identifiable variation between one country and the next, although general patterns can be detected.

In Romanesque times, the wood used was

while others were free-standing. A massive example (*c.*1200) at the Cathedral Museum, Halberstadt, is painted both inside and out with the figures of saints.

Simple stools with turned legs were commonplace. However, in a feudal society ruled by strict orders of precedence, more elaborate versions served as status symbols: the eleventh-century Bayeux Tapestry shows three of box-like construction – varying in design but all carved with animal

board and footboard, and boards at the sides; this type, too, was hung with draperies. Both kinds could be knocked apart so that in an emergency they could be transported from one place to another, but more customarily only the drapes were taken on journeys, being removed and packed in chests. Also frequently mentioned in inventories are truckle beds, mounted on wheels, and trussing beds, which folded up.

In the medieval hall a large household sat down on stools and benches to eat at trestle tables which were set at right angles to a more formal table, raised on a dais, where the lord and his lady sat on chairs. After the meal, the tables could be dismantled to make space for entertainment. In the ninth and tenth centuries there were also semicircular dining-tables which were draped with curtains hung from rails. This range of furniture survived in many areas until long after the arrival of the Gothic style in the twelfth century.

WALNUT HUTCH
(HIGH CHEST), MID-
13TH CENTURY

The words Ave Maria Gracia Plena *are incised between the two rows of Romanesque arches. The stiles are chip-carved with roundels and pierced with open arches.*

usually a local one: cypress was rarely employed north of the Alps; walnut was confined mainly to Italy, Spain and parts of France and Germany; oak predominated in Britain, the Netherlands, much of France and Germany; and pine and fir generally held sway in Scandinavia. Local stone and iron were also put to use.

Numerous types of chests were made. These included the primitive dug-out, which was made by hollowing out a log; the ark, which had a gabled detachable lid; the dome-topped 'standard'; the boarded type, or six-plank chest, which was made by nailing boards or planks, front and back, to solid ends, and adding a lid; and the high hutch, which had front boards housed in wide vertical corner posts (stiles) and, often, framed-up sides. Chip-carved roundels and Romanesque arches were used in Britain and Europe to decorate furniture and these forms persisted in some areas until about the end of the sixteenth century.

Some armoires were built-in fitments

heads and feet – as the thrones of, respectively, William the Conqueror, Edward the Confessor and Count Guy. The X-shaped stool, known in medieval times as a faldstool or cathedra, implied even more authority. The 'chair of estate', reserved for the lord and master, was likewise often of folding-X form for use both in the home and when travelling or campaigning. Sometimes it was made of iron; if made of carved wood it might be embellished with precious materials.

Box-seated armchairs were known, but the posted type, constructed with turned verticals ('posts') into which holes were bored to receive cross-members, was more usual. An armchair and a settle of this type, *c.*1280, together with a slope-top desk of about the same date, are in Vallstena Church, Gotland, Sweden. All three are decorated with carved arcading and applied turnings.

The posted bed was similarly constructed with turned columns. From these were hung curtains, so that the bed became like a room within a room. Another type had a head-

GOTHIC

The term 'Gothic' was first used by Giorgio Vasari (1511–74) as one of abuse. Vasari was extolling the architecture of the Renaissance at the expense of medieval buildings which, in fact, owed nothing whatsoever to the Goths. These were Germanic people who conquered Rome, reached the peak of their power in sixth-century Spain and finally lost it in AD711 – more than four hundred years before Abbot Suger built the first 'Gothic' church, at St Denis in France, in 1140–44. To achieve results, the Abbot extended the use of lay labour so that ordinary workmen acquired skills that had hitherto been jealously guarded by the monks. This practice spread widely during the fourteenth and fifteenth centuries as the Gothic style slowly replaced the Romanesque throughout most of Europe. Many buildings – and, indeed, many pieces of furniture – show both influences at work, because no style ever replaces another at a stroke; there is always a transitional phase – sometimes a long one.

Gothic differed from Romanesque in several important ways, of which perhaps the most notable was a pervasive elegance which had been absent from the Romanesque. The pointed arch, deriving from Saracenic buildings seen in the East by the Crusaders and in Sicily by the Norman invaders, largely replaced the rounded Romanesque type. The spaces within the arch were filled with tracery and fretted patterns of animals and foliage, rendered more naturalistically than before.

The woods used for Gothic furniture were much the same as those used during the Romanesque. Iron, both wrought and cold-cut, was used to strengthen and decorate. Dovetailing was crude; mortise-and-tenon joints, secured by pegging, were employed for the framework of panelling. Turning, carving and painting were excellent, but few painted pieces retain more than a trace of their original pigments.

The importance of Gothic chests (or *coffres*) was such that, in 1254, their makers were allowed by the Provost of Paris to form their own guild, separate from that of the carpenters — a decision which was to have a major effect on the future of French furniture-making. Some of the finest French chests were of the housed construction which had been popular during the Romanesque and were elaborately bound with scrolled ironwork; a good example, dated *c*.1200–50, is in the Musée des Arts Décoratifs, Paris. Similar examples have been found in English churches. These may have been private possessions left in the vaults for safekeeping, as was the custom. Chests with three locks — one for the priest and one for each of two wardens — were probably meant for church use; an example is the hutch-type chest with framed ends, dated *c*.1480, in the Chapel of the Pyx, Westminster Abbey, London. Many are carved with arches and tracery and a few with jousting scenes, such as a fourteenth-century tilting chest in the Victoria and Albert Museum, London.

Italian chests (*cassoni*) were very different. Delicately carved gesso surfaces featured, or there might be panels of intarsia (inlay of coloured woods). However, the Gothic style never really took firm root in Italy.

Grand chairs of the period include the late-fourteenth-century throne of King Martin of Aragon, given to the cathedral at Barcelona after his death in 1410, which is of solid silver and has three sharply pointed arches surmounting the back. The Coronation Chair at Westminster Abbey is one of the few medieval pieces that can be firmly attributed to a known maker, Master Walter of Durham, working to the order of Edward I. It has a sharply pointed arch to the back, downward-curving arms carved below with Gothic arches, and a space under the seat to accommodate the Stone of Scone, which had been taken from Scotland in 1296. The chair

OAK STOOL, ENGLISH, 16TH CENTURY *(above left)*

The carved understretcher of this stool is secured with wedges — a common method of construction during the Gothic and early-Renaissance periods.

OAK COFFER, FRENCH OR ENGLISH, 14TH CENTURY *(above)*

This coffer is carved with a scene of knights fighting or perhaps only tilting — a popular sport among gentlemen in the Middle Ages. Chests carved with this kind of subject were probably fairly plentiful in medieval times, but very few examples survive.

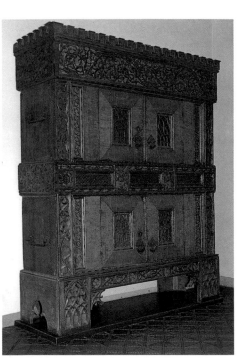

PAINTED CUPBOARD, GERMAN, LATE 15TH CENTURY *(left)*

Like so much Gothic furniture, this cupboard was probably painted all over in vivid colours, traces of which still remain. For this reason, various types of wood were used in its construction. The carving is in the style of Gothic church architecture.

has four 'lion' supports, added in 1509. These were chairs for royalty.

More usual in England, France and the Netherlands was the box-seated chair with high back and enclosed arms, constructed with panels bevelled at the edges, fitting loosely into rebates in the frame. Examples dating from the fifteenth and early sixteenth centuries were often carved with 'linenfold' or 'parchmen' patterns.

A popular type of stool from the fifteenth and early sixteenth centuries had two slab supports which were shaped on their edges, slightly splayed and joined either by a wide stretcher set vertically under the seat or by two boards nailed to the outside edges of the ends. Simple chairs without arms but with a support for the back are known as backstools.

Some of the most impressive Gothic armoires were made in Germany. A late-fifteenth-century type, of architectural design with a crenellated cornice above a deep, richly carved frieze and four doors with carved panels, is at the Bayerisches Nationalmuseum, Munich.

During the early Tudor period in England a type known first as an aumbry (from 'armoire'), later as a livery cupboard, stood in the bedchamber to store the overnight ration of food and refreshment deemed necessary to sustain the British metabolism until morning. A celebrated example is in the Victoria and Albert Museum, London; it is said to have belonged to Arthur, Prince of Wales (Henry VIII's elder brother), who died in 1502. The armoire is carved and pierced with Gothic-style openings for ventilation (although some authorities believe that these are not original). The tendency in late-Gothic England was towards a plainer style of armoire (and, indeed, of furniture in general). In France, by contrast, and more especially in the rich dukedom of Burgundy and its possessions in the Netherlands, the trend was to an ever-increasing grandeur.

Two distinct types of buffets held sway during the fourteenth and fifteenth centuries. One was a large construction of stepped tiers for the grandiose display of silver, the number of tiers being specified according to rank: for example, Marie of Burgundy displayed five, the Countess of Amiens only

WALNUT PORTABLE DESK, c.1525

This desk is covered in leather and painted with the royal arms of Henry VIII and his first wife, Katherine of Aragon. Other subjects include Mars and Venus, profiles of Helen of Troy and Paris, and putti sounding trumpets – showing distinct signs of Renaissance influence.

three and Henry VIII as many as ten. A French commentator at a royal marriage in 1486 described one of these as a 'buffet', while an English guest at the wedding called the same article a 'copeborde'.

The other type of buffet was smaller. Its several tiers were not stepped. However, the owner's rank permitting, the tiers were topped by a canopy (a status symbol sometimes placed also over thrones and beds). This second form of 'cup-board' evolved into the sixteenth-century court cupboard, which was initially open but then gradually came to be enclosed by doors and panels.

In addition to the trestle type, which developed massive supports on cruciform bases, a variety of other tables came into use during the late fifteenth century. Most notable of these was the circular table with a central support.

In France and England the full-tester bed developed from the Romanesque prototype and the canopied kind into the grand state bed. The popular term 'four-poster' is used for these beds, but often it is inaccurate because many examples, while they had two posts at the foot, had the tester (an overhead frame) supported at the other end by a high panelled headboard.

In Italy, with beds, as with all forms of furniture during this period, the story was a little different. The Ospedale del Ceppo, Pistoia, has a fourteenth-century bed which has no tester but which does have a head-board and footboard decorated with paintings of religious figures. The decoration of Gothic furniture, in Italy as elsewhere, was seldom far removed from the influence of ecclesiastical architecture and Christian iconography. Some beds are said to have been painted with figures from classical mythology in anticipation of the Renaissance revival of ancient Greek and Roman styles, but may have been repainted in this way.

THE RENAISSANCE

During the fourteenth century there was an artistic and cultural revolution. The main and urgent thrust of this revolution, which started in the city-states of northern Italy, was a revived confidence in the power and dignity of Man, coupled with a profound study of contemporary Man's place among the artists and thinkers of classical antiquity. Beyond Italy, throughout northern Europe and the Iberian peninsula, this interest in a revival of the classical ethos and its meshing with a vigorous medieval culture were apparent in many ways. There was a passion for realism, fostered by the leading artists working for Philip the Bold at the Burgundian court and at the great Carthusian monastery of Champmol. The artist began to be admired as an inspired creator and his place in society was given added status by the patronage extended by popes Alexander VI, Julius II and Leo X to Michelangelo and others in Rome.

The 'universal' or 'Renaissance' man was well read in the classical texts; he could also master the complexities of engineering, science and military works. Growing attention to anatomy and perspective allowed artists, sculptors and architects to fashion three-dimensional forms with greater assurance than ever before.

While Renaissance style was replaced gradually, from the 1520s onwards, by the style of Mannerism, with its deliberate contradiction of classical rules, enough had been done already to change the patterns of patronage, which underpinned all artistic effort.

In the search for an alternative to the entrenched Gothic spirit the glamour of the new Italian achievement became irresistibly appealing throughout all Europe.

DETAIL OF INLAID CABINET, LORENZ STROMAIR, AUGSBURG, 1560–5

The art of inlaying various fruitwoods, known as intarsia, is carried to perfection in this cabinet. The inside is as rich as the outside. The decoration shows the advances made by the Renaissance perspectivists and the skilled use of a wide repertoire of engraved sources for architectural detail.

ITALY

In the Florence of the early fourteenth century the vision of a new art began to dominate the minds of Italian masters. This vision was concerned with human standards and achievements, overlaid by ideas and forms drawn from what was known of the vanished civilizations of ancient Greece and Rome. The first to set out all the theoretical principles was the architect and theorist Leon Battista Alberti (1404–72), who defined beauty as 'the harmony and concord of all the parts, achieved in such a manner that nothing could be added or taken away or altered except for the worse'. Ornament he regarded as giving an additional brightness and improvement to beauty. By further stating that the principal ornament in all architecture was the column, Alberti was asserting afresh the ancient supremacy of the architectural orders. In using columns balanced by the whole range of architectural features in his buildings he not only established important systems of proportion, by the relation of one part to another, but inspired many – among them, furniture-makers – to try blending columns, pilasters and pediments with motifs from the rich and varied classical repertoire into their lavishly decorated constructions.

Every aspect of the commercial life of the typical late-medieval Italian city-state had been dominated by guilds. Self-perpetuating and self-regulating, these tended to be so restrictive in attitude that they inhibited development, and thus came increasingly under attack from those jealous of their power. Moreover, often active outside the jurisdiction of the guilds were a number of important artists who had turned aside from painting religious scenes on wood panels to the lucrative task of decorating elaborate *cassoni* (marriage chests). These were made, often in pairs, to contain a bride's trousseau and were decorated not only with the coats of arms of her family and those of her intended husband but with relief ornament, swags of fruit, panels of mosaic in patterns (intarsia) or paintings of religious subjects. These gilded and carved gesso objects, the

symbols of dynastic patronage and achievement, were replaced in the later sixteenth century by *cassoni* made for brides in general rather than for a specific bride. In carved and polished walnut, these *cassoni* were fashioned in the form of antique sarcophagi, all their surfaces being patterned with acanthus foliage around reliefs of classical scenes.

Along with beds, chairs and benches, *cassoni* were principal objects of interior furnishing. Their surroundings were rich and brilliantly coloured, featuring Turkish table carpets and Alexandrian silk cloths, leather wall hangings with stamped gold patterns and luxurious damask hangings.

CARVED WOOD
AND GESSO
CASSONE,
FLORENTINE,
c.1472

This marriage chest is an elaborate example of the painter's and gilder's art with narrative panels painted in tempera on gesso, with parts subsequently gilded. The sources for the paintings were taken from the Bible and classical mythology.

richly decorated testers. Very few of these beds have survived.

Indeed, while all the skills of the furniture-maker or silversmith might be found in a single lavish casket of this age, such achievements were rare. Even in the greatest of the sixteenth-century palaces, the rooms, while they gave a dignified impression, were sparsely furnished, albeit with pieces of great elaboration. Some of these pieces incorporated *pietre dure* (hard stones). In 1580 Francesco I de'Medici summoned craftsmen from Milan to set up in Florence a hard-stone workshop, the Opificio delle Pietre Dure. The English diarist John Evelyn visited this

During this early period Italian houses did not have dining-rooms and furniture was made to be easily movable so that it could be set up wherever seemed convenient – although the *credenza* (sideboard), previously just a rough table draped with a cloth, took on a more elaborate architectural form, with columns or pilasters holding up a cornice. Such features appeared sometimes on monumentally designed state beds which had posts in the form of caryatids as well as

workshop in 1644 and saw 'divers incomparable tables of Pietra Commessa, which is a marble ground inlayed with several sorts of marbles and stones of divers colours, in the shapes of flowers, trees, beasts, birds and Landskips like the natural'. It was a process that was to interest subsequent visiting Grand Tourists.

As well as the elaborate furniture, the room itself, often featuring panelling that displayed fine profiling and carved foliage,

CARVED WALNUT
SGABELLI, ITALIAN,
16TH CENTURY
(above)

STUDIOLO OF
FEDERIGO DA
MONTEFELTRO IN
THE PALAZZO
DUCALE, URBINO,
1470S *(above right)*

*The amazing intarsia
decoration of this study,
in which manuscripts
were kept, is by an
unknown designer
working with the
architect, Luciano
Laurana (d.1479).*

THE DREAM OF ST
URSULA, VITTORE
CARPACCIO, 1495
(right)

*The saint sleeps in a
bed with turned posts
and elaborate tester
hangings. A small table
is covered with a cloth
and a stool is set by it.*

could represent a major example of the
intarsia-worker's art. For example, the
studiolo of Federigo da Montefeltro, *c.*1470,
in the Ducal Palace at Urbino, has superb
intarsia decoration by an unknown artist.
Intarsia attracted its own groups of craftsmen: in 1478 Florence had no fewer than
eighty-four workshops of *intarsiatori* and
other wood-decorators. The Renaissance
painter and chronicler Giorgio Vasari referred to perspectives of buildings as having
been the earliest subjects represented in
intarsia. Perhaps the most important of this
type are the inlays of the choir-stalls of Siena
Cathedral (1503) and the doors of Raphael's
Stanze in the Vatican (1514–21), both by one
of the best masters, Fra Giovanni da Verona,
with assistance on the Stanze doors from the
carver Giovanni Barile. Together with his
brother Antonio, Giovanni Barile was a
superb maker of carved and gilded frames for
altars and paintings. Intarsia decoration,
important in itself, had a considerable influence on the decoration of furniture.

CARVED WALNUT CUPBOARD, ATTRIBUTED
TO HUGUES SAMBIN, FRENCH, *c.1570*

Term figures, published by Sambin (1572), appear on several sixteenth-century cabinets.

ENGRAVING OF A BED, JACQUES ANDROUET
DUCERCEAU, *c.1560*

FRANCE

In the Middle Ages construction of all types of furniture had been simple, most of it being made in oak. Oak does not carve easily, and the new taste for Italian ideas – which, through the patronage of important families like the Dukes of Burgundy, had reached France before the start of the sixteenth century – demanded the use of a darker, smoother wood, such as walnut. This is an oily wood with a fine grain, and was in plentiful supply in France. The use of walnut allowed carvers to depict felicitously elaborate forms of Mannerist decoration, such as composite capitals, carved heads, palmettes, acanthus leaves, caryatids, 'strapwork' (taking the form of cut and interlaced straps of leather), polished bosses, masks and flowing arabesques.

In 1525 the return of Francis I to France after his captivity in Italy gave a boost to sumptuous decoration, as the restored king turned his attentions to his depleted palaces. In 1530–32 he invited two important Italian artists, Giovanni Battista Rosso (Rosso Fiorentino) and Francesco Primaticcio, to come to work for him at the palace of Fontainebleau, a few miles outside Paris. The achievements of these men and those of the many talented artists who worked for them soon changed the prevailing style, first from French to Italian, and then, in the reign of Henry II, from 1547 onwards, back to French but with the addition of many classical overtones.

Architects and decorators – particularly Jacques Androuet DuCerceau (*c.1520–84*), who published important engravings of furniture in 1550 – were concerned to show objects with these classical ideas of proportion but to overlay them with geometric patterns and representations of exotic human and animal figures. These included sphinxes, griffins, eagles, lions, sea-horses and attenuated figures which were made even more popular by the important sculptures of Jean Goujon (*fl.1540–68*). Joiners and carvers in the Île-de-France, the Loire Valley, Burgundy, Provence and elsewhere went beyond the pattern-books to ransack

popular mythological stories for scenes to represent. The architect, sculptor and furniture-maker Hugues Sambin (*c.1515/20–1601/2*), who worked at Dijon in particular, published a book on the diversity of the term figures used in architecture; Sambin's book, in conjunction with DuCerceau's engravings, had a profound effect not only on the appearance of many sculptural pieces of furniture but on the development of carving in low and high relief.

Inside a French house of the sixteenth century there would be several dominant pieces of furniture. Since medieval times the chest had been important both as a receptacle for storage and, in a developed form, as a travelling trunk. Now, however, with the need for more storage within rooms, the dresser was introduced; this had an upper part, raised on column supports, enclosed by two or more doors that were decorated in low relief. From the 1550s onwards this upper stage became more architectural in overall appearance, and incorporated the carved animal or human forms made popular by DuCerceau and Sambin. Some fine walnut examples were made, particularly in Dijon.

The armoire, a precursor of the wardrobe, usually had only one large door. While there is the constant difficult problem of defining what actually constitutes a 'cupboard' (for the armoire could be fitted into the panelling of a room), it was certainly a very useful item of furniture.

Few examples of sixteenth-century upholstered furniture survive from any country, but we know that it was not uncommon, since it was often shown in the paintings and engravings of that time. Velvet would be held in position by brass studs nailed through intricate braids. The movable table, with its elaborate supports connected by stretchers, was usually covered with a carpet or with fabric matched to the room's decoration. Chairs could be either portable or heavy and throne-like. A new type was the *lit de repos*, or day-bed, which had a raised back for daytime reclining. Some chairs were given arms; others, such as the gossiping chair (or *chaise caquetoire*), had seats of trapezoidal form. The backless bench was popular, as was the stool (*sgabello*). A variant,

CARVED OAK
DRESSER, FRENCH,
c.1524 *(left)*

*In the early sixteenth
century the dresser
retained the rectangular
or hexagonal form. The
upper stage of this
dresser has two doors,
but the lower central
door is flanked by
panels.*

INLAID CABINET,
LORENZ STROMAIR,
AUGSBURG,
1560–5 *(right)*

*Intarsia decoration was
well suited to free
ornament and often
included views of
imaginary buildings,
representing the
unfulfilled ambitions of
contemporary
architectural taste.
Various woods were
stained to achieve
coloured effects.*

By contrast, in the south of the country – in Catholic Bavaria, for example – softwoods such as lime were in common use. To give it life lime is a wood which needs to be painted or inlaid with contrasting woods. It was well suited to the work of sculptors and altar-makers such as Tilman Riemenschneider (c.1460–1531) of Würzburg, who had one of the largest workshops, employing no fewer than twelve apprentices. There were also many intarsia-workers settled at Augsburg. These craftsmen drew their inspiration from such books as Lorenz Stöer's *Geometria et*

Perspectiva (1567), with its array of precise perspective views.

Standards of living rose steadily throughout the sixteenth century. As houses became more comfortable, new kinds of furniture were needed. Beds were given larger canopies, raised on posts, so that they became more prominent and, as the bedroom became a place for reception as well as for rest, served as indicators of status. Chests were always useful, their long panels being well suited to carved or intarsia decoration; it was not long before the practice of placing one chest upon another led to the development of a spacious cupboard which could be mounted on a stand. Nuremberg was noted for making cupboards of many types while, to the south, Augsburg specialized in elaborate writing-cabinets. The latter of these were often combined with desks containing many drawers and compartments and which were constructed as showpieces of the art of

covered with tapestry and known as a *placet*, allowed one to sit almost on the floor, as if on a church hassock. This item of furniture remained popular at the French court well into the seventeenth century.

GERMANY

The pervasive influence of the Italian Renaissance was most evident, as we might expect, in the work of the many German sculptors, carvers and designers who had earlier been to Italy. Although Hans Holbein the Younger and Albrecht Dürer both visited Italy, it was in the woodcuts of people such as Peter Flötner, who had likewise been there, and the cabinet-maker known only as the Master H.S. that

the richest decorative effects were displayed. Working from the centres of Nuremberg and Augsburg, in which the influence of the guilds was all-powerful, they and others provided many vivid examples in which a variety of classical architectural motifs were blended with cavorting putti, animal masks, weird grotesques and arabesques.

Craftsmen north of the Alps who had no direct experience of the new decorative features derived from Italy relied on the work of engravers such as Flötner to stay level with not only their southern competitors but also those craftsmen who, working at the princely or ducal court or for a powerful abbot, were free from both guild restrictions and undue concern with costs. The north of Germany at this time was marked by its great conservatism and stolidity: although there was some use of lime, ash and walnut, oak furniture was preferred by patrons in this region.

OAK AND ASH CUPBOARD, FROM A DESIGN BY PETER FLÖTNER, 1541 (above)

Flötner was active as a sculptor, draughtsman, wood-engraver and cabinet-maker. His artistic education almost certainly took place in Augsburg; he is one of the leaders of the Renaissance in Germany.

OAK AND MAPLE TWO-STAGE 'MARRIAGE CABINET', GERMAN, 1590 (above right)

Commemorating a marriage in the family of Closen-Nothaft, this inlaid cabinet shows a keen appreciation of architectural forms.

marquetry, intarsia and metal-work.

In 1577, the city of Augsburg demonstrated the skills of its artisans in a most flamboyant way when it presented a chair of chiselled steel made by Thomas Rucker (and now in Longford Castle, Wiltshire) to the Emperor Rudolf II. Chairs for everyday use were less exotic than this and, while sturdy, usually lacked arm-rests. Comfort was supplied by the use of loose cushions – although these could not be fastened easily to the many benches, stools and Italian-style folding chairs that were now in use in all European countries. Chairs could be drawn up easily to the large dining-tables (usually a board on trestles) or to the many small elaborate tables which came into general use during the Renaissance period. Much more guild and craft concern was focused on the making of elaborate ebony cabinets, inlaid with precious stones so as to form a *Kunstkammer* or *Wunderkammer*.

THE LOW COUNTRIES

In the same way that the German master-craftsmen assembled at Augsburg and Nuremberg and thereby gave their guilds and cities prominence, those in the Low Countries gathered in Antwerp, with the result that the city soon enjoyed international acclaim as a centre for the making of veneered and painted cabinets. These were worked in ebony or with ebony veneers, with some painters specializing in the depiction of mythological or classical scenes on the panels. These cabinets were exported to France, England, Holland, Austria and Portugal. Such lavish creations apart, furniture-makers in the northern Netherlands – where there was a strong guild system that encouraged local styles but perhaps inhibited innovation – were adept at making several kinds of cupboard, including marriage presses designed for the storage of linen. The best of these have carved figures on the door panels, flanked by caryatid supports. Intarsia techniques, too, came from Italy to the Netherlands, and *trompe-l'oeil* perspectives and vases of flowers were featured as a principal type of decoration.

The spread of Renaissance ideas into the Netherlands seems to have owed its origins to the visit of the painter Jan Gossaert, called Mabuse, to Italy in 1508. However, it was the ready availability of engravings, many of them by Cornelis Bos and the sculptor Cornelis Floris (Cornelius de Vriendt), which allowed the Fontainebleau/Italianate type of grotesques and strapwork to trickle down to the level of the many furniture-making shops in the Netherlands. Patrons coveted the 1539 Flemish translation of Sebastiano Serlio's *Fourth Book of Architecture*, or acquired relevant engravings with which to instruct. Craftsmen had merely to satisfy their guild that they were not stepping outside their prescribed divisions of labour, and that they had the requisite seasoned wood and veneers to render, if possible, what their patrons' engravings showed.

Dutch seafaring tradition encouraged the import of exotic materials. Ebony was used extensively to decorate plain oak furniture or for the more elaborate veneered cabinets which were exported principally to Britain, France and Portugal.

Chairs from the Netherlands were usually made in walnut; a few were made in ebony, which was exceptionally strong and hard and, because thinner sections could be used, was cost-effective despite the fact that it was a much more expensive wood. Chair-legs were of vase-shaped section, and the back uprights typically terminated in lions' heads. The chairs of the Netherlands – upholstered in leather, velvet or cloth held by large-headed brass nails – broke away from their Italian and Spanish inspirations in terms of construction, but nevertheless there were definite similarities, even if the arm-rests did terminate in highly individualistic carved animal heads or tightly curved volutes. In the back splats architectural elements were evi-

dent, perhaps through one arch being superimposed above another, or through the separation of each carved layer of the splat and top-rail by a number of turned baluster-form spindles.

Tables were generally of oak and, when extra ornament was required, inlaid with ebony. Some were made so that extra leaves could be drawn out from beneath to double the length of the top. The bulbous legs, connected by inlaid stretchers, and the strapwork brackets between frieze and legs were based on the precise engravings in Hans Vredeman de Vries' *Differents Pourtraicts de Menuiserie* (c.1580), soon available also in Germany, England and Sweden. A customer could refer to this book to show his joiner what was needed; later two similar volumes were published in 1630 by Hans's son, Paul Vredeman de Vries, so that designs were available for all the common types of furniture – even down to towel-horses.

SPAIN AND PORTUGAL

WALNUT WITH MARQUETRY *VARGUEÑO*, SPANISH, FIRST HALF OF 16TH CENTURY

The reliefs are in boxwood. The drop front opens to reveal small doors and drawers with reliefs on a velvet ground.

By the end of the fifteenth century both Spain and Portugal were wealthy. The Moors had finally been expelled in 1492, America had been discovered in the same year and was now being exploited, and Mexico and Peru had been conquered. At the start of the sixteenth century Portugal enjoyed successful trade with the Orient and had extended its land possessions through the Persian Gulf to Goa and as far as Siam and Japan. Lisbon was the wealthiest capital in Europe. Spain had profited from the long reigns and acquisitions of Charles I (the Holy Roman Emperor Charles V) and Philip II. Artistic activity flourished, late-Gothic and Moorish (Mudéjar) influences blending with those of the Italian Renaissance to give an impetus through the decorative use of antique heads, urns, cherubs, masks, grotesque figures and trophies. These motifs were carved in deep relief. The most popular wood was walnut, but chestnut, poplar, oak,

orangewood and pine were commonly used, and exotic woods such as ebony, rosewood, jacaranda and mahogany were readily available as imports from the overseas colonies. A plentiful supply of Peruvian silver from the mid-sixteenth century was useful for the making of furniture mounts, such as ornate hinges and clasps.

The original contributions of the Spanish to Renaissance furniture-making included various kinds of chairs and the fall-front cabinet known since the nineteenth century as the *vargueño*. Upholstery was applied lavishly to many sturdy chair-frames but rarely to the folding hip-joint chair, which had semicircular curved legs, connected by stretchers, and curved arm-rests supporting shaped arms which were attached to a rectangular back. Coloured leather (*guad-amecil*) from Cordova was used on the type of chair known as the *sillón de fraileros*, or monk's chair. This was of medium height, with square legs, stretchers and bracket feet, and a fretted front splat below the seat to which the leather was attached using large ornamental studs. The two upright back-rails, which terminated in metal balls, had leather or upholstery either covering them completely or fastened so that the frame was visible; velvet or brocade, with heavy fringes, was substituted acceptably for leather. However, it was those chairs with the coloured tooled leather that came to be highly regarded throughout Europe as a 'distinctive Spanish invention'.

Many common forms of Spanish and Portuguese furniture evolved from the pieces which were used in church sacristies to house the altar-plate and vestments. Cabinets which were high enough on their stands so that one could conveniently see into them and which had fall-fronts that could be supported on pull-out stays, soon became popular. Such cabinets are known as *vargueños* or, without the fall-front, as *papeleiras*. The profusion of drawers and the small central cupboard within were often decorated lavishly with inlaid wood or ivory on a ground of velvet, and some had an architectural appearance, with arches, columns and pediments surrounding or sur-

mounting relief portrait-heads.

The furniture of Portugal was much influenced by French and Spanish forms. An active group of furniture-makers and turners was based in Lisbon. These craftsmen mostly used walnut, sometimes chestnut. The influence born from Portugal's trading partnership with the Orient encouraged the copying of lacquered and gilt furniture. There were also ready supplies of silver, ivory, mother-of-pearl and precious stones and these were frequently set into ebony. However, little of this sixteenth-century output has survived the destructive effects of wars and the great earthquake of 1755.

The union of Spain and Portugal under Philip II in 1580 had the artistic result that, although the earliest influences of the Renaissance had come into Portugal from Italy and France, those of the fully-formed style flowed from Spain alone.

The dominance of the guilds reached out even to Mexico, so that the joint Iberian influences were strong enough there that a Mexican furniture-maker of the late 1560s would be required to be able to make a *vargueño*, an inlaid hip-joint chair, and a turned bed and table, almost as if he were practising his craft in Toledo or Lisbon.

BRITAIN

The medieval period persisted longer in the countries of the British Isles than anywhere else in Europe, not only because of their isolation, but also because of a natural conservatism on the part of their inhabitants.

The Classical Revival, c.1525–75

In 1511 Henry VIII brought the Florentine sculptor Pietro Torrigiano (1472–1528) to London to work on his father's tomb for Westminster Abbey and it was he and his countrymen, and later the German painter Hans Holbein (1497/8–1543), who brought to a wider English audience their first glimpse of classically inspired ornament.

The first engraved and printed designs followed hard on the heels of these isolated works, providing new models for British craftsmen. The architectural pattern-books of Sebastiano Serlio (1475–1554) were translated into Flemish and made available in Britain before the middle of the century, closely followed by others such as Hans Vredeman de Vries' *Das Erst Buch* of 1565.

By 1540 some classical motifs such as 'Romayne' portrait panels and elaborate 'grotesque' ornament, closely based on Italian originals, had already appeared superficially on British buildings, architectural woodwork and furniture, and they were soon followed by orders of columns. However, the linenfold panel survived in use throughout the sixteenth century and even the tail-ends of Gothic tracery appeared half-heartedly for another few years.

During the Middle Ages, the craft guilds had developed through three centuries into an efficient structure governing the training, workmanship and behaviour of their members and regulating the price and quality of manufacture. With the Reformation and the dissolution of the monasteries, the guilds were thrown into upheaval and were eventually disbanded.

Yet the craftsmen themselves were still functioning and the market was offering expanding opportunities in exciting new fields, following the enrichment of the ruling classes and the growth of a new affluent middle class of merchants and yeomen-farmers. In order to serve these new masters, the tradesmen reorganized themselves and received new charters under Elizabeth I and

later James I. In place of the guilds were the new trade companies, a development that resulted in the dominance of the joiners, who formed their company in London in 1570.

The Age of the Joiner

During the latter half of the fifteenth century these craftsmen developed framed-panel joinery as a practical technology. The furniture was assembled as a strong framework of tenon-jointed rails and stiles, the joints held securely with pegs. The spaces created by the frames could be left open, producing a flexible range of lightweight chairs, stools and tables, or they could be filled with panels of riven oak, held loosely in grooves or rebates around the inner edge of the framing, to make enclosed chests, boxes and settles or large areas of wall panelling. The final technical breakthrough came in the 1540s with the development of the true mitre, which considerably simplified the manufacture of moulded framing.

Although the bulk of the surviving furniture from this period is made of oak, walnut was generally the most favoured timber in richer homes, and a number of other native hardwoods are mentioned as being in com-

WALNUT CENTRE TABLE, 1560–1600 (above)

The 'sea-dog' supports are based on designs by Jacques Androuet DuCerceau. It may have been made for the English royal household.

ROSEWOOD AND BRAZILIAN PADOUKWOOD STOOL WITH WALNUT TOP, c.1580 (left)

Possibly made for the original Elizabethan house at Chatsworth, this stool was the latest novelty in imported exotic timbers.

ASH GREAT CHAIR, 16TH CENTURY (above left)

This chair was made by a turner in a style derived from medieval forms; this style persisted into the eighteenth century.

mon use. Softwoods were less accessible in sixteenth-century Britain than in the rest of mainland Europe, although the native yew was highly prized.

The middle years of the sixteenth century saw the full technical evolution of joiner-made furniture and by 1575 all of the forms and techniques which were to characterize the next century of English furniture production had been established. Apart from the later adoption of the dovetail joint, the developments which took place between 1575 and 1675 were almost entirely stylistic rather than technical.

Decoration

Around the primary trades evolved a whole series of specialist craftsmen who supplied decorative and functional components, mostly serving the needs of joiners, who included turners, inlayers, painter-stainers, blacksmiths, brassfounders and upholders (the guild name for upholsterers).

Turned decoration became the most widely used feature in the vocabulary employed in joiner-made furniture. Turned balusters had been used as early as 1535 by the Italian craftsmen working on the great screen at King's College Chapel in Cambridge, but it was not until the 1560s that turned decoration started to be used so distinctively on English furniture. The great majority of open-framed pieces made after this had their legs and other supports turned in the solid, and often modelled on the simple columns or balusters of classical architecture.

Despite this development, carving remained unchallenged as the most significant means of decorating furniture. In the Middle Ages, much furniture and architectural woodwork was painted, both for the sheer love of colour and as a measure of protection.

Sixteenth-century Britain saw the introduction of inlays of coloured woods, using a restricted palette of dark and light timbers and green or red stains. Inlaid panels and rails of very high quality were used in a fairly restrained way in fashionable Elizabethan furniture and during the next century in more robust form on vernacular pieces from the north of England.

Elaborate hardware was fairly rare on British-made furniture. Perhaps the only exceptions were the richly sculpted and enamelled bronze finials sometimes seen on upholstered chairs.

Loose cushions had been used on chairs and stools from the earliest times, but in the sixteenth century came the development of fixed upholstery, especially in the form of padded seats. Most upholders bought their chair-frames from local joiners and completed in their own workshops the complicated task of webbing, padding and covering upholstery with turkeywork, embroidery, leather, velvets and other fine cloths.

Gloriana and Mannerism

During the sixteenth century, English explorers and merchant adventurers, along with the Dutch, Spanish and Portuguese, spread through most of the known world, establishing contacts in Russia, Turkey, Persia, India, Japan, China and the Americas. Always hungry for novelty, London became the gateway through which came a vast range of exciting new products. Rare, exotic timbers including padouk, rosewood, ebony, mahogany and lignum vitae, were occasionally used in inlays or even in the solid. But only the Oriental cultures exercised any stylistic influence on English furniture-makers, who were immediately entranced by the lacquer ware imported from China and Japan.

A new sense of stability, unity and enterprise fired the Elizabethans to set their jaw against the world, to trade or plunder as the opportunity presented itself. This burst of vitality expressed itself in a flowering of the arts of literature, music, architecture, interior design and conversation. The aristocracy threw their resources into consolidating their new estates, whether by building new houses incorporating the latest planning ideas or converting the old monastic piles into manageable shape. Considerations of comfort, privacy and even efficiency began to influence the layout and equipment of some houses.

An appreciation of comfort and style also began to filter down the social order. Not only gentlemen, but also yeomen-farmers, tradesmen and craftsmen were able to equip their homes with fine (or at least substantial) furnishings and accessories.

The concentration of furniture production in provincial centres – such as Norwich, York, Bristol and Exeter – quickly led to a polarization. The joiners responded to the preferences and demands of local markets, so

that, in sharp contrast to the internationalism of the patrician market, a clear pattern of regional styles began to emerge.

At a more 'polite' level, small-town merchants eagerly followed the trends from London. Mainstream furniture design adopted the European Mannerist style, dictated by the demands of architecture and interior decoration and informed by the models published in the pattern-books. A number of these, produced in France, Flanders and Germany, now became available to the English carvers, including those by Jacques Androuet DuCerceau the Elder and Hans Vredeman de Vries.

Form and Symbolism

Most pieces of medieval furniture had a static function and often took a simplified form so that they could serve a number of different uses. Chests frequently doubled-up as tables or beds and some types of seating might incorporate a box-base for storage.

In the sixteenth century a greater mobility

OAK TESTER BED, c.1580

The 'Great Bed of Ware', mentioned by Shakespeare, is a prodigy among English furniture. It was possibly made by a German immigrant in London or Southwark for a rich London client.

occurred. The old box-base master's chair, fixed in its appointed place on the dais (high table), gave way to lighter open-frame armchairs. These could more easily be moved about the room and indeed the house, as occasion demanded. The panelled back of an armchair was a prime site for prestigious decoration and this often took the form of the owner's coat of arms or a cartouche of carving or inlay in the latest style.

Chairs made by the turners continued in use. They included a type of chair without arms known as a backstool. These were not made by joiners until late in the sixteenth century and even then the earliest joined

versions were probably intended to be upholstered. The usual seat for individuals was the single backless stool – longer versions were known as forms or benches.

Long dining-tables still persisted, but were now more often mounted on a framed base rather than on removable trestles. A new development was the withdrawing-table, in which extra leaves could be pulled out from under the top to accommodate extra company. The long table was supplied with matching sets of stools or benches, with an armchair for the master and sometimes one for his wife. The great tables were supplemented by a multiplicity of smaller side-tables used for specific purposes, such as the serious business of eating oysters.

Storage was always a problem in a busy household and special pieces evolved in which the contents could be closed away behind doors. These were at first called by their older names of 'aumbry', 'press' or 'locker', but when they began to enclose the open cup-boards with doors, they became known as 'close cupboards' and this term soon contracted to 'cupboards'. A feature of the family parlour was the great press cupboard, which acted as a focus of decoration in the room, vying for importance with the fireplace and its elaborate overmantel. From continental Europe came the idea of a small cupboard or cabinet to stand on a table.

Lidded chests were still by far the most common means of storage and were used for everything from linen and clothes to documents and books. Almost every inventory listed chests, coffers, trunks and boxes of all kinds and sizes, especially in bedchambers. The distinctions between these names are not always clear although, according to one contemporary writer, chests generally had flat lids whereas coffers and trunks had domed lids.

The most important and costly piece of furniture was the bed, although the expense could often lie in the elaborate curtains, valances, coverlets and trimmings rather than in the wooden bedstead itself. Middle-class houses had simpler tester bedsteads, with turned posts and plain panelling, or a roofless version which had a low headboard and turned pinnacles at the foot.

THE
BAROQUE

The period in which the Baroque style was prominent began early in the seventeenth century in southern Europe and extended into the first third of the eighteenth century in northern Europe. When studying the arts of this period it is necessary at the outset to appreciate two aspects of seventeenth-century Europe. Firstly, there was a large and complicated trade in exotic and luxury goods with the Far East and with the colonies which the European powers had established in the Americas and in Africa. Secondly, the power of the Roman Catholic Church diminished during the period while the concept of the sovereign state and absolute monarchy developed.

During the seventeenth century art was often produced with the sole intention of enhancing the prestige of a pope or a monarch. This was less true in the northern states, where there already existed an established merchant class and a powerful aristocracy, particularly in the Netherlands and in Britain, where art and luxury objects therefore tended to be aimed at the wealthy private citizen.

In many respects Baroque furniture shared characteristics of style with Baroque paintings and architecture, displaying an element of theatricality, and strong contrasts of light and dark. The highly sculptural qualities of Italian furniture related to the quieter and more naturalistic carving of Dutch Baroque furniture in the same way that Caravaggio's paintings represented the power and vigour of the southern Baroque while those of Rembrandt revealed the quieter northern style, with its greater interest in realism. Moroever, Baroque furniture shared with architecture of the era an interest in the contrast of textures and shapes, as illustrated by the designs of the lavish show-cabinets created during the Baroque era, which were made from a dazzling array of exotic materials.

WALNUT-VENEERED CABINET-ON-STAND, c.1675

All of the interior facings to drawers and doors on this English cabinet are lined with contemporary needlework depicting conventional subjects.

SPAIN AND PORTUGAL

Geographically, the Iberian peninsula is isolated from the rest of Europe, an isolation reflected in its decorative arts. In terms of ornamental design, furniture from Spain and Portugal is more abstract than other European furniture. Both countries demonstrated the influence of Oriental and exotic cultures with which they had long had economic and political ties.

At the beginning of the seventeenth century Spain was the most powerful European nation, but Spanish power waned as the population of the country decreased and its *per capita* wealth likewise fell. By the end of the seventeenth century Spanish furniture design had lost much of its vitality: the country's craftsmen turned first to Portuguese and then to Anglo-Netherlandish and French designs for inspiration. The influence of Portuguese furniture spread farther afield than Spain, affecting also the design of furniture in Britain and Holland, its two chief trading partners at that time.

José Churriguera (d.1725) can be taken as representative of one stream of Iberian design and Francisco de Herrera (1622–85) as exemplifying another, athough no furniture has been positively attributed to either man. Churriguera was an architect/designer, the 'Churrigueresque' style featured the combination of human figurative elements with architectural and purely decorative features; the resulting effects were often fantastic. De Herrera enjoyed success as a painter, architect and designer. He may also have been related to Philip II's architect, Juan de Herrera. From Seville, he introduced a classical style of Baroque design into Spain as a result of his studies in Rome.

In the sixteenth century Spanish furniture played an influential role in the rest of Europe, and many of the forms developed then carried over into the seventeenth century. To generalize, the Spanish furniture of this period was frontal and formal in design, and the basic shapes of chair, table and chest had changed little since their introduction in

WALNUT *VARGUEÑO*, EARLY 17TH CENTURY

This Spanish vargueño *has bone-fronted drawers and is decorated with architectural designs.*

the late Middle Ages. Decorative forms in Spanish art tend to be abstract, owing to the long-lasting influence of Moorish culture: interlacing, non-representational forms are frequent in ornament. In addition, Spanish furniture has since its earliest days been designed to relate to the interiors in which it was to be placed. During the sixteenth century the Spanish developed the idea that side-tables and cabinets-on-stands, as well as chairs, should be used in specific positions within a room to define its architectural space. This concept was to become central to the design and function of European Baroque furniture. The formal nature of Spanish interiors was further emphasized by the court fashion for black dress with the contrast of white. This fashion for using black and white together spread throughout Europe during the seventeenth century.

The small, portable document boxes of earlier periods continued to be made in the first years of the seventeenth century. Other forms of cabinet furniture included reliquaries, which were usually richly decorated with architectural motifs and lavish materials.

Side-cabinets developed from the medieval chest, being rectangular in shape and frequently decorated with carved geometric panels; often made of oak, with doors and iron fittings, side-cabinets were functional pieces of furniture.

The cabinet-on-stand, known since the nineteenth century as a *vargueño*, represents one of the major contributions of Spain to European furniture history. It could be placed on a carved stand or on top of another box-shaped cabinet to make a chest-on-chest. In the sixteenth century the *vargueño* was developed as a luxury item, and during the Baroque era became more widespread as a furniture type. In the seventeenth century *vargueños* continued to be made of wood, often of walnut. Many examples had decorative, pierced metal mounts on the exterior of the fall-front and a number of small drawers with decorated fronts of carved bone, ivory, or hardwoods. Early-seventeenth-century cabinets tended to have more abstract decoration; later in the century architectural motifs such as broken pediments, balustrading and Baroque twisted columns became more common. In the second half of the seventeenth century Spanish cabinet-makers, in response to developments in northern Europe, began to use ebony veneer with ivory and tortoiseshell.

The Spanish practice of arranging an interior with a rectangular side-table gave rise during the Baroque era to the European console table, a form which continued well into the nineteenth century. There are numerous examples of Spanish side-tables with turned legs and distinctive curved iron stretchers attached to the cross-bars between the front and back legs. Many of these examples seem to have been folding tables — easily transported along with *vargueños* and therefore functional items of furniture. They were made of oak, walnut or chestnut. One such side-table, now in the Victoria and Albert Museum, London, dates from the final quarter of the seventeenth century and is remarkable for its painted chinoiserie decoration, in colours and gilt, which seems to reflect the influence of Oriental lacquer design. To judge by its distinctive and delicately patterned ornament, this particular

FOLDING TABLE
WITH IRON
STRETCHERS, LATE
17TH CENTURY *(left)*

*The chinoiserie
decoration of this
Spanish table imitates
Oriental lacquer.*

CHESTNUT CHAIR,
*c.*1675 *(right)*

*This type of Portuguese-
style Spanish chair,
with its embossed
leather seat and back,
inspired English and
Dutch seat furniture at
the end of the century.*

table may have been designed with a specific interior scheme in mind.

Another form of side-table which was typical of seventeenth-century Spain had either boldly carved trestle supports at each end or four turned legs joined by stretchers; it also had an overhanging top and a long, horizontal silhouette. Often two good-sized drawers with pendent metal drawer-pulls would be included, the drawer-fronts being decorated with carved abstracted versions of European Mannerist strapwork. The continued use of Mannerist ornament in Baroque furniture, although found in all European countries, was particularly evident in northern Europe and the Iberian peninsula.

The typical early-seventeenth-century Spanish chair was severe and frontal in design, with squared or block-shaped uprights and horizontals and upholstered in simple leather bands which formed the seat and back; they are sometimes called 'monks' chairs', and examples can be seen in various Spanish Baroque paintings. A later and more sophisticated form of chair was directly inspired by Portuguese seat furniture. Its back, in the shape of a scrolled medallion or cartouche, was separated from the seat.

Often these chairs, made of chestnut and walnut, had a seat and back in embossed leather, which frequently came from Cordova, a city of southern Spain famous for its Moorish leather-work.

Later in the century French-style scrolled or gently curving arm-rests came into fashion, while pierced front stretchers, featuring scrolls and leaf-carving, were inspired by Portuguese crested decoration. The old form of Spanish and Portuguese legs, with turned decoration and twisted column forms, gave way to the newer combination of block and baluster forms. By the end of the century the influence of the Iberian peninsular on European furniture forms and decoration declined in favour of new decorative forms from the Netherlands and France.

The *contador* (or Portuguese cabinet-on-stand) consisted of an upright rectangular cabinet mounted on a stand which could have many legs and which might or might not have been made for the cabinet it supported. Elaborate *contadors*, with many small, locking drawers, were made during the second half of the seventeenth century; the fronts of the drawers were often decorated with a distinctive ripple-cut motif called

tremido carving. These *contadors* were executed in ebony or rosewood. Legs could be simple twisted-column supports, or saucer-like sections could be added to the legs and stretchers. This type of decoration later became popular in Spain.

Rosewood side-tables, in imitation of Spanish models, were made in Goa, Brazil and Portugal itself. Legs and stretchers were composed of bulb and saucer shapes made by turning the wood on a lathe. Portuguese craftsmen produced splendidly turned and decorated bedsteads, or *camas*, during the seventeenth century. An important example of this type of Portuguese furniture, thought to have been made by Portuguese craftsmen working in Spain, is now in the Museo de Artes Decorativas, Madrid.

Portugal had long-established trading links with the East, and a number of fascinating examples of seventeenth-century furniture were produced in Goa (Portuguese India). Ebony chairs made there were highly prized in Europe. Ebony was a luxury material which was imported into Europe from tropical countries either in its raw state or in the form of furniture that had been made in colonies such as Goa where there were skilled craftsmen. Ebony wood, being naturally dark in colour, was in keeping with the Baroque interest in dramatic contrasts of dark and light. Being a very hard wood, ebony can be polished to a high sheen and it is extremely durable; thus a surprising amount of this furniture has survived, although it is difficult to date precisely. Because of its hardness, ebony was usually carved in low relief in small-scale repeated geometric patterns that reflected Eastern influence. Goanese chairs are characterized by twisted-column legs and stretchers.

A typical feature of Portuguese furniture was the use of carefully arranged and richly carved vine and leaf scrolls. (These appeared

EBONY CABINET-
ON-STAND, *c.1675*
(left)

With its ebonized wood, pietre dure panels and agate columns, this Portuguese cabinet was inspired by contemporary Italian examples. The panels may even have been imported from Italy.

EBONY CHAIR,
SECOND HALF OF
THE 17TH CENTURY
(far left)

The legs and carving of this Indo-Portuguese chair demonstrate Portuguese forms rendered in an abstract, Eastern style.

around the seat-rails of Goanese chairs.)

A school of stylized but lively leaf-carving was developed in northern Portugal. At the top of the back of the Portuguese chairs these scrolls formed a rounded pyramid shape often referred to as 'cresting', perhaps because family crests were commonly carved here. Cresting and leaf-scrolls are two features of Portuguese furniture which were adopted by Dutch and British craftsmen during the seventeenth century.

THE
NETHERLANDS

In 1581 the seven United Provinces of the Netherlands – northernmost and Protestant – had declared themselves independent of Spanish rule; the ten southern provinces of the Netherlands remained under Spanish control. In these southern provinces was Antwerp, which during the seventeenth century continued to have a large export trade in art objects and luxury goods, including magnificent, showy furniture made from the exotic materials that were being imported from Africa and Asia. In due course Antwerp was replaced in importance by Amsterdam, which during the second half of the seventeenth century became the most important port in Europe

and the centre of world trade.

By the middle of the seventeenth century the Netherlands had emerged as an important area in terms of the production of furniture. By about 1640 Antwerp, in particular, had become famous for its lavish ebony- and tortoiseshell-veneered cabinets, which were exported all over Europe. Veneering and marquetry were used extensively by Netherlandish craftsmen, and towards the end of the century Dutch cabinet-makers working in Amsterdam were producing the most spectacular examples of pictorial floral marquetry.

The Spanish Netherlands

In Antwerp the production of Baroque cabinets as showpieces for the houses of the wealthy had by mid-century grown into a large industry. Before then craftsmen had

been veneering small box-like cabinets made out of ordinary woods like oak and pine with luxurious veneers of imported ebony: early (c.1620) examples are sometimes called 'table-cabinets', since they were made to rest upon separate side-tables or stands. Such cabinets usually had two doors which opened outwards to display highly decorative drawers or compartments.

By mid-century the small table-cabinets made in Antwerp had developed into spectacular cabinets-on-stands with ebony and tortoiseshell veneer and, often, no doors to cover the lavish decoration displayed on their fronts. Doors became less common on cabinets as the century progressed.

In many of these mid-seventeenth-century 'Antwerp cabinets' the drawer-fronts were decorated with large, convex oval shapes called bosses, a decorative motif associated with Mannerist ornament.

Many Flemish cabinets of the 1640s and 1650s had stands with six legs of ebonized wood (wood painted black to resemble ebony). An open, rectangular stretcher reinforced the legs, which rested on bulb- or bun-shaped feet. Later examples from the 1660s had carved stands with caryatid or supporting figures which were either wholly or partly gilded. Gilding could enhance the dark-light contrast that was so distinctive a feature of Baroque furniture.

A spectacular example of this later type of 'Antwerp cabinet', now in the Rijksmuseum, Amsterdam, has a stand with front-supports showing four carved and partly gilded black slaves. The slave trade was an unpleas-

ant fact of life during this period and 'blackamoors' appeared frequently in some types of furniture, such as ebony cabinets and ebonized and gilt *torchères*.

Lavish tables were made in Antwerp during the mid-seventeenth century. In many of them, only three sides were decorated, since the fourth side would be placed against a wall. Some tables were extremely colourful, with ivory, ebony and wood inlaid into a red tortoiseshell veneer. Tables of this

TORTOISESHELL AND EBONY CABINET-ON-STAND, MID-17TH CENTURY *(above)*

EBONY TABLE-CABINET, *c.*1625 *(top left)*

This Antwerp cabinet is made up of ebony veneer, ebonized wood and oil panels showing scenes from the life of Cupid.

BLACKAMOOR STAND, ANTWERP, *c.*1650 *(above left)*

type have been associated with the Flemish-born cabinet-maker Leonardo Van der Vinne (*fl.1662–93*), who was *marqueteur* in the Grand Ducal workshop of the Medici family in Florence between 1667 and 1693.

More common were tables made of carved oak for everyday use. Draw-leaf tables were popular because their tops could be enlarged by drawing out two leaves. Plates published by Crispin de Passe, son of a Utrecht cabinet-maker of the same name, illustrate draw-leaf tables among a number of other practical items of furniture. A number of these tables had large bulbous legs and an open, rectangular stretcher. A table of this type, with Mannerist 'cup-and-cover' supports and carved strapwork, can be seen in Peter Paul Rubens' house in Antwerp. The simple joined wood furniture used in humbler Netherlandish interiors is readily seen in the many genre paintings of artists such as Jan Steen.

During the Baroque era the seat furniture produced in the Spanish Netherlands remained largely similar to that from the northern Netherlands.

The United Provinces

Amsterdam's period of great wealth came after that of Antwerp and Dutch Baroque furniture developed its distinctive characteristics during the second half of the seventeenth century, after Flemish Baroque furniture had had its heyday.

Among the designs published in 1642 by Crispin de Passe the Younger was one for a cabinet sometimes known as a 'Utrecht' cabinet. De Passe had worked with his father in Utrecht before moving to Amsterdam in 1639; the name of the Utrecht cabinet may be a reflection of this. The cabinet is upright in shape and has attached columns, raised panels or bosses on the front drawers and spherical or bulbous feet. Usually these cabinets were made of contrasting rosewood with ebony veneer and had three large horizontal drawers. An alternative type featured two large hinged doors which opened outwards. Often blue-and-white pots were displayed across the top. The function of these cabinets was probably to store linens

and textiles for the household.

Dutch craftsmen expressed the regional fascination with nature, and spectacular translations of floral still-life painting began to appear in wood marquetry. A splendid floral marquetry cabinet-on-stand in the Rijksmuseum has been attributed to Jan van Mekeren (*fl.c.1690–c.1735*), a craftsman who was known to have had a large business in Amsterdam during the final years of the

seventeenth century. At least three other surviving examples of large floral marquetry cabinets-on-stands are thought to be his work. Just as the Forchont (also known as Fourchoudt) firm had earlier exported tortoiseshell and ebony cabinets from Antwerp, the van Mekeren firm exported floral marquetry cabinets to other European countries. The Dutch also collected 'Antwerp' cabinets, as illustrated in a painted interior by Hieronymus Jansen.

Floral marquetry was not confined to cabinets. Suites of furniture in the French manner consisting of side-tables flanked by two *torchères* were also made in floral marquetry. A richly decorated side-table (*c.1680*), adorned with floral marquetry in rosewood veneer, is in the Victoria and Albert Museum, London. It has baluster legs of Louis XIV type with tassel forms carved in wood and partly gilded. The most striking aspect of its design, however, is the use of black-and-white edging, made of ebonized

wood and ivory in a pattern resembling classical egg-and-dart moulding. There developed simultaneously a more Dutch type of table, featuring rich, naturalistic carving. A design for a table with legs in the form of large scrolls was published by Crispin de Passe the Younger as early as 1642, although it is much less richly carved than one example (*c.1680*) in the Rijksmuseum. This distinctively Dutch type of carving was reflected in

WALNUT TABLE, c.1640 (left)

With its simple, columnar legs and bulb feet, this Flemish table influenced contemporary French examples.

DUTCH INTERIOR SCENE, ATTRIBUTED TO PIETER DA HOOCH, c.1660–70 (above)

Note the use of the Oriental table carpet, the backstool and the Utrecht cabinet.

MARQUETRY CABINET-ON-STAND, ATTRIBUTED TO JAN VAN MEKEREN, c.1690 (left)

Van Mekeren's Amsterdam workshop produced floral marquetry of outstanding quality.

WALNUT CHAIR, c.1690 (right)

Rich carving on this Dutch chair suggests an important commission. The elongated back with pierced scrollwork and crested back-rail are in the manner of Daniel Marot.

Britain in the elaborate and often minutely detailed work of the renowned Grinling Gibbons (1648–1721), himself born in Rotterdam, and his imitators.

A variety of seat furniture was used for everyday use, including simple joined stools and 'backstools'. These are depicted in contemporary Dutch paintings, commonly with plain tan leather upholstery on the seat and a leather band across the back-frame of the chair. Owing to Portuguese influence, in the 1660s and 1670s new medallion-backed chairs became fashionable in the Netherlands and exotic woods such as ebony and rosewood began to be used.

More sumptuous seat and cabinet furniture developed during the final quarter of the seventeenth century after the arrival of the French Huguenot designer Daniel Marot (c.1663–1752), who had moved to the United Provinces after the Revocation of the Edict of Nantes in 1685. Marot was a nephew of the French court cabinet-maker

Pierre Golle (fl.1644–84) and brought the French court style of the 1670s to northern Europe. He worked for the Prince of Orange and his English wife, Mary, both before and after they ascended the English throne. He subsequently worked for them in Britain before settling in the United Provinces. Marot was conservative in his approach to design: he never adopted the Rococo style, instead working throughout his career in the style of Louis XIV's court. Thus, by the time that Marot's designs were fashionable in Holland and Britain, they were already becoming outdated in France.

The new style of seat furniture associated with Daniel Marot is illustrated by a group of chairs made of walnut with richly carved elongated backs, of c.1690. A wealth of sources is evident in the decoration of one of these chairs now in the Victoria and Albert Museum. Several features in the ornament refer back to Portuguese furniture of the 1660s and 1670s, such as the crested shape of

the back-rail and the profusion of controlled, deeply cut leaf-scrolls. The overall shape of the back is that of a pierced cartouche; in it is displayed a rather clumsily carved Renaissance-style bust framed by two 'C' scrolls. Elsewhere on the back are a large carved shell and bandwork reminiscent of sixteenth-century ornamental designs as reinterpreted by the French designer Jean Bérain (1640–1711), who worked for Louis XIV as Royal Designer from about 1679. The form of this chair's legs, with wooden tassel shapes, is likewise French in inspiration, but the feet, shaped like stylized chrysanthemum flowers, seem to represent an early instance of Western designs borrowing directly from Japanese forms. Despite the great mixing of sources evident in this design, the chair is unmistakably late seventeenth-century Dutch because of its elongated back (only British chairs were taller at this time), the rich use of naturalistic sources for the ornamental carving and its rather rigid upright silhouette.

THE GERMAN AND BALTIC STATES

As the United Provinces of the Netherlands grew wealthier during the seventeenth century, the German and Baltic states declined. Often, eastern European furniture displays a naïve 'folk' quality, now highly prized by some collectors. The sophisticated court furniture produced in Germany during the seventeenth century came chiefly from the south. Augsburg, a rich banking city until the end of the preceding century, had many fine craftsmen during the seventeenth century who produced magnificent cabinets in precious materials – as did the craftsmen in Würzburg and Munich.

The great exception to this regional decline was Sweden, which emerged as the most powerful nation in the Baltic area. Charles XI of Sweden, who came to the throne in 1655, particularly admired the autocratic style of government practised by Louis XIV of France, with its sensational programme of building and patronage that made Versailles the undisputed centre of European art and design during the final quarter of the seventeenth century. Charles XI sent a Swedish architect, Nicodemus Tessin the Elder (1615–81), to the French court to study the building of Versailles and to report on important artistic developments. The result was that, within the circle of the Swedish court, Baroque furniture worthy of Versailles was produced.

Like Sweden, Bavaria was an important regional centre during the seventeenth century. Indigenous forms of furniture, particularly richly veneered cabinets and large carved cupboards or *schränke*, continued to be made, exported and copied by the provincial cabinet-makers of other regions.

During the sixteenth century the cabinets made in southern Germany, especially those from Augsburg, were highly prized luxury items. Small cabinets veneered with ivory and amber, placed on a stand or a small table,

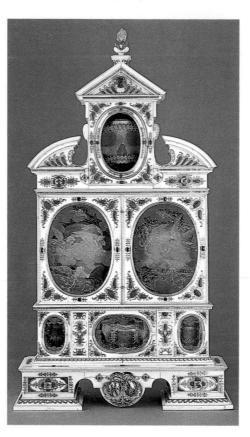

IVORY RELIQUARY CABINET, 1642

This cabinet was made in Munich and features gems, amber bosses and etched glass panels.

gave rise to the veneered seventeenth-century cabinet-on-stand. A beautiful reliquary cabinet, now in the Royal Residenz in Munich, was made in that city in 1642 and reflects the continuation of the cabinet-making tradition of Bavaria into the seventeenth century. It was veneered with ivory and decorated with gems and amber bosses set into scrolling gilt mounts which curiously suggest the Rococo style of the following century. The large oval panels on the front, decorated with angels, are of etched glass and through them one views the relics contained in the cabinet. The whole design is surmounted by a broken pediment with a projecting cupola, terminating in an urn on a pedestal decorated with angels.

Centralized, architecturally based designs are a consistent feature of Baroque cabinets, but German cabinets show the greatest interest in the use of materials. Flemish cabinets used rich combinations of tortoiseshell and ebony, but those from Germany in particular used every conceivable material available to the cabinet-maker, including glass.

In the middle of the seventeenth century the region of Egerland (now in Hungary) emerged as a centre of production for cabinets which had many drawers or compartments and a pair of exterior doors decorated with finely carved low-relief panels. These often showed allegorical figures such as the Four Seasons, a popular theme in contemporary Anglo-Dutch prints. At the less expensive end of the scale, Egerland exported large numbers of boxes and gaming pieces. Eger cabinets featured finely carved panels in hard, closely grained lustrous woods, notably box, with surrounding ripple-cut borders and sometimes with contrasting ebony veneer or ebonizing.

A German cabinet-on-stand with chinoiserie decoration, now in the Schloss Charlottenburg in Berlin and dating to c.1690, has japanned decoration on a white ground. It was made for Friedrich Wilhelm, the Elector of Brandenburg, and has been attributed to Gerhard Dagly (fl.c.1687–1714), Friedrich Wilhelm's Director of Ornaments. White or ivory cabinets were well established in Germany by the beginning of the seventeenth century. The Berlin cabinet had a simple coved top and two front doors which opened to reveal a central compartment surrounded by small drawers. The stand of this cabinet had twisted columnar legs and bulb feet, reinforced by an H-shaped stretcher with a central disc, on which a porcelain pot could be placed.

Undoubtedly the most typical form of furniture produced in the German and Baltic regions was the *schrank*, or cupboard, which could have a variety of storage functions. A number of finely carved walnut clothes-cupboards were made in southern Germany during the seventeenth and early eighteenth centuries. Some of these cupboards were boldy carved or painted in a strongly vernacular style. This group of furniture is perhaps closest in spirit to the Dutch Utrecht cabinets, or to French provincial armoires.

CABINET-ON-STAND, ATTRIBUTED TO GERHARD DAGLY, *c.*1690 *(left)*

Dagly worked in Berlin, specializing in japanned furniture.

SILVER TABLE, *c.*1690 *(below right)*

This Swedish table is based on the silver furniture designed for Versailles and seen by Swedish designer Nicodemus Tessin in 1687.

The influence of French furniture design became pronounced in this region during the last quarter of the century. A number of items of German furniture were decorated in a technique of metal marquetry known as Boulle work, named after André-Charles Boulle. German craftsmen made Boulle marquetry furniture with a brass veneer over a wood carcase, tortoiseshell and mother-of-pearl being inlaid into the brass sheet. Friedrich Luchtenstein of Düsseldorf was one craftsman working in this technique early in the eighteenth century.

In the countries of northern Europe the Baroque style lasted well into the eighteenth century. Partly responsible for this in Germany was the guild system of training cabinet-makers, since the guilds insisted that young craftsmen had to produce presentation pieces built according to traditional specifications. A remarkable example of this work was a late-Baroque cabinet, now in the Victoria and Albert Museum, which was made in 1716 by two journeymen in Würzburg, Jacob Arend from Koblenz and Johannes Wittelm from Vienna, both of whom were working as apprentice-journeymen for the court cabinet-maker Servatius Arend.

In about 1588 a Flemish designer, Hans Vredeman de Vries (1526–1604), published designs for tables and these were used by European cabinet-makers throughout the seventeenth century, particularly in the German and Baltic regions, where design tended to be more conservative. That the designs for these tables were derived from the sixteenth century is evident in their rectangular shapes, bulbous cup-and-cover legs and flat, open rectangular stretchers. The Mannerist cup-

OAK CENTRE
TABLE, c.1700

*This two-leaved
Russian table has an
inlaid top and ebonized
panels. A similar
example is in the
Hermitage, Leningrad.*

and-cover shape was a frequent feature of northern European furniture during the Baroque era. German examples could be made of woods like maple, which had a distinctive, marbled grain – in keeping with the Baroque craftsman's interest in rich textures. Sometimes these rectangular tables were hinged to reveal, for example, a well with gaming pieces for chess or backgammon.

Primitive but nonetheless fascinating examples of Baroque table furniture were made as far afield as Russia. Sophisticated designs from the major European centres were exported into relatively remote regions, where they could be executed by local craftsmen.

During the seventeenth century German and Baltic seat furniture tended to follow either French or Anglo-Netherlandish models. An engraving by Eric Graf Dahlberg, depicting the meeting of the kings of Denmark and Sweden in 1658, shows the royal families seated on upholstered and fringed backstools with arm-rests that are virtually indistinguishable from contemporary French and British examples. At the end of the century, the new Anglo-Netherlandish chair with a tall splat back derived from Chinese furniture found its way into northern Europe.

In Rosenborg Castle, Denmark, is a silver throne made in Augsburg in about 1715 for Frederick IV of Denmark. This throne chair has the elongated back, the domed top section and the loosely scrolled arm-rests

that might be expected in a French Baroque chair of 1700. However, the front legs of the throne consist of tapering fluted sections resting on two sphinx supports; the back section is surmounted by a coat of arms with the crown and two lions as supports.

ITALY

During the seventeenth century Italy, like the German states, comprised a region rather than a country. It was made up of semi-autonomous city-states, principalities and duchies; the country's highly regional character was reflected in its art. Venice, Rome and Naples were the important centres for the production of furniture. The vicinity of Rome was dominated by the Vatican and the authority of the Catholic Church: Roman design reflected the city's classical heritage. Southern Italy – including Naples and Sicily – was under Spanish control until the middle of the century: Spanish influence was evident most notably in the black-and-white cabinets produced in Naples for the Spanish aristocracy. The region of Piedmont and its largest city, Turin, had close ties with neighbouring France: northern Italian furniture frequently used French models. The remnant of Floren-

tine and Venetian wealth of the early Renaissance lingered on: in Florence the Grand Duke of Tuscany patronized workshops where magnificent inlaid panels of stone called *pietre dure* were produced and shipped throughout Europe for use in furniture.

By 1600 Neapolitan craftsmen were making magnificent ebony and ivory cabinets for well-off Spanish patrons. The severe contrast of black against white suited Spanish Baroque taste, since it was the fashion of the Spanish court to dress in black. A splendid example of a Neapolitan cabinet made of ebony and engraved ivory panels in the Spanish style, now in the Victoria and Albert Museum, has the form of a rectangular box and black-and-white decoration of architectural character.

By the middle of the century the ebony cabinets made in Naples had become larger in size and were made with accompanying stands or supporting lower sections. Table-cabinets were less common after mid-century. Two ebony cabinets made in Naples around 1650 are now in the collection of the Palazzo Barberini in Rome. Although they retain a strongly architectural character, the influence of Flemish design is evident in the use of both tortoiseshell veneer to contrast with the ebony and painted panels to decorate the drawer-fronts. Flemish design is equally evident in the cabinets produced in Florence in the middle of the seventeenth century. These ebony-veneered cabinets-on-stands had elaborate arrangements of small drawers and compartments in which precious or collectible objects could be kept. Florence had become the production centre for inlaid stone panels (*pietre dure*); these panels often featured stylized scenes of birds or flowers, and were exported from Florence in great numbers as luxury objects. Often *pietre dure* panels were mounted on the fronts of ebony cabinets-on-stands. It is indicative of the status of Flemish craftsmen at this time that the Grand Ducal workshop in Florence, where *pietre dure* was produced, was run by a Fleming, Leonardo Van der Vinne (*fl.*1662–93). This workshop was patronized by the powerful Medici family.

It was in the area of tables, seats and decorative carving that seventeenth-century

Italian craftsmen excelled. In Turin a splendid Baroque room, the Audience Chamber in the Palazzo Reale, demonstrates the phenomenal skill of Italian carvers. It was designed and executed between 1659 and 1663. In this chamber is one of the Palazzo Reale's many carved and gilded side-tables made during the final quarter of the seventeenth century which displays the influence of contemporary French court furniture, most notably in the use of pilaster-like legs with exaggerated bulging sections in the basic form of Ionic volutes.

These richly carved Turin side-tables form an interesting contrast to a side-table in the Palazzo Spada, Rome, which features two large carved eagles, wings outspread, as supports for a marble top. A number of these Roman tables seem to have been made at the end of the century and their impressive but austere design inspired the British eighteenth-century Palladian designers. Around 1700 a new type of side-table emerged in Rome which was richly carved and gilded and ornamented with vigorous but carefully controlled leaf-scrolls and classical masks.

Frames for paintings and looking-glasses constituted an important aspect of the carver's trade in Baroque Italy. In the Palazzo Brignole, Genoa, are a fantastic three-dimensional pier-table and looking-glass, carved as one, with putti, leaf-scrolls and shells. They have been dated to about 1700

WRITING-TABLE, *c.1700 (above)*

Inlaid with ivory and illustrated with hunting scenes, this Piedmontese table takes its form from the French writing-bureau.

EBONY CABINET-ON-STAND, GIOVANNI BATTISTA FOGGINI, 1707–9 *(left)*

This Florentine cabinet has pietre dure *panels, gilt-bronze mounts and red marble pilasters. Foggini trained as a sculptor in Rome.*

EBONY, IVORY AND PALISANDER WOOD TABLE CABINET, *c.1600 (above left)*

This piece is attributed to Giacomo Fiammingo, a Fleming working in Naples, possibly for a Spanish patron.

and attributed to the sculptor Domenico Parodi. Looking-glasses were considered luxurious additions to the Baroque interior, since glass was very expensive. In Murano, the glass-making centre in Venice's Lagoon, a number of decorative looking-glasses were produced for export.

One of the most outstanding carvers that Italy produced was a Venetian, Andrea Brustolon (1662–1732). He carved a wide variety of furniture, including frames, tables and a famous stand carved for the Palazzo Venier, made of ebony and boxwood and depicting a blackamoor standing on a tripod base that had three dragons. However, it is as a maker of seat furniture that Brustolon has become most famous. In the 'Brustolon Room' of the Ca' Rezzonico, Venice, are examples of the armchairs he carved around 1700 of boxwood and other hardwoods in a vigorous, organic matter which antici-pates somewhat the later Rococo style. In

CARVED AND GILT THRONE-CHAIR, ATTRIBUTED TO ANTONIO CORRADINI, c.1720

overall shape, Italian seat furniture at the end of the seventeenth century showed the influence of French forms but, in the boldly carved frames of these throne-like armchairs, Italian furniture-makers diverged radically from their French counterparts.

FRANCE

During the seventeenth century French mercantile power and gen-eral prosperity were considerable. Henry IV had enacted the Edict of Nantes in 1598 which, generally, provided freedom of worship for Protestants. The population of France was large – about three times that of Britain and four times that of the Dutch United Provinces. The market for goods was likewise potentially large. France was thus prosperous and stable in 1661 when the young Louis XIV came to the throne. Two dates in Louis XIV's reign were of special importance for the arts. In 1666 the French Academy in Rome was founded by the government minister Jean-Baptiste Colbert. The Academy sent French artists to study in Italy and thereby strengthened the ties between these two Catholic countries. More important, though, was the fact that in 1685 Louis revoked the Edict of Nantes, which resulted in an exodus of Protestant mer-chants and craftsmen to other countries, especially to the Netherlands and Britain.

The furniture created in France during the reign of Louis XIV is often considered the quintessential Baroque furniture, and the forms established in the Gobelins workshops by the court designers influenced all of Europe. It must be remembered, however, that a surprising number of the craftsmen and designers working at the French court were foreign-born. Thus the great Baroque furni-ture created in France under Louis XIV is international in character and inspiration.

The French word for cabinet-maker is ébéniste – literally meaning someone who works with ebony, a material introduced into Western furniture-making by the skilled craftsmen of Spain, Portugal and, most

importantly, the Spanish Netherlands.

French cabinet furniture in the first half of the seventeenth century showed the unmis-takable influence of Flemish designers, most notably in the adoption of ebony-veneered cabinets-on-stands to replace the older armoires à deux corps which were popular in the previous century. A number of ebony cabinets-on-stands, based on Flemish mod-els, were made in Paris between about 1640 and 1660; examples of these are in the Louvre, the Victoria and Albert Museum and the Danish castle of Frederiksborg. The name of Jean Macé (fl.c.1640–60) has been associ-ated with the cabinet in the Victoria and Albert Museum. Macé, a Frenchman, trained in Antwerp before settling in Paris in the early 1640s and, by 1644, he had been granted a workshop in the Palais du Louvre. He is known to have made ebony furniture for Anne of Austria, the Regent for the young Louis XIV. The Victoria and Albert Museum's cabinet was decorated with ripple-cutting and polygonal medallions skilfully carved in low relief to show classical scenes from the myth of Endymion.

Such French ebony cabinets-on-stands can be distinguished from Flemish examples by the fact that they are entirely black, no tortoiseshell or contrasting materials having been used. Also, French decoration of this date tended to be more restrained and less three-dimensional than that found on popu-lar Flemish furniture.

In 1663 the Gobelins workshops were founded by Colbert to produce the furniture and other decorative objects required for the series of spectacular residences which were being prepared for the new king, most notably Versailles. In 1682 Versailles was finally ready to receive the French court. The designer Charles Le Brun (1619–90) was appointed first director of the royal manufac-tory at Gobelins. The chief furniture designer was Jean Le Pautre (1618–82), a Parisian engraver, and it is primarily through the many engraved designs Le Pautre published that we know about the sumptuous Baroque furniture and interiors he created.

Le Pautre may have provided the inspira-tion for a group of remarkable marquetry cabinets-on-stands which feature boldly carved three-dimensional figures in various attitudes supporting upper structures composed of many small drawers richly decorated. The larger pair of these cabinets features muscular, turned figures in blowing drapery, while the smaller two rest on frontally placed term figures. Once thought to have been the work of André-Charles Boulle (1642–1732), the group is now sometimes attributed to Pierre Golle (fl.1644–84), a Dutch craftsman and *marqueteur* who was in the Louvre workshops by 1644. There has been speculation as to whether Boulle developed his famous metal marquetry under Golle's tutelage at the Gobelins workshops. Certainly metal marquetry appeared in Flemish furniture of the third quarter of the seventeenth century, and Golle and Domenico Cucci (1635–c.1705) both used the technique in the furniture they produced for the French court. However, it was Boulle's genius for this technique which

INTERIOR OF DRUMLANRIG CASTLE, FEATURING MARQUETRY CABINET-ON-STAND, ATTRIBUTED TO PIERRE GOLLE, c.1675 *(above)*

With tortoiseshell, gilt-bronze mounts and ebonized and gilt figures, this cabinet is believed to have been a present from Louis XIV to Charles II of England.

EBONY CABINET-ON-STAND, ATTRIBUTED TO JEAN MACÉ, c.1640 *(left)*

The interior of this Parisian cabinet is composed of stained-wood marquetry. The exterior is carved with scenes from the novel L'Endymion *of 1624.*

ENGRAVED DESIGN, JEAN LE PAUTRE, c.1675 *(above)*

developed a distinctive type of decoration that is still known today as Boulle marquetry. Simply defined, Boulle work features designs cut out of brass and pewter and inlaid into a tortoiseshell-veneered panel, often framed by ebony veneer.

Boulle was born in Paris, the son of a Flemish cabinet-maker whose surname was probably spelled 'Bol'. In 1672 he received the important position of *ébéniste du Roi*, and was thereby entitled to accommodation in the Louvre. Eight plates of designs by him were published in the 1720s by the French publisher Mariette; subsequently they were published in Nuremberg, and then several times during the nineteenth century when Boulle work was much admired and copied. His early furniture seems to have demonstrated the heavy, formal style of Le Pautre. Boulle later came under the influence of the court designer Jean Bérain and he began to design more delicate marquetry, decorated with the new, lighter arabesques which foreshadowed the Rococo. Boulle retired in 1718, but a disastrous fire in 1720 destroyed most of his possessions and so he seems to have returned to work, probably with his sons, who themselves produced furniture until the middle of the eighteenth century under the name 'Boulle fils'.

Despite his reputation, only two items of furniture can be certainly assigned to Boulle: a pair of magnificent commodes, now in Versailles, which were made about 1708–9 for the Grand Trianon. These commodes have a distinctive, rounded coffer shape, their four legs have gilt-bronze winged-female terms with lion-paw feet. Only slightly less certain in its attribution to Boulle is a group of armoires in ebony and tortoiseshell veneer with brass and pewter inlay and gilt-bronze mounts. Several examples are in the Musée du Louvre, Paris, and a simpler and more restrained example is in the Jones Collection of the Victoria and Albert Museum and another in the Wallace Collection, London. These cabinets almost certainly date from the early years of the eighteenth century.

Before the advent of the sumptuous Baroque furniture produced at the Gobelins workshops, French interiors had featured fairly simple furniture, designed according to the geometry of the cube and made rich by the use of expensive textiles. For example, designs published by the Parisian Jean du Breuil in the middle of the century showed simple joined wood tables of rectangular shape with simple columnar legs, an open rectangular stretcher and bulb feet – a type of table which clearly derived from the Hispano-Netherlandish side-table of the first half of the seventeenth century. For a rich effect, such tables could be entirely covered by a textile, as illustrated in du Breuil's book. *Perspective Pratique* of 1649. These observations apply equally well to the block-like beds illustrated by du Breuil. During the first part of the seventeenth century, in more modest Baroque interiors, beds might be in almost any room of a house, since their heavy curtains ensured a degree of privacy for their occupants.

Later in the century, tables became more sumptuous, reflecting the influence of the new court taste. A richly carved and gilded side-table (c. 1680) in the Hôtel Lauzun, Paris, displays features of Netherlandish Baroque design, most notably in the use of naturalistic flower garlands and swaying female term

EBONY ARMOIRE, ATTRIBUTED TO ANDRÉ-CHARLES BOULLE, c.1700 (above left)

This armoire is one of a pair and is decorated with tortoiseshell and metal marquetry including figures representing Wisdom and Religion.

EBONY COMMODE, ANDRÉ-CHARLES BOULLE, 1708–9 (above)

This commode is one of a pair made in the Gobelins workshops.

supports on scrolled brackets. Elegant little side-tables made in Boulle marquetry began to appear at the beginning of the eighteenth century. One example, formerly in the collection of the Duchesse de Talleyrand, had a veneer of tortoiseshell coloured green with inlaid brass arabesques and figures clearly derived from the designs of Bérain – the legs had the form of double-scrolled brackets resting on a curved H-shaped stretcher.

Another form of table developed during the later seventeenth century, possibly at Gobelins, was the so-called 'Bureau Mazarin'. These did not appear until after the death of Cardinal Mazarin (1661), but the term is sometimes used to mean a writing-desk with drawers, a central kneehole section and a central locking drawer supported on scrolled bracket legs with a variation of the H shaped stretchers and inverted baluster feet. During the 1680s a group of these luxurious writing-tables was made in brass and tortoiseshell.

Small stands were an important part of the Baroque interior, particularly for the placement of candles. Baroque stands commonly had a tripod base with scrolled bracket feet, a baluster-shaped central support, and a small round or polygonal top. Jean Le Pautre is

credited with creating the French Baroque 'ensemble', composed of a side table with a matching mirror flanked on either side by two stands, designed *en suite*. The proximity of a mirror to stands with candles would help to magnify the light in an interior.

The state bed and state bedchamber represent an important aspect of Baroque furniture and interiors. They developed around the rituals of kingship created for the court of Louis XIV. The Baroque concept of state apartments is almost incomprehensible to the twentieth-century observer, since it involved great expenditure on a sequence of rooms which were essentially non-functional but contained the most lavish furnishings of a Baroque residence. State apartments were intended primarily to impress and were rarely used, a fact that may have helped ensure their survival, together with much of their furniture.

The simple cubic proportions of beds of the first half of the seventeenth century gave way, during the final quarter of the century, to spectacular carved and draped beds which were taller and more imposing in silhouette. Swags of drapery resembling clouds decorated the testers of a type of French Baroque

CARVED AND GILTWOOD ARMCHAIR, *c.*1700 *(below)*

This example displays typical late-Baroque legs and scrolled arm-rests, the tall back indicating a turn-of-the-century date.

METAL MARQUETRY WRITING-BUREAU, *c.*1685 *(left)*

The tortoiseshell used on this piece is backed with various pigments. The arms are those of the di Porcia family of Milan.

ENGRAVED DESIGNS, JEAN DU BREUIL, 1649 *(left)*

These designs show the importance of geometry to early seventeenth-century interiors.

CHERRY MAHOGANY (BRAZILIAN
BULLETWOOD) ARMCHAIR, c.1617 (right)

*This piece bears the arms of Nicholas Roope of
Dartmouth, England, who imported the batch of
timber from which it was made from the Amazon.*

OAK CHEST, EARLY
17TH CENTURY
(right)

*This elaborate middle-
class chest uses elements
of Franco-Italian
Classicism in a purely
English manner.*

state bed called a *lit d'ange*, literally an angel's
bed. One such example was sketched by the
Swedish architect Nicodemus Tessin during
a visit to France in 1687.

French seat furniture in the first half of the
seventeenth century consisted primarily of
joined wooden stools and backstools, both
designed according to the proportions of the
cube, with simple upholstered seats and
separate upholstered backs. Unless in use,
these were formally arranged against a wall
of the room. X-frame stools (*tabourets*) were
also used. In the 1660s a type of armchair
evolved which became the classic French
Baroque chair. The arched or rectangular
backs and the seats of these were upholstered
and usually fringed, with a pair of loosely
scrolled arm-rests and scrolled bracket or
upright carved legs as well as some variant of
the H-shaped stretcher. Slightly later, legs in
the form of obelisks or flat-sided columns
began to be fashionable and, by the turn of
the eighteenth century, backs had become
taller although curves had begun to overtake
the outline, particularly on the back. Wooden
frames could be either entirely gilded or
left plain.

BRITAIN

The power and character of the Elizabethan age lasted long after Elizabeth's death in 1603. There was little
detectable change in furniture during the
reign of James I of England, VI of Scotland,
although the ground was laid for some
profound developments. The reign of
James's son, Charles I, was illuminated by the
work of the architect Inigo Jones (1573–
1652). Jones studied in Italy with the great
collector Lord Arundel and returned home
with a deep insight into the work of Andrea
Palladio. Jones became Surveyor of the
King's Works in 1615. His buildings, especially the Queen's House at Greenwich
(begun in 1616, but not developed until
1629–35) and the Banqueting House at
Whitehall (1619–22), were novel to the
British, involving previously unencountered
classical planning and detail.

Jones was responsible for other radical
buildings (most no longer extant) and for
developing their interiors for use by Charles I
and the court. He had an early training as a
joiner, and a few drawings survive with
designs for furniture, mostly large and elaborate cabinets, but we do not know whether
these were ever made. Indeed, it is not clear
how his pristine Italianate rooms were actually furnished. Some grand pieces were
imported from Europe: the inventories of
Charles I, compiled at his death in 1649, are
rich with continental pieces in fine materials
such as giltwood and marble.

In looking for suitable English-made
equivalents of the Jonesian style of furnishing we find likely candidates in the form of a
group of furniture loosely associated with
Archbishop Laud. Laud commissioned a
number of works at Lambeth Palace (including the recently restored Chapel Screen) and
his Oxford college of St John's. These are
clearly in sympathy with the aesthetic pur-
sued at Greenwich and Whitehall. One
cabinet is very similar to another now at
Arbury Hall which bears Laud's coat of arms
while he was Bishop of London (1628–33)
and is remarkable in Britain for its date, in
terms of both its continental-type construction (dovetailed boards with carved and
applied decoration) and its clear Palladian

ENGRAVED DESIGN FOR A CUPBOARD,
JOHANN JAKOB EBELMANN, PUBLISHED BY
JOHANN BUSSEMACHER, 1598 (left)

DETAIL OF OAK
CUPBOARD,
c.1628–33 (left)

*The cartouche frames on
these doors are copied
from the German
engraving (far left)
although the general
form owes more to
Palladianism.*

OAK GATE-LEG
TABLE, c.1660 (below)

*This table, with a ball-
turned frame, is recorded
in the inventory of
Colonel Richard Pickering
of Willow House,
Darton, Yorkshire.*

OAK TESTER BEDSTEAD, c.1612 (left)

*This bed, now in Montacute House, has intricately
carved and painted Mannerist decoration. It was
made for a Devon family and bears the royal arms of
James I, his son Henry, Prince of Wales and
Frederick, Count Palatine of the Rhine.*

inspiration. Even here, though, there is an element of English compromise and opportunism, for the two elaborate frames on the doors are taken with minimum adaptation from a German pattern-book published about thirty years previously in 1598.

These German designs, by Johann Jakob Ebelmann, were part of a series published by Johann Bussemacher of Cologne. Many designs in the series were a source of inspiration to the 'Laudian' group. They made free use of the architectural themes which were becoming the stuff of the Baroque, combining classical columns, pilasters and arches with anthropomorphic supports, fantastic strapwork, carved bands, scroll brackets, cartouche panels and elaborate crestings. But, as always, the British version is characterized by a balance and restraint often lacking in continental versions. A drawing for a cabinet by Inigo Jones, now in the Radcliffe Library, Oxford, reveals a familiarity with the same designs.

A further indication of the growing influence of foreign craftsmen in London was the construction by indigenous makers of dovetailed boards. This technique, despite a long history on the Continent, had never previously been favoured by British joiners. The trade companies were still able to keep the 'strangers' at arm's length, but the talented craftsmen from abroad were set to erode the monopolies of the Englishmen.

The reign of Charles I was marked by a new spirit of artistic patronage. Charles presided over a brilliant and sophisticated court, and sent his agents abroad to acquire single works and whole collections of paintings, sculpture and furniture to decorate his palaces. Artists came from Italy, France and the Low Countries to work on interiors, and woodwork took on a more successful architectural character, generally in a more restrained manner than that proposed in the pattern-books. Panels of much larger sizes than before became frequent, although they were still broken up by applied surface ornament and shallow three-dimensional devices such as the cartouche frame and the perspective arch.

Except in the more conservative areas of the country, where the old exuberance of

OAK SIDEBOARD, c.1665–85 (left)

This East Anglian table is of unusual design, displaying strong Dutch influence. It also reveals close parallels with a contemporary group made by East Anglian settlers in Essex County, Massachusetts.

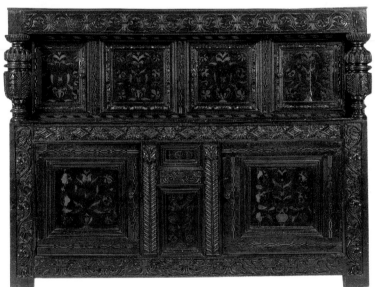

OAK PRESS CUPBOARD WITH INLAY, c.1675 (left)

The earlier fashion for German-style inlaid decoration persisted in the more conservative areas of northern England, as this cupboard from Halifax, Yorkshire, demonstrates.

Elizabethan taste persisted, the zest for elaborate carving declined considerably. A more sophisticated restraint was shown, plain and ornamented surfaces being contrasted and laid out with a keen sense of harmony and proportion. Flat areas could be divided and articulated by schemes of applied mouldings mitred together. Another device which became increasingly popular was to split a small turned spindle down its vertical axis and then glue the flat backs of the resulting halves to a plane surface such as a panel or joint-block. The decorative impact of these turned elements was often emph-

asized by painting them black, in imitation of ebony. In short, the detailing of furniture was starting to reflect the influence of Dutch styles, a tendency which later became even more obvious.

The changing tastes were accompanied by a further expansion in the range of furniture types, reflecting a preference for more intimate social conventions. Upholstered furniture came into more common use; it was covered with textiles or leather, the chairs and backstools typically with low square backs and the armchairs with scrolled wooden arms, or with straight arms padded and covered to match. Settles or settees appeared *en suite* with armchairs, and some inventories list dozens of matching stools.

Joiner-made panelled backstools, in sets for use at the dining-table, started to appear, and a variety of presses and livery cupboards were made for use in the dining-parlour, supplemented by small side-tables and candlestands on cruciform feet.

The Civil War and the Interregnum

Much of the artistic and technical progress achieved under Charles I was severely interrupted by the Civil War, which started in 1642. The future Charles II escaped to Paris and then Brussels, leaving England in the hands of Oliver Cromwell. The Puritans introduced a number of reforms aimed at encouraging a sobriety in cultural life, such as closing the theatres, but it would be wrong to think that a complete cultural embargo hung over Britain during the period of the war and the Interregnum.

In 1646 Inigo Jones was pardoned for having previously associated with royalty. He worked with his pupil John Webb (1611–72) for the parliamentarian Lord Pembroke on the influential new interiors at Wilton House, including the double-cube room.

Neither was extravagant ornament restricted to buildings. A great deal of brightly-coloured needlework survives from this time, including table-boxes, pictures and mirror frames. A distinctive group of chests-of-drawers dates from the 1640s and 1650s; they have vibrant decoration comprising inlays in bone and mother-of-pearl. Both the decoration and the form were innovative; the few drawers known from before this date were usually plain-fronted and hidden behind doors, but in most of this group the fronts of the chests were exposed to view and served as the vehicles for the decoration.

The Restoration

Charles II returned from exile in 1660. His travels in France and the Low Countries had reinforced his appreciation of continental styles, and the new court encouraged a revolution in English taste.

House-plans were developing rapidly, with the rules of symmetry and harmony gaining precedence, as was a simpler taste for large fielded panelling for rooms. Social life became much more informal, and a new appreciation of gaiety, luxury and creative

OAK BACKSTOOL, CANDLESTAND AND GLASS SHELF, ALL LATE 17TH CENTURY

Furniture and accessories of this kind are recorded in enormous numbers in ordinary English household inventories of this period.

enjoyment opened the way to further novelties in furniture. Walnut became the preferred wood for a much wider social group, and other timbers such as cherry, cedar, olive, yew and laburnum were favoured for their rich graining and high polish. The expansion of trade interests made imported furniture more readily available. A new influx of craftsmen from Europe brought with them novel forms and techniques, such as veneering, spiral turning, bun feet and the Chinese idea of caning for the seats and backs of chairs. This latter style arrived in 1664 and was immediately in fashionable demand.

Gate-leg dining-tables were first mentioned by Samuel Pepys in 1660, and the convention of dining at a long table quickly gave way to a new fashion for eating in intimate groups of six or eight persons at gate-leg tables, with as many as eight or ten tables in a large room. Small folding tables, designed for occasional use and easy storage, likewise proliferated.

Purpose-built dressing-tables, glazed bookcases, writing-bureaux, bureau-bookcases and long-case clocks all made their first appearance at this time. Case furniture was now enlivened by the use of brass rather than wrought-iron hardware.

In 1665 London was still a great medieval city of timber-framed buildings. The houses were mostly cramped, insanitary and inefficient, difficult to modernize for new tastes, and land for redevelopment within the City

skills from those offered by the joiner and the turner, and rich patronage looked elsewhere. Instead of the visible structures of rectangular framed-panel construction, the new taste demanded the suave, smooth surfaces offered by the cabinet-maker and his dovetailed boards. These surfaces could be defined by mouldings and enriched with a choice of two-dimensional all-over finishes which were not constrained by the forms of

was almost impossible to come by. Then, in 1666, came the Great Fire of London. In addition to 13,000 houses, a great many churches and public buildings were destroyed, including St Paul's Cathedral, the Royal Exchange, the Guildhall and the halls of many City companies, as well as most of fashionable London. If the importance and prestige of the capital were to be maintained, these buildings and their contents would have to be replaced and improved all within a few short years.

The opportunity was not to be missed. The Great Rebuilding Act of 1667 provided revolutionary new conditions for the crafts to get on with the work of creating anew the

world's greatest city. The Act permitted 'stranger' craftsmen to work in London for seven years entirely free of the old restrictions imposed by the trade companies, and further granted freeman rights thereafter for life to any artificer who took full advantage of this ruling. In 1669, under the same Act, the architect Christopher Wren (1632–1723) was appointed Surveyor General of the King's Works.

As the process of rebuilding continued, the London furniture-making trades entered a gradual and inevitable period of change, as profound as the reorganization experienced a century before, although the companies survived. High fashion demanded different

the structural framing. The continental skills of quartered veneering and floral marquetry became freely available in London and, inspired by imports of Chinese and Japanese lacquer wares, japanning began a return to favour, along with other Chinese ideas such as the splat-back chair, the 'bended-back' chair and the cabriole leg.

The upholders also benefited from the increase in trade during this time. They and the cabinet-making trade emerged in a powerful position in 1675. The carvers — boosted by the popularity of Grinling Gibbons (1648–1721), who was 'discovered' in 1671 — allied with the cabinet-makers, and an associated trade, that of the separate chair-maker, began to emerge. The cabinet-makers were seen as specializing in providing case furniture, tables and stands whereas the joiners provided architectural woodwork and domestic necessities such as bedsteads and the cheaper forms of 'wainscot' furniture. The stage was now set for the appearance of the integrated firms of 'Cabinet-makers & Upholsterers', who came to dominate the trades during the eighteenth century.

success without being ostentateous. Cabriole-legged chairs, no longer needing stretchers, might be embellished with a little carving or they might rely on the graceful curves of their backs and legs for their decorative appeal. Claw-and-ball or pad feet were most usual, while seats were often drop-in.

Case furniture was as functional as it was elegant. The earlier chest-on-stand had evolved into the bureau-cabinet. The upper

THE UNITED STATES

English settlement in North America took many years to establish itself. No permanent colony survived until Jamestown was founded in Virginia in 1607 and the arrival thereafter of the Pilgrim

WALNUT-VENEERED COLLECTOR'S CABINET, c.1700 (left)

The upper cabinet is fitted with forty-four drawers, some hidden behind the central door, and is designed to house a collection of curiosities.

OAK ARMCHAIR, c.1675 (right)

Made in Essex County, Massachusetts, this chair owes much to English design, but it is nevertheless one of a distinct American group.

William and Mary

Dutch influence on English furniture had been strong for decades when William and Mary arrived from Holland in 1688, bringing with them the designer Daniel Marot. His chief impact was on beds and their hangings and, through them, on the development of upholstery. The Flemish designer, Gerret Jensen, had already established royal patronage and continued to create his distinctive marquetry pieces for William and Mary.

At this time, England enjoyed a period of relative peace and prosperity and the newly-affluent middle classes favoured a simple, elegant style that declared their worldly

stages of the grandest examples had two doors enclosing various arrangements of shelves and drawers and terminated in domes or pediments. Beneath the upper sections were fall-front writing-bureaux with drawers beneath.

Convenience spawned many smaller pieces of furniture, such as the kneehole writing-desk, reflecting the growing preference for more intimate surroundings.

Tables were equally varied and made for a multitude of purposes. Walnut remained the preferred wood, but oak continued to be used, especially in rural areas. For luxury pieces, decorative effects were achieved with oyster or burr veneers.

Fathers at Plymouth, Massachusetts in 1620.

In Virginia, little attempt was made during the seventeenth century to establish any degree of self-sufficiency or autonomy. The plantation-owning classes turned to England for many of their furnishings and luxuries. Indeed, the production of sophisticated goods was hampered by English law, and the rural economy failed to throw up any towns of consequence. The colony was then made up of the usual crew of agents, adventurers, mercenaries and other entrepreneurs, manipulating a labour force of native and criminal slaves and usually channelling all the profits back to the old country.

New England, though, was different. It

Oak chest-of-drawers, Essex County, Massachusetts, 1678 *(left)*

Oak chest, Connecticut, late 17th century *(below)*

was unique among the English colonies of this period in that, from the first, the population consisted almost entirely of ordinary men, women and children who had come to build a new society for themselves. The settlers were a mixture of ambitious and under-privileged farmers, craftsmen and small merchants, mostly trying to escape from disadvantage or religious oppression.

Pilgrim Furniture

The early myths about furniture being brought from England on the *Mayflower* and other ships are just that – myths. Chests were used for storage and packing, but otherwise there was little space on these early vessels to carry furniture. It was far more efficient to carry a craftsman and his box of tools.

Turners in particular had the prospect of a bright future in the New World, since they were able to work with green (unseasoned) timber; this goes a long way to explaining the popularity of turned chairs in the early colonies. Joiners, on the other hand, needed a store of dry seasoned timber for proper use, and such stocks could not be built up quickly.

The virgin timber forests were one of the great bonuses waiting for the settlers to exploit. Some woods, like white oak and American ash, were familiar but others, such as red oak and hickory, were not. All were available in the wide boards which had long since disappeared in Europe.

In 1642 the joiner Edward Johnson noted that the Massachusetts towns were fast turning into civilized communities, and that the 'wigwams, huts and hovels the English dwelt in at their first coming' had been transformed into 'orderly, fair and well-built houses, well-furnished many of them'. These houses were constructed in the image of the timber-framed and weather-boarded farmhouses of eastern England, with plastered smoke-hoods, brick chimneys and clapboard panelling to keep out the harsh New England winters. Their furniture likewise closely followed the styles of provincial England, using the same construction and motifs of decoration. Boston, however, was only a few weeks' sailing away from the advanced stylistic influence of London, and here social manners and domestic arrangements largely paralleled those in England. As

one might expect, the traditional styles persisted rather longer in the small ports and townships in areas such as Essex County (north of Boston), Plymouth and New Haven.

That these areas were initially English provinces is reflected in the furniture produced in them before 1675. A group from Essex County, for example, is very clearly derived from a parent style found in South Devon, England, using complex leafy patterns set within arches. The transmission of this style can probably be traced to the joiner William Searle, who was trained in Ottery St Mary, South Devon, and who by 1663 was working in Ipswich, Massachusetts, making chests and chairs in the style he had learned at home. In 1668 another joiner, Thomas Dennis, moved to Ipswich and married William Searle's widow. He continued to make very similar pieces.

The New Haven furniture does not exhibit the same excellent quality as the Essex County pieces, but their carved patterns are likewise clearly derived from models prevalent in the English West Country and East Anglia, the areas which were the main sources of emigration to New England.

As colonization spread northwards along the Connecticut River, second-generation joiners developed their own styles of carved details which increasingly owed less and less to specific British originals. Although the distinctive and simple scheme of tulip heads and leaves found in a group of chests and boxes from the area around Hadley, Massachusetts, has some parallel in England, another group of chests and press cupboards from around Wethersfield, Connecticut, bears a sunflower motif and exaggerated split turnings in a form which seems to be truly original to the colony.

These trends were already pointing towards the period after 1675, when North American furniture began to escape from the close ties of its English roots, when Boston consolidated its importance, and when centres linked by the coastal trade each developed their own special forms of cabinet-making and decoration.

When Charles II came to the British throne, new design ideas survived from Europe: late-Mannerist and early-Baroque notions from France and the Netherlands affected British taste and, thereby, North American taste during the first quarter of the eighteenth century. On her marriage to Charles II in 1662, Catherine of Braganza brought with her Portuguese and Goanese furniture as part of her dowry, providing popular models for contemporary furniture designers. Increased trade with China led to a vogue for Oriental styles, including chinoiserie decoration. In 1689, further new concepts were introduced by William and Mary. Traditional heavy oak furniture gave way to lighter and more elegant designs. The new style, Mannerist in approach, emphasized taller and more attenuated furniture forms.

William and Mary, c.1690–1725

The shift in design towards lighter, taller pieces necessitated new and more sophisticated construction techniques. Finely cut dovetails were used to join drawer-sides and the cases of furniture; this technique differed radically from the earlier joining and pegging of oak panels and nailed oak drawer-

MAPLE AND BURR WALNUT FLAT-TOP HIGHBOY, EARLY 18TH CENTURY *(far left)*

Made in Boston, Massachusetts, this highboy reflects contemporary Dutch and English preferences, equally well understood in fashionable Boston society.

sides. Thin sections of crotched or burled walnut or maple veneer were applied to drawer-fronts and façades. This change in construction methods allowed more freedom of design; the term 'cabinet-maker' replaced 'joiner' in the colonial vocabulary.

As more specific and structured social roles emerged there came into being new attitudes towards room design and, consequently, towards the functions of furniture. Specialized forms of furniture such as the day-bed, dressing-table, easy-chair, spice chest and highboy came into being.

Boston was one of the first cities to begin working in the new style. Cabinet-makers here began to make a new form of case furniture: the high chest-of-drawers, or highboy. Highboys were supported on trumpet-turned legs with Baroque-inspired

stretchers and ball feet. The taste for taller and more attenuated furniture also affected chair-backs, which became higher and were sometimes caned or leather-covered; occasionally the crests were carved with stylized leafage and 'C' scrolls. These chairs, constructed of maple, were based on British beechwood models, and they remained popular throughout much of the eighteenth century. They were made in large quantities, many being shipped down the coast to other North American cities.

During this period a Portuguese influence became apparent on chairs in the form of 'paintbrush' feet, sometimes referred to as 'Spanish' or 'Braganza' feet.

Increased literacy caused the fall-front desk to emerge. In New York there appeared an upright desk which was sometimes inlaid with vine and berry motifs. Cedar and gumwood, along with walnut, were used occasionally in New York. Painted furniture was a feature of New England and in the upper Connecticut River valley, near Hadley, Massachusetts. The panels of chests and court cupboards were painted in polychrome within a geometric framework. As elsewhere, designs were slow to change and Hadley-type chests were made with traditional nailed construction until at least 1730. In New York, grisaille-painted wardrobes appeared ornamented in *trompe l'oeil* style; fruit and foliate motifs were used in shades of grey and beige.

In coastal Connecticut and eastern Massachusetts, pine, tulipwood or maple chests-of-drawers, their emphasis on vertical proportions, were sometimes ornamented with polychrome scrolled leafage and fleur-de-lis motifs. The style of these differed from that of the chests made in Philadelphia or Chester County, Pennsylvania, which usually had walnut as the primary wood. In Chester County the façade was organized in geometric panels, and vine- and berry-inlaid tulip motifs were used.

Boston became a centre of japanning, which involved covering flat surfaces with layers of gesso, goldleaf and paint to match the Oriental taste. The designs, in common with their European antecedents, depicted flowers, pagodas, birds and exotic beasts.

THE ROCOCO PERIOD

The Revocation of the Edict of Nantes in 1685 had a dramatic and long-term effect on the applied arts. Large numbers of Huguenot craftsmen left France and sought refuge in friendly Protestant countries such as Holland, England, Switzerland and certain German states. During the eighteenth century other designers and craftsmen, not necessarily Huguenots, likewise travelled from France to work in the courts of fashion-conscious European monarchs, while, conversely, many went from abroad to Paris to immerse themselves in the French taste and artistry. European furniture of the first half of the eighteenth century, at least, was thus dominated by French designers and craftsmen; however differently the Rococo style was interpreted in other countries, its initial development was a French phenomenon.

It is difficult to determine where Baroque ends and Rococo begins, for the one grew out of the other by a gradual process. The term 'Rococo' was a nineteenth-century invention, a combination of 'rocaille' (shellwork) and 'barocco', used at first as a term of abuse for an outmoded style, possibly associated with the name of the painter Federico Barocci (1528–1612). It was not until the 1940s that the term assumed its present association with the prevailing decorative forms of the first half of the eighteenth century.

Rococo ornament on furniture developed in three distinct stages. The first stage was influenced by Jean Bérain (1637–1711), Louis XIV's chief designer in the last years of the seventeenth century. Bérain was among the first to adopt a new delicacy in his decorations, drawing heavily on the grotesque ornament of Renaissance Italy – in turn a revival from ancient Rome – and his later designs, for brass-inlaid furniture, chimney-pieces, ceilings and wall panellings, are airy confections in which classical gods, fanciful beasts and occasionally Chinese figures are surrounded by symmetrical arrangements of

MADAME DE POMPADOUR, F.-H. DROUAIS, 1763 (DETAIL)

The naturalistic detail on the dress and the floral mounts on the furniture are staples of Rococo decoration. However, the Vitruvian scrolls anticipate popular Neoclassical forms.

swirling arabesques and lacy borders of strapwork and foliage. Bérain's career as a royal designer was reinforced in 1711 by the publication in Paris of a collection of his engraved designs, *Oeuvre de Jean Bérain, recueilliés par les soins du Sieur Thuret.*

Claude Audran (1657–1734), who was responsible for the decoration in several royal palaces, gave a new freedom to grotesque ornament, in some of which he incorporated monkeys among the fabulous beasts – hence the term *singeries*. Pierre Le Pautre (1648–1716) was another draughtsman at the royal court whose playfully informal and often asymmetrical designs may be seen as a reaction to the ponderous Louis XIV style.

This leavening of the Baroque gathered momentum during the early years of the eighteenth century. In 1715 the Sun King died, leaving his five-year-old great-grandson, the future Louis XV, as his heir. This heralded the second stage of Rococo furniture design, During the period of the Regency (1715–23) under Philippe, the duc d'Orléans, which followed, the new phase of the French Rococo, the Régence style, came into full flower.

Classical elements gave way to fantastic mythical beings, frolicking Chinese figures and playful animals. Flowers and plants were also used to emphasize sinuous lines which tended more and more towards the asymmetrical. Whereas the grotesque ornament of Bérain, however extravagant, had tended to be arranged in symmetrical panels, the designers of the Régence period, led by Gilles-Marie Oppenord (1672–1742), followed the lead given by Pierre Le Pautre in abandoning symmetry in favour of a perpetual motion of C- and S-shaped curves, uneven rockwork, carefully imbalanced sprigs and garlands and delicately poised figures.

By the 1730s the Régence style was further developed into the *genre pittoresque*, a more extreme – and more frivolous – form of the Rococo. This was the third of the three distinct stages in the development of the Rococo. Its major exponents were Nicolas Pineau (1684–1754), Germain Boffrand (1667–1754) and Juste-Aurèle Meissonnier (*c*.1693–1750), and their designs carried the Rococo into its most spirited phase. Rocky caves were inhabited by dragons and other improbable reptiles; cascading waterfalls were embellished with shells and waving plant fronds; chubby putti disported themselves among naturalistic festoons and *bocages* – all of these wildly romantic compositions being intertwined and edged by scrolling cartouches and wavy-edged leaves.

Design books and engravings by the most prolific and influential French decorators ensured that the new style was successfully marketed throughout Europe. Among these publications were the volumes of engraved designs by Jean-Bernard-Honoré Toro (1632–1731), published in Paris between 1716 and 1719, which included tables and other furniture as well as cartouches, arabesques and Rococo motifs. Another set of volumes was the published *Oeuvre* (1734) of Juste-Aurèle Meissonnier, whose designs for architecture, furniture and metalwork inspired Rococo craftsmen all over Europe.

Nicolas Pineau was one of the most influential of all Rococo designers. He spent the early part of his working life in Russia, where, around 1720, he designed carved wood panelling (*boiseries*) for Peter the Great. His engraved designs covered all aspects of interior decor, furniture and bed-hangings as well as wall decoration and were much copied. Jean Pillement (1728–1808) made his mark on all aspects of the decorative arts. He did so rather later than Pineau, but no less internationally: in the course of his career he worked in France, Spain, Portugal, Italy, Austria, Poland, Germany and England, making chinoiserie his speciality. The architect Jacques-François Blondel (1705–74), who published his two-volume *De la Distribution des Maisons de Plaisance* in 1737–8, affirmed the Rococo architect's concern with all aspects of domestic design – with the distribution of rooms and their arrangement, and with the furniture that went into them.

The frivolous anti-classical tendencies of the Rococo were inevitably offensive to the serious-minded few, even in France, and there was a parallel 'anti-Rococo' movement which upheld the rules of Classicism, particularly in architecture. In France this took the form of a conservative adherence to the Baroque among some furniture designers, but in England, where the Palladianism of Richard Boyle, the third Earl of Burlington, had taken root before the importation of the Rococo, a classical style in furniture-making was of greater importance. William Kent (*c*.1685–1748) was at the forefront of the movement. He designed hefty Palladian-Baroque furniture which pleased the purists while at the same time making ornamental concessions to the encroaching Rococo.

BEDROOM DESIGN, JACQUES-FRANÇOIS BLONDEL, 1737–8 *(above)*

HÔTEL SOUBISE, PARIS, ARCHITECT GERMAIN BOFFRAND *(right)*

In the 1730s the decoration of the Hôtel Soubise, the Prince de Rohan's town house, became a talking point among Parisian decorators and cabinet-makers.

The first half of the eighteenth century saw unprecedented advances in the quality of furniture workmanship and in the development of the applied arts generally. During the eighteenth century the upholsterer rose in importance from being a mere artisan to the status of a highly regarded craftsman, whose prestige was at least level with that of the cabinet-maker. Techniques did not so much change as develop a greater finesse, textiles being used, as before, for grand effects. Beds and their furnishings were the most important items in any household and state beds of the early eighteenth century had vast sums lavished upon them. However, the most marked developments took place in upholstery. This, with the increasing informality of the Rococo, was expected to be more comfortable than imposing. Chairs were thickly stuffed, with rounded contours and down cushions. This is not to say that they were inelegant: they were given colourful refinement by close-nailing, carved and often gilded woodwork, and coverings of silk damask.

VERNIS MARTIN COMMODE, *c*.1745 *(below)*

The gilt-bronze mounts on this piece are stamped M. Criaerd and L.B. The bombé shape and the 'C' scroll floral mounts are typical of late French Rococo.

KINGWOOD AND TULIPWOOD BUREAU, *c*.1740 *(left)*

The parquetry on the exterior and the marquetry on the interior demonstrate the mid-eighteenth-century love of elaborate wood decoration.

were likewise marble-topped commodes with sumptuously crafted gilt-bronze mounts. Some of Gaudreau's commodes were designed by Sebastien-Antoine Slodtz who, with his two brothers, Paul-Ambroise and René-Michel, was an important royal designer during the middle years of the century. The gilt-bronze mounts of Gaudreau's most grandiose pieces were the work of Jacques Caffiéri (1678–1755), who was probably the greatest of all *fondeur-ciseleurs* of the Rococo period.

Bernard van Risen Burgh was a somewhat shadowy figure, probably of Dutch origin, whose *estampille* 'B.V.R.B.' perplexed furniture historians until as late as 1957, when he was identified as the maker of some highly important commodes and tables and of a number of small but exquisite pieces. These included a writing-table and a bedside table for Madame de Pompadour and a *vide poche* (a small rimmed bedroom table for the contents of a man's pocket) owned by the painter François Boucher. The creator of superbly crafted furniture in exotic woods with gilt-bronze mounts, van Risen Burgh also favoured decorative panels of Japanese and European lacquer, and he was the first *ébéniste* known to have decorated his furni-

ture with porcelain plaques, a practice that was to become popular later.

Prominent among other famous names in French *ébénisterie* at this time are those of Pierre Migeon (1701–58), a specialist in small pieces, Louis Cresson (1706–61), a maker of chairs and upholstered furniture, Jacques Dubois (*c*.1693–1763), a specialist in highly-decorative lacquer pieces, the chair-maker Jean-Baptiste Tilliard (1685–1766), and the influential royal cabinet-maker Gilles Joubert (1689–1775).

An important development in the use of japanning coincided with the Rococo age. The Martin brothers, Guillaume (*d*.1749), Etienne Simon (*d*.1770), Julien (*d*.1783) and Robert (1706–65) refined and perfected an imitation lacquer to which they gave their name, *vernis Martin*. Taking as their basis the recipes for oil lacquers developed and published by the Italian Father Filippo Bonanni early in the eighteenth century, they succeeded in making both copal and amber oil lacquers of such quality that *vernis Martin* became synonymous with all French japanning in the Rococo style, especially that popularized during the nineteenth century. In 1730 the brothers were granted a monopoly for making imitations of Chinese and

Japanese lacquer in relief, but their smooth lacquer, often on a base of papier mâché (which they also developed to a new strength and durability), was the type mostly associated with their products. The decoration – on gleaming surfaces of green, grey, blue or mauve – was sometimes painted in polychrome, not necessarily in the Chinese style, and sometimes merely consisted of gold speckling in the Japanese manner. All kinds of objects, from wall panelling, carriages and commodes to snuff-boxes and fans, were decorated with *vernis Martin*, and many examples were snapped up by rich and fashionable tourists to Paris and so found their way into other parts of Europe.

The Evolution of Furniture Types

The royal court's tendency away from pomposity during this period, as expressed so often in the relaxed informality of the Rococo style, was given practical effect by the use of smaller, intimately comfortable rooms rather than great chambers of state. This led to a burgeoning of new furniture types, many of them of a feminine delicacy and practicality. French cabinet-makers were by now respected as artists and they lavished

LOUIS XV WALNUT
SIDE CABINET *(left)*

*This French provincial
piece adopts Rococo
motifs, but the cabriole
legs and the end panels
are reminiscent of earlier
Louis XIV pieces.*

LOUIS XV
GILTWOOD CHAIR, IN
THE MANNER OF
CRESSON *(far left)*

*This type of chair is
known as* à la reine
*because its flat-backed
shape was favoured by
Queen Marie Leczynska.*

their ingenuity and decorative talents on an array of small tables (for games, needlework, flowers, coffee, writing and the toilet), *secrétaires* (*en pente, en tombeau, à abattant, à cylindre* or *de voyage*), display cases, jewel cabinets, firescreens and mirrors. The *bonheur-du-jour* was born at this time, as was the *table de chevet*. Among larger pieces, the armoire was important and several sorts of bureau were developed. Beds and chairs came in a vast array and the general trend towards greater comfort meant that upholstery was pre-eminent.

Regional Styles

As one might expect, the furniture of the areas around Paris – Île-de-France, Anjou, Touraine and Orléans – shows most influence from the capital, whereas more remote places, such as Provence, the Basque region, Burgundy and the Auvergne, generally developed more individual styles; surprisingly, perhaps, the furniture of Normandy, too, showed a marked independence of style. However, plenty of provincial makers emulated the forms as well as the craftsmanship of the capital and sometimes their work can be mistaken for that of Parisian cabinet-makers. Pierre Nogaret of Lyon, for example, made chairs in the most fashionable style. The fact that he stamped his work helps to prevent confusion. For country furniture generally, oak was used predominantly in the north of France, while furniture from the more southerly districts was generally of walnut. Fruitwood was an alternative in many areas, particularly in Normandy, the Auvergne and Burgundy.

As usual with country-made furniture, styles were conservative: the distilled Baroque of Louis XIV persisted for much of the eighteenth century in most areas, while makers in the Auvergne region clung to even more archaic forms. It was only relatively late in the eighteenth century that Rococo elements – cartouche-shaped door panels on armoires and *dressoirs*, cabriole legs on cupboards, commodes and chairs, wavy apron panels and friezes, and scrolling escutcheons and handles – came to be imposed on well-established furniture forms.

Brittany and the north-eastern regions of Lorraine and the Franche-Comté adopted a more 'folksy' style than most areas, with flowery carved decoration lightening flat surfaces. Carving was typical in the southerly Basque country, too, but here it took the form of geometric roundels and zigzag patterns of a distinctly Moorish flavour.

Provençal furniture, almost always of walnut, shows the provincial craftsman at his most confident and inventive. Among the specialities of the region were the *buffets à glissants* (a cupboard with a superstructure fitted with lateral-sliding compartments) and a sturdy but graceful version of the armoire – an all-time furniture classic.

ITALY

Considerable inspiration for the French Rococo had come originally from Italy, indeed, Italian influence on French furniture had been strong throughout the sixteenth and seventeenth centuries. By the early eighteenth century, however, the tide was flowing the other way and French fashions were affecting Italy as much as anywhere else in Europe.

Much Italian furniture of the eighteenth century was distinctly conservative in style during the 1730s and 1740s, but, in certain areas of the peninsula – still a collection of independent states rather than a single country – the Rococo style, as developed in France under the Régence, was taken to its most ebullient extreme. In Turin, for example, the Sicilian architect Filippo Juvarra (1678–1736), who had earlier designed furniture in the grand Baroque manner, worked with Pietro Piffetti (c.1700–77), cabinet-maker to the King of Savoy from 1731, to create a dazzling triumph of Rococo. Every available surface was loaded with ornament: walls were covered with mirrors framed with carved and gilded garlands and cartouches, painted panels overflowed with flowers and furniture was embellished not only with weighty gilt-bronze mounts (many by the French-trained sculptor, Francesco Ladatte [1706–87]), but with a profusion of inlays in ivory and rare woods.

Many different furniture forms, too, fell victim to this unbounded exuberance, with top-heavy cabinets surmounting side tables whose exaggerated cabriole legs looked as though they might simply crumple to their knees under the strain. Unlike much Italian furniture of this period, which was made with more concern for effect than for quality of execution, Piffetti's was superbly crafted in every respect, even if the richness of ornament can be a trifle indigestible.

Regional Styles

In Lombardy and Tuscany, fruitwoods, chestnut and walnut were the timbers most widely available to cabinet-makers. Inlays of ivory, pewter and mother-of-pearl, as well as of exotic woods, were still used. The typical Baroque ornament of classical gods and goddesses was sometimes replaced by frivolous putti or Chinese figures and the surrounding swirls of plant and shell motifs were adapted to suit the new freedom of movement and asymmetry of design. Furniture shapes began to swell and curve with greater vivacity.

In the Venice area a fat form of the *bombé* shape was favoured as nowhere else and while inlaid furniture was produced, painted and lacquered effects were a speciality of the region. The furniture surface (generally of pine) was built up with layers of gesso to

MARQUETRY CABINET, PIETRO PIFFETTI, 1731

Commissioned by the King of Piedmont for the Palazzo Reale, Turin, this cabinet for the Queen's closet shows the extremes of full-blown Rococo. Ebony, fig, acacia, boxwood, ivory and mother-of-pearl are used in the marquetry.

GILTWOOD SIDE-
TABLE, c.1720
(right)

*The term legs are joined
by an X-form stretcher
and the apron consists
of a series of stylized
foliate scrolls. The
scagliola top is
nineteenth century.*

PAINTED CHEST-OF-
DRAWERS, c.1750
(below right)

*The Italian technique of
lacca contrafatta is
used to great effect on
this mid-eighteenth-
century piece.*

LACCA COMMODE,
c.1740 (bottom left)

*In both shape and
decoration this commode
is characteristic of
Venetian furniture. The
delicate, lively painting
and the high-bosomed
bombé shape enjoyed
great popularity in the
mid-eighteenth century.*

form playful and often crowded chinoiseries in relief. These were invariably gilded, while the backgrounds might be plain (usually black, green, red or yellow) or, especially later, painted in tempera. Venetian lacquer from the middle of the eighteenth century is typified by delicate relief-gilded scenes of figures in landscapes framed with garlands and bouquets of flowers painted in polychrome on a light ground.

Oriental lacquer – or *lacca*, as Italian japanning was known – was the loose inspiration for another, cheaper form of decoration particularly associated with Venice. This was *lacca contrafatta* (also called *arte povera*), in which paper scraps or cut-out prints were stuck onto the furniture surface and covered in layers of varnish. While the effect is hardly deceptive, it is gay and colourful, especially when, as is often the case, the background is painted in a bright or light colour.

Painted furniture was a speciality in the mountainous regions of northern Italy, while *lacca* was produced in many parts. That of Piedmont and Liguria tended to be more restrained in style and, like most of the furniture in this part of Italy, of better quality than that from other parts of the peninsula. The influence of neighbouring France was most noticeable in the furniture of Piedmont, an area with a tradition of inlaid work, since

the Huguenot craftsmen who settled both here and in Liguria brought French styles and standards of craftsmanship with them.

The furniture of Emilia Romagna, the area south of Venice, is characterized by a robust solidity not found in many other regions. Here oak was used as well as walnut. Typical decoration consisted of metal florets and studs, arranged in geometric patterns, and turned wooden roundels.

Spanish influence can be seen in the furniture made around the port of Genoa, where imported woods such as palisander were used alongside the native walnut. The Spanish connection is evident also in the furniture of Sicily, where ivory inlaid cabinets modelled on the Spanish *vargueño* were produced. Painted pieces were also typical and the use of woods such as olive or poplar may indicate that a piece is of Sicilian origin.

The painted furniture of Umbria and Tuscany tended to greater restraint and elegance than that of Venice, while Florence's long celebrated and very expensive speciality – furniture decorated with hard stones (*pietre dure*) – continued to astonish and delight the eighteenth-century world. Colourful panels for tables and cabinets were made more accessible to Grand Tourists and Italians alike by the development in the middle of the century of an effective imitation in scagliola.

SPAIN AND PORTUGAL

Dynastically speaking, Spain was connected with both France and Italy, and most of the influences on the country's furniture in the first half of the eighteenth century came from these two quarters. Ornately carved and gilded console tables with marble tops, surmounted by large mirrors, were considered essential furnishings for palatial interiors. To supply the

ROSEWOOD CHAIR, c.1750

The pierced and carved decoration on this chair shows how French and English influences were assimilated and adapted in Portuguese furniture of this period.

demand for these mirrors, Philip V established a factory at San Idelfonso in 1736. The commode began to oust the traditional Spanish *vargueño* as a principal item of furniture, but until the second half of the century Spanish commodes, made of solid wood with carved, sometimes parcel-gilt, decoration, were far removed from the sophistication of their French inspirations.

Portugal's furniture styles were influenced by her mercantile agreements with England and her long-standing trade in the East Indies and South America. Large numbers of English cane-seated chairs and japanned bureau-cabinets were imported during the first half of the century, and English Queen Anne and later Chippendale chair styles were reinterpreted in an unmistakably Portuguese way, sometimes in hard jacaranda wood from Brazil rather than in walnut.

Even when, towards the middle of century, the French Rococo influence crept into Portuguese furniture, it was adapted in a restrained form and with many English elements. It was only at the royal court of John V that the Rococo style was embraced in its full richness.

GERMANY AND EASTERN EUROPE

At the beginning of the eighteenth century, the Baroque style, which in one form or another had flourished for many years in Germany, held sway in most states of the Holy Roman Empire. From the late seventeenth century the influence of Louis XIV style was paramount, and it was to persist for many years to come, especially in the north. The early eighteenth-century German version of this style was perhaps most spectacularly embodied in the numerous published designs of Johann Jakob Schübler (1689–1741), which included all kinds of household furniture as well as church furnishings, garden ornaments and various mechanical inventions.

Vienna, as capital of the Empire, was a major artistic centre, drawing craftsmen and influence from Italy as well as developing talent within her own boundaries. Magnificent Baroque palaces were built in Vienna, Pommersfelden, Prague and Würzburg, and the solid qualities of the Baroque appealed also to the rich merchant classes, whose

furniture, if less sumptuous than that of the princely courts, still tended to the grandiose. The monumental panelled and corniced *schränke* (cupboards), typical representatives of German opulence, continued to be made in many parts of Germany, notably Frankfurt, Aachen and Würzburg, well into the eighteenth century.

However, the developing French styles gradually had an influence and by the 1720s new fashions were percolating into certain areas, particularly Bavaria, whose Elector employed two architects, Joseph Effner (1687–1745) and François Cuvilliés (1695–1768), who had studied in Paris before returning to Munich thoroughly versed in Louis XV Rococo. The French style permeated the area also as a result of the proliferation of published engravings available to German designers from the early eighteenth century onwards. The consequence was an 'outbreak' of Rococo in the churches and palaces of southern Germany which outdid almost anything seen anywhere. The work of Cuvilliés in and around Munich from the 1730s onwards provided both a yardstick and a stimulus for would-be Rococo designers all over Germany, and his published designs – for ornament and furniture – spread his influence far beyond.

In Saxony, the Elector Augustus the Strong, also King Augustus II of Poland, had in 1710 established the Meissen porcelain factory, whose products became the embodiment of the Rococo style in ceramics. As a result, Rococo furniture-makers of the highest calibre were inevitably drawn to his court.

Würzburg, Mainz, Ansbach, Bayreuth, Mannheim, Berlin and Potsdam were other major centres of courtly Rococo furniture. The furniture produced under the direction of Frederick the Great's court architect, Georg Wenzeslaus von Knobelsdorff (1699–1753), for his master's palaces in Berlin and Potsdam is outstanding for its sophistication and craftsmanship. Among the cabinet-makers employed by him were Johann August Nahl (1710–85); the two Spindlers, Johann Friedrich (1726–c.99) and Heinrich Wilhelm (1738–c.99), both of whom had previously worked at Bayreuth; the brothers Hoppenhaupt, Johann Michael (1709–c.55)

WALNUT SECRETAIRE CABINET, ATTRIBUTED TO FRANZ ANTON HERMANN, c.1758 *(left)*

The curved exterior surface of the writing leaf, moulding around the doors, bold cresting piece and symmetrical marquetry are typical features of cabinets produced by the Mainz guild in the mid-eighteenth century.

KINGWOOD CABINET, MARTIN SCHNELL, c.1730 *(right)*

The monogram contained in the cabochon moulding supported by two female figures is that of Augustus the Strong for whom this cabinet was made. This piece demonstrates the popularity asymmetrical forms enjoyed throughout the Rococo period.

WALNUT BUREAU, c.1740 *(below right)*

The somewhat restrained nature of this German piece contrasts with elaborate French bureaux of the same period. The gently curving lines are enhanced by the beautiful grain of the wood.

and Johann Christian (1719–86), and Johann Melchior Kambli (1718–73).

Berlin was already famous for the products of Gerhard Dagly (fl.1687–1714), a native of Spa, Belgium, whose imitations of Oriental lacquer in the seventeenth and early eighteenth centuries were unrivalled during this time. His pupil, Martin Schnell (fl.1703–40), was among several outstanding japanners who went to Dresden and worked for Augustus the Strong and his no less Rococo-obsessed prime minister, Count Heinrich von Brühl.

Not surprisingly, in an area as vast and diverse as the German states, regional variations in vernacular furniture were considerable. In the north the main influence was from Holland, whereas in the south certain features, like the shapes of *bombé* commodes, owe more to Italy. Likewise, in southern Germany painted furniture was typical, just

as it was in northern Italy and Switzerland.

English furniture was highly regarded in many parts of Germany. Its best-known promoter was Abraham Röentgen (1711–93), who spent the early years of his career in England and eventually, in 1750, set up a workshop in Neuwied which was to become one of the most celebrated in all Europe. Much of his work was done in walnut or fruitwoods, but he made a speciality of marquetry, using, in addition to exotic woods, brass, ivory and mother-of-pearl.

Inlays of such materials, which are difficult to work, had been a German speciality for more than a century and the practice persisted particularly in Brunswick. During the middle years of the eighteenth century a type of bureau-cabinet, or *schreibschrank*, of serpentine form and with walnut veneers decorated in elegant curlicues of inlaid ivory, was produced there.

THE LOW COUNTRIES

For most of the first half of the eighteenth century, Dutch and English furniture had much in common; indeed, English furniture was so admired in Holland that some Dutch craftsmen, striving for prestige, called themselves 'English cabinet-makers'. Walnut was favoured for high-quality pieces and oyster veneers were used for the decoration of surfaces like the doors of cabinets or the tops of tables – these might be of laburnum, acacia or other exotic woods as an alternative to walnut. The double-domed bureau, originally an English invention, had by the beginning of the eighteenth century evolved into a form familiar in both countries. Chairs with veneered vase-shaped splats and cabriole legs with carved knees were made in the two countries with only minor stylistic variations and canework was extensively used for the backs and seats of chairs and settees.

Japanning provided a more colourful decoration than figured woods, however exotic, and in the Low Countries it was developed on many levels. Spa, in Belgium, had been famous for the production of imitation Oriental lacquer for the past century, and its products, ranging from large cabinets to small snuff-boxes, were popular throughout the eighteenth century with tourists who came to take the medicinal waters of the resort. Japanners elsewhere in the Netherlands also reached a high degree of skill. Dutch japanning of the late seventeenth and early eighteenth centuries usually consisted of sparsely arranged chinoiserie in gold on a black ground.

As in England, the Rococo style had little effect on Dutch furniture before the 1740s, at which time *bombé* and serpentine shapes grew more exaggerated and carved, and applied embellishments began to twitch and scroll with an exuberant delicacy. Now French influence once more re-exerted itself, and the demand for luxurious ormolu-mounted commodes resulted in some fine home-produced examples, whose outstand-

WALNUT CHAIR, c.1720

This chair, with its inlaid vase-shaped splat and cabriole legs, is typically Netherlandish.

ing feature, predictably, was floral marquetry. More typically Dutch was a form of tallboy consisting of a low-bellied *bombé* commode and a shelved clothes cupboard with two doors. The curvaceously shaped top was customarily fitted with ledges so that china could be displayed.

RUSSIA AND SCANDINAVIA

One of the first forays into the Rococo outside France was in Russia, where the French designer and Rococo pioneer Nicolas Pineau worked between 1716 and 1726. Fashionable French and German furniture was imported into Russia and copied by native craftsmen and the circulation of published designs enabled

the Russian nobility to keep abreast of the latest decorative taste.

By the middle of the century the predominating mood of the Rococo style, as adopted in Russia, was distinctly Germanic in its appearance. Its major exponent, the son of an Italian sculptor, was Count Bartolommeo Francesco Rastrelli (c.1700–71), chief architect at the Russian court, whose rich and gaudy interior schemes – notably at Tsarskoe Selo and the Winter Palace at St Petersburg – included furniture and ironwork, as well as plasterwork and elaborate carved wall decoration.

The enormous demand for timber following the Great Fire of London (1666) resulted not only in increased prosperity and cultural growth in Scandinavia but also in closer links with England, whose furniture styles became most influential in the late seventeenth and eighteenth centuries. The connections with English and Dutch furniture gave Scandinavian furniture an 'Anglo-Dutch' feeling. As in some other parts of Europe, chair-making and cabinet-making were quite separate crafts, the chair-makers being much more conservative than the cabinet-makers. Indeed, Queen Anne and early Georgian chair styles remained extremely popular in Scandinavia long after they had given way to the Rococo in England.

During this period Denmark and Norway were politically and culturally joined, and their interests and geography linked them closely with northern Germany; inevitably, furniture-makers drew much inspiration from that direction, and it was the German form of Rococo that was eventually adopted in Norway and Denmark. The guilds in these countries were modelled on those in Germany and similar types of furniture were produced including *schränke* and swollen-fronted commodes.

In Scandinavia as a whole the Rococo was chiefly a courtly introduction during the 1730s and 1740s. It was seen at its most sophisticated and francophile in Sweden, most of whose leading architects and furniture designers had trained in Paris. It was much later in the eighteenth century that Rococo ornament became a common feature of Scandinavian bourgeoisie furniture.

BRITAIN

By the reign of Queen Anne, Dutch influence had been thoroughly assimilated and English furniture set off on a separate course of development which was to be influential in many parts of Europe during the eighteenth century.

The London furniture trade was concentrated around St Paul's Churchyard. Although it is known that the industry was booming, few individual makers can be identified. Occasionally pieces appear today bearing makers' labels such as those of the firms Coxed & Woster, Hugh Granger, William Old & John Ody, or Giles Grendey, and they cause excitement among furniture historians, but such superficial and easily faked clues must be regarded with caution. Another important firm was that of John Gumley & James Moore, which supplied looking-glasses and other furnishings to the royal household between 1714 and 1725. Gumley's 'Glass Gallery' in the New Exchange was well known among fashionable Londoners of the early eighteenth century and his glass factory in Lambeth fiercely rivalled that of neighbouring Vauxhall where, from 1700 onwards, large looking-glass plates were being made and supplied to the makers of carved and gilded frames. The widespread use of mirrors, over fireplaces or on the piers between windows, is easy to understand: they reflected the contents — and occupants — of rooms and enhanced both natural light and candlelight.

Gilding was used extensively, not only for mirror frames but, from the 1720s onwards, increasingly for other furniture. This was largely due to the influence of William Kent (1684–1748), architect, painter and designer of practically anything, whose influence on furniture was enormous. His chief patron, Richard Boyle, the third Earl of Burlington, was the main English protagonist of the Palladian style of architecture, and it was Kent who provided the furnishings to go with it. His furniture was architectural and ponderous, laden with classical ornament and best suited to the palatial buildings of the nobility. His most famous furnishing

schemes were at Chiswick House (for Lord Burlington) and at Houghton Hall (for Sir Robert Walpole), but his designs — for cabinets, console tables, settees, pedestals, mirror frames and chairs — were copied by some of the most prestigious cabinet-makers of the 1730s and 1740s and his architectural style was much emulated for more ordinary furniture. Among the most important of his contemporaries were John Vardy (d.1765), and the royal cabinet-maker Benjamin Goodison (c.1700–67). Much Kentian furniture was parcel-gilt: the decorative scrolls on the pediments of cabinets or the capitals of their flanking columns, the carving on mirrors or the knees of chairs and stools, or the embellishment of table-legs and friezes might be picked out thus to give a more sumptuous effect. Even richer were the wholly gilded console tables with marble tops that stood beneath the piers of grand rooms. Like the gilded looking-glasses above them, these console tables were usually of

WALNUT WING CHAIR, c.1720 *(above left)*

Contemporary gros and petit point *needlework on this piece indicate a characteristic Rococo interest in elaborate, overblown naturalism. The inviting cushioned seat reflects the emphasis on comfort prevalent during George I's reign.*

GILTWOOD SIDE TABLE, c.1750 *(above)*

Although the marble top of this table is supported by characteristic Rococo 'C' scrolls, the use of other decorative elements such as the mask and the Prince of Wales feathers show signs of the onset of classical influences typical of furniture in the Kent style.

STATE BED, CALKE
ABBEY, EARLY 18TH
CENTURY

*The elaborate design of
the headcloth looks to the
engravings of Daniel
Marot, popular during
the early years of the
eighteenth century,
although the straight lines
of the tester reflect the
taste for more
architectural designs of
the second decade of the
century. The remarkably
vivid colours of the
chinoiserie embroidery
hangings indicate that
they were seldom used.*

beechwood or pine, which could be elaborately carved and finally gilded, and they were complemented by gilded chairs, stands and centre tables. The softwoods used were a prey to woodworm, and only a small proportion of gilded furniture has survived; it was probably much more common than the number of extant examples might suggest.

By the 1730s walnut was being superseded as the chief cabinet-making wood by mahogany, a timber from the West Indies which had dark richness and great strength and versatility. Mahogany was well suited to furniture in William Kent's architectural style, with its crisply carved classical borders and strongly defined ornament, and it was

also ideal for chairs, which could now be strong as well as decorative. The gradual introduction of mahogany into English furniture-making coincided with a new breath of foreign air – that of the French Rococo style. This came about partly because of the numbers of immigrant or visiting artists and craftsmen who brought the new lighter mood across the Channel and partly as a result of the fact that, whatever the political climate, matters of fashion were still ultimately dictated from France.

The influential Rococo painter Jean-Antoine Watteau had come to England as early as 1719 and during the next decade his style was emulated by painters who, like Philippe

(or Philip) Mercier and Pieter Angellis, had already settled there. Engravers, the most famous of whom was the French immigrant Hubert Gravelot, did much to popularize the *genre pittoresque* during the 1730s, and French, Italian and German pattern-books and engravings were widely available. The designs of Pineau, Bérain, Toro, Meissonnier, Brunetti and Cuvilliés were borrowed freely by craftsmen in many fields.

The St Martin's Lane Academy, founded by William Hogarth in 1735, was the chief centre for the promotion of the Rococo style in England. Here the beauty of the serpentine line and the importance of nature in ornament were inculcated in the rising generation by such teachers as Gravelot, Francis Hayman and Louis-François Roubiliac. The replacement of St Paul's Churchyard by St Martin's Lane as the chief furniture-making area of London was important for the development of English Rococo furniture. The proximity of the Academy meant that the Rococo style in art was quickly assimilated by cabinet-makers.

It was in silver, particularly that by George Wickes and the Huguenot Paul de Lamerie, that the Rococo first began to show itself in the applied arts, but carving and furniture were not slow to follow. Soon there was a proliferation of design books proclaiming the Rococo in its peculiarly English form. Among the first were *The Gentleman's or Builder's Companion* (1739) by William Jones and *The City and Country Builder's and Workman's Treasury of Designs* (1740, with subsequent editions in 1745, 1750, 1756 and 1770) by Batty Langley with engravings by his brother Thomas. While the designs in both books were in a predominantly Palladian style, Rococo elements borrowed from Europe are also discernible.

The teacher and master-carver Matthias Lock (*fl.c.*1740–70) was probably the most important exponent of the Rococo style in English furniture. His *Six Sconces* (1744) and *Six Tables* (1746) were followed by other ornamental design books including *A New Book of Ornaments in the Chinese Taste* and *The Principles of Ornament*. Lock's designs were based on asymmetrical 'C' scrolls, cartouches and wavy acanthus foliage, but watery elements, rock work, animals and rustic tree-trunks also featured regularly.

By the 1750s both Chinese and Gothic elements had been added to the Rococo vocabulary; often they were mixed together in a hotch-potch of romantic fantasy, but equally they might be the dominating theme. Lock collaborated with Henry Copland (first recorded work 1738, d.1761), a notable Rococo engraver, to produce *A New Book of Ornaments* (1752), which included designs for chimneys, sconces, tables, stands, girandoles, chandeliers and clocks.

A still lighter form of the Rococo was evident in the designs of Thomas Johnson (1714–c.1778), published during the 1750s. Johnson, like many other English Rococo artists and patrons, was a member of the Anti-Gallican Society, founded in 1745 'to extend the commerce of England and discourage the introduction of French modes and oppose the importation of French commodities'. By responding to the public taste for what was originally a French style, Rococo artists and craftsmen in England clearly felt that they were upholding the Anti-Gallican philosophy. Johnson's culminating publication was *One Hundred and Fifty New Designs* (1761), which set out a whole range of carvers' pieces in a most lively Rococo form. He included chinoiserie, rustic compositions, animals, birds and fish, and scenes from Aesop's *Fables*, all of which he placed among sparkling fountains and splen-did waterfalls, arching foliage and exaggerated scrolling cartouches.

Another engraver, Matthias Darly (*fl.*1750–78), published *A New Book of Chinese, Gothic and Modern Chairs* in 1750–51 and *A New Book of Chinese Designs* in 1754, but he was better known for his collaboration with Thomas Chippendale (1718–79) in *The Gentleman and Cabinet-maker's Director* (1754, with subsequent editions in 1755 and 1762), for which he engraved most of the plates. He contributed also to two other important Rococo pattern-books, Ince and Mayhew's *The Universal System of Household Furniture* (1759–63) and *Household Furniture in the Genteel Taste for the Year 1760 by a Society of Upholsterers, Cabinet-Makers etc.* The last of the English Rococo pattern-books (apart from many reissues of earlier publications) were those of the cabinet-maker Robert Manwaring (*fl.*1760–66): *The Cabinet and Chair-Maker's Real Friend and Companion* (1765) and *The Chair-Maker's Guide* (1766).

Of them all, however, Chippendale's *Director* was undoubtedly the most important. It was the first design book to cover all kinds of household furniture and its success was so great that 'Chippendale' became the generic label for practically all mid-eighteenth-century mahogany furniture. Chippendale himself was merely one among many businessmen and cabinet-makers from whose workshops in and around St Martin's Lane furniture of consistently high quality

MAHOGANY DINING CHAIR, *c.*1755 *(above)*

Like many chairs based on those included in Chippendale's Director, *this chair is not entirely faithful to one design.*

DESIGN FROM *A NEW BOOK OF ORNAMENTS*, MATTHIAS LOCK, 1752 *(right)*

DESIGN FROM A COLLECTION BY THOMAS JOHNSON, 1758 *(far right)*

These clocks are a fine example of Johnson's imaginative and vivid furniture designs.

MAHOGANY
CABINET, JOHN
CHANNON, *c.*1740
(left)

*Though somewhat
reminiscent of
contemporary German
cabinets in its strong,
almost architectural
shape, the bold gilt-
bronze mounts reflect
mid-eighteenth-century
English taste.*

GILTWOOD PIER-
GLASS, *c.*1760
(right)

*The scrolling sides and
chinoiserie motifs of this
piece are characteristic
of English Rococo.*

JAPANNED *BOMBÉ* COMMODE, *c.*1750 *(right)*

*The restrained bombé front, together with the
characteristically English treatment of the japanning,
indicate that this commode was made in the mid-
eighteenth century.*

emanated during the 1750s and 1760s. The *Director* was, in fact, less a collection of original designs than an overview of the range of furniture and the variety of styles available to the gentry during the middle years of the eighteenth century.

Chairs were more decorative than ever. Typical of the period were those with carved back splats, surmounted by gracefully serpentine top-rails, as well as carved knees and cabriole legs. The carved decoration might take the form of Rococo cartouche shapes and scrolling acanthus or might incorporate 'Gothick' arches, Chinese fretwork or interlacing ribbons. 'French' chairs, with upholstered backs as well as seats, had carved cartouche-shaped backs and crisp leafy decoration on legs and seat-rails. In some the lustrous dark mahogany was contrasted by colourful upholstery, while others were enriched with gilding. At this time the trade of upholsterer equalled that of cabinet-maker in importance; there were just as many upholsterers as cabinet-makers, and many firms advertised themselves as both 'upholders' and cabinet-makers.

Chinoiserie was introduced in the fretted galleries around tables or the pagoda-like tops of cabinets, while the carving of legs and stretchers might be embellished with curling plant forms or clustered into 'Gothick' columns. 'Gothick' tracery formed the glazing bars on cupboard doors, and mock-medieval pinnacles surmounted them.

Carcase furniture fell under the Rococo spell to varying degrees. At the top of the market were lacquer-embellished or inlaid 'French' commodes of *bombé* shape, richly ornamented with gilt-bronze mounts, made by the French immigrant *ébéniste* Pierre Langlois (b.1738). Others included the impeccably constructed mahogany cabinets with serpentine lines and crisp carving made for Queen Charlotte by William Vile (c.1700–67) and John Cobb (c.1710–78) and the massive brass-inlaid writing-tables and cabinets of John Channon (fl.1740).

Other important cabinet-making names of this period include William Hallett (1710–81), James Whittle (fl.1742–61), Samuel Norman (fl.1754–66) and John (d.1796) and William (d.1763) Linnell, all of whom have

DESIGN FOR A CHAIR, JOHN LINNELL, *c.1750 (above)*

Linnell's design shows the adaptation of Oriental characteristics to suit European tastes and furniture types.

YEW AND ELM BURR-WOOD WINDSOR ARMCHAIR, *c.1760 (above)*

This is a particularly grand example of a provincial form, with its pierced, vase-shaped splat, scrolling arm supports, sturdy cabriole legs and pad feet.

been identified through the royal accounts or the archives of noble houses. None of them, any more than Chippendale, was in the habit of marking his furniture, and it is only through documentary records such as bills and inventories that definite attributions to particular cabinet-makers can be made. The similarity to a Chippendale or a Linnell design does not, in itself, confirm that a piece was made in their workshops. Most of the furniture produced in the eighteenth century was anonymous and none the worse for that. There were literally hundreds of cabinet-makers, in the provinces as well as in London, turning out well-made furniture of enduring usefulness and elegance.

Country furniture on the other hand was relatively unassailed by changes in fashion and the Rococo, a style concerned mostly with ornament, was hardly likely to make much impact on furniture whose design was dictated primarily by function and economy. However, the Windsor chair, a type in general usage from the 1730s onwards, often had 'Gothick' arches in the back and a cresting rail shaped in the curving style associated with Chippendale chairs typical of the 1750–60 period.

THE UNITED STATES

The 1685 Revocation of the Edict of Nantes had brought numerous French Protestant craftsmen to England, altering English taste and imbuing it with Continental influences. Britain's rising influence all over the world, spurred on by the Treaty of Utrecht (1713), increased its exports of household textiles and furnishings – particularly, of course, to its colonies.

The two editions of the *Oeuvres* of the French designer Daniel Marot, published in 1702 and 1712, had a major effect on taste in Britain and subsequently in North America. Marot's designs introduced the cabriole legs and utilized shells and scrolls. The S-shaped line became an important constituent of the

'Queen Anne' aesthetic. In his publication entitled *Analysis of Beauty* (1753) William Hogarth stated that such an S-shaped line suggests motion and, as he observed, 'leads the eye on a wanton kind of chase, and from the pleasure that [it] gives the mind entitles it to the name of Beautiful'.

Queen Anne

Furniture design in the North American Queen Anne period (c.1725–60) was, as earlier, largely dictated by contemporary design in Britain, especially England. An attempt was made at this time to design furniture to adapt to and fit the needs and comfort of the human body. This concern was shown in the backs of chairs, which became serpentine-shaped, to fit the back of the sitter, and lower in height. Case furniture became more graceful and delicate, due to the introduction of cabriole legs and pad, slipper or trifid feet, replacing the more unstable-looking legs of the William and Mary period. While only straight cornices had been evident previously on the top section of highboys or secretaries, the Queen

Anne period introduced S-shaped bonnets mounted by carved or turned finials. Walnut and mahogany were the main primary woods used during the period, but maple, cherrywood, gumwood and cedar featured to a lesser degree. Secondary woods were pine, tulipwood, maple, chestnut and ash.

Early in the period veneered surfaces were incorporated on case pieces, but after the middle of the century solid sections of mahogany and walnut were preferred. Façades were designed with a careful balance of plain surfaces to ornament, which usually consisted of carved or gilt shells, acanthus leaves, 'C' scrolls and veneered crossbanding.

The Queen Anne period is sometimes called the 'Age of Regionalism'. As growth and sophistication increased, the settlements, founded by diverse ethnic groups, developed their distinctive styles of furniture. These differences were influenced and enhanced by local materials, inherited traditions and the demands of patrons. Newport, Boston, New York and Philadelphia grew into distinct design centres, each reflecting the popular taste of its region.

During the first three-quarters of the

eighteenth century Boston was a thriving and prosperous commercial centre and it emerged as a style centre, too, influencing other nearby cabinet-making towns such as Salem, Newburyport and Portsmouth. By 1740 there were 160 warehouses along the Boston harbour and by the time of the Revolution there were at least 150 cabinet-makers, chair-makers and carvers active in the city. Numerous sophisticated pieces were made and often commissions involved the work of several artisans – the cabinet-maker, turners, inlay- and veneer-makers, a carver and, sometimes, gilders and japanners. The degree of elaboration was most often dictated by the wishes of the person ordering the piece. Typical of Boston furniture are tray-top tea-tables with cyma-shaped skirts and delicate pad feet. Block-front furniture was produced on a large scale and, frequently, cases were inlaid with stellar devices and herringbone veneers. New England chairs were of a tall form and fitted with turned stretchers.

Newport, a large flourishing seaport, produced the Quaker families of cabinet-makers, the Goddards and the Townsends,

MAHOGANY CARD-TABLE, BOSTON, c.1740 *(left)*

A fashion for card games during Queen Anne's reign led to the development of many kinds of card-tables.

WALNUT SIDE CHAIR, c.1760 *(right)*

Shell carving and claw-and-ball feet on this regional 'Queen Anne' chair are characteristic of the New York school.

who were renowned for their unique block-front and shell-carved dressing-tables and secretary-bookcases.

In Connecticut, several well-known cabinet-makers worked in local cherrywood; their styles were highly original, featuring elaborate and eccentric carving. Often these pieces show the design influences of other cabinet-making centres, including Newport and Philadelphia.

The influence of Dutch settlement in New York had a strong effect on furniture and design in that city. The furniture tended to be generously proportioned, with flatter carving and less detail than was seen in other areas. Increased trade with the Orient brought about design changes, such as the vase-form splat on chair-backs: in New York, the splats and seats were lower and wider than elsewhere, and usually joined by turned or flat stretchers.

The integration of the S-curve was never achieved more fully or successfully than in Philadelphia. Chairs, in particular, showed a careful mastery of design, with balloon-shaped seats and inward-curving stiles and legs. Distinctive construction details, such as

exposed mortises at the back of the rear legs and distinctive joinery of the seat, are further signs of chairs from this region, although exceptions to this rule do exist. Two of the better known cabinet-makers working in Philadelphia at the time were William Savery (1721–88) and John Elliott (1713–91). Among the many new forms introduced were the tilt-top candlestand and tea-table with birdcage attachment, the rectangular mixing-table and the folding card-table.

Secretaries, highboys and chests-on-chests were now fitted with a broken-arch pediment. With increased prosperity in the colonies came a demand for elegance and comfort which was satisfied by new forms of upholstered furniture, including generous wing chairs and sofas.

The Chippendale Period

The colonial rivalry that existed during the eighteenth century between France and Britain resulted in the French and Indian War of 1754–63. With the signing of the Treaty of Paris in 1763, the French gave up their control in Canada and ceded future owner-

ship of the region to Britain. The colonists were generally ecstatic: for the first time their destiny seemed secure. As their military dependence on Britain diminished, the colonies entered an exciting new era of self-confidence and independence.

The furniture trade in eighteenth-century North America was a lively business. Household effects, and especially furniture, accounted for a much greater proportion of a person's net worth than they do today. Some furniture was imported from Britain and sold through upholstery and cabinet shops in the South; in the North (with the exception of mirrors) this trade was virtually negligible. North American dependence on British taste, design and culture chafed many of the colonists, who strongly advocated the development of an indigenous culture, but it was to be a while before this came about.

Thomas Chippendale, in his first edition of *The Gentleman and Cabinet-maker's Director* (1754), offered the most up-to-date furniture manual for urban colonial cabinet-makers. The book was enlarged, revised and reissued in 1762. Chippendale's published drawings combined three major design elements:

EDWARD STILES'
DRAWING-ROOM,
1762

Chippendale interiors of this type were not uncommon among wealthy Philadelphians. All of the furniture is mahogany and exhibits carved acanthus leaves and 'C' scrolls typical of the Philadelphia school. The bonnet-top highboy by Michael Gratz is a Philadelphian form.

MAHOGANY BONNET-TOP HIGHBOY,
PHILADELPHIA, c.1760

Flamboyant Rococo pieces of this nature indicate American cabinet-makers' assimilation of designs included in Chippendale's Director. Both the carved knees and the intricate openwork on the pediment reflect Chippendale's influence.

Chinese (adapted from Oriental objects), medieval Gothic style and the refinement of Rococo. They influenced a whole generation of North American cabinet-makers. The fact that a thirty-year period of North American furniture-making has been named after this enlightened businessman is testament to his enormous influence.

Native woods – walnut, maple, cherry, white pine and tulip poplar – were readily available and extensively used. As a result of the 'Triangle Trade', West Indian mahogany was also easy to come by. The preference for solid woods rather than veneers stemmed not just from their ready availability but also from the fact that they better withstood the rigours of the climate. Moreover, it did not cost very much to set up a cabinet shop (at least, relative to the expense that would have been involved in Europe), while shipping bulky pieces across the Atlantic was obviously expensive. All of these factors meant that North American furniture generally cost less than its imported British counterparts.

As very little eighteenth-century furniture was either signed or labelled, little is known about its makers. Most cabinet shops were small – consisting of the master, one or two apprentices and one or two journeymen. Apprentices were bound for a fixed time, usually seven years, and journeymen came and went at will. As there was no strict guild system, any individual piece could be the product of a diversity of participatory hands. Nevertheless, we have information about some of the makers. In Philadelphia William Savery produced a wide range of chairs employing a variety of design and construction techniques and these he subsequently labelled. John Townsend (1732–1809) of Newport, a member of that city's renowned Goddard-Townsend family of cabinet-

makers, carefully signed and/or labelled a wide variety of pieces over four decades; moreover, it is often possible to attribute Townsend's work, even when not signed, since it displays consistent and individual design and structural techniques.

While so little North American furniture can be documented in terms of its maker, recent scholarship into design techniques and the woods used in construction has often made it possible to identify the region in which a piece was made. For example, the shape of a chair's claw-and-ball foot can almost certainly indicate whether it was made in Philadelphia or in Boston, while a side-rail extending through the rear leg of a chair to create a through-tenon is an absolute signature of the Philadelphia school of cabinet-making. From the science of wood microanalysis and our knowledge of where specific native woods were available and

used, it can be determined whether the pine used in the construction of a drawer-side was from the Middle Atlantic states (*Pinus taeda*) or New England (*Pinus strobus*). This research has also helped clear up some questions as to whether specific pieces are of North American, English or Anglo-Irish origin.

The principal cabinet-making centres during this period were along the Eastern seaboard. The forms – the highboy (high chest-of-drawers) and its companion lowboy (or dressing-table), chests, gaming- or card-tables, chairs (both upholstered and straight), beds, secretary-bookcases, tall-case clocks and round tea-tables – changed little during this period. A few new furniture styles, such as the Pembroke or small drop-leaf table, were introduced in the Chippendale style.

In terms of ornamentation, the emphasis was on carving rather than on inlay. The carved detail was often applied, rather than hewn from the solid. Mahogany, when available, was the wood favoured in most urban centres.

Some of the most sophisticated North American furniture produced during the third quarter of the eighteenth century was made in Boston and its immediate environs. Here two distinctive styles, neither of them influenced by Chippendale's *Director*, flourished. These were the block-front and *bombé*. Chests-of-drawers, secretary-bookcases and chests-on-chests often employed the design enhancement of shaped drawer-fronts, a frequent feature of block-front furniture. The most distinctive group of furniture produced in Boston during this period had a *bombé* form and showed a curious and essentially American mixture of French and English styles. First appearing in Boston in the 1750s, the kettle shape was in demand for chests and other case pieces through the 1780s, long after it had passed out of fashion abroad. Often the wood used in the construction of these pieces was of a particularly high quality and figure.

With the exception of the block-front, the Boston style did not have any great influence on the other major colonial cabinet-making centre, Newport, Rhode Island. It was in Newport, starting in the 1740s, that a local school of cabinet-making emerged which was to be renowned for its originality of design. Like Boston, Newport had a large and lively cabinet-making trade by the middle of the century, but it was thanks to two intermarried Quaker families – the Townsends and the Goddards – that the city became so important in the history of furniture-making. John Goddard (1723–85) owned a copy of Chippendale's *Director* but, as in Boston, this had no direct effect on his furniture-making. In Newport the Boston block front was further elaborated with a lobed shell to create a distinctly North American style, and for nearly thirty years John Townsend made block-and-shell case pieces of almost unchanged design. This shell appeared as an ornament on the crest-rails and legs of chairs as well as on the interiors of desks. Constructed of the finest Honduras mahogany, the furniture was available to Newport's mercantile elite.

With the exception of certain chair models produced during the Queen Anne period, the cabinet-making of New York City could not have been less like that of Rhode Island. New York cabinet-makers followed British practice. Because of the predominance of Loyalists, New Yorkers wanted their furniture to look strictly like that of the old country and thus the proportions tended to be broad and heavy. The highboy, with its tall cabriole legs, was rarely made in New York during this period, the more British chest-on-chest being favoured. The most successful furniture form produced in New York during the third quarter of the eighteenth century was the card-table, with its distinctive serpentine top and sides, carved apron, five cabriole legs and claw-and-ball feet. Much New York furniture of this period has survived, despite the fires of the 1770s, which destroyed large portions of the city. However, it was not until the Federal period that the city really came into its own as a cabinet-making centre.

The influence of Chippendale's *Director* was most pronounced in the Philadelphia of the 1760s and 1770s. London-trained craftsmen arrived here – it was then North America's wealthiest and most populated city – in full force. Benjamin Randolph, Thomas Affleck (1740–95), Hercules

Courtenay and Thomas Johnson were all at work in the full Chippendale style – resulting in, among other things, applied Rococo carving to ornament case pieces, acanthus-carved knees on cabriole legs, and claw-and-ball feet. Thanks to the extraordinarily successful commercial growth in the area, a number of individuals could afford the finest furniture these craftsmen had to offer. Among them was General John Cadwalader, who between 1769 and 1771 built one of the grandest houses in Philadelphia. Cadwalader received a bill dated 13 October 1770 from Thomas Affleck which gives us a very accurate idea of what this house's drawing-room must have looked like. A number of pieces of furniture, all with a history of ownership in the Cadwalader family, have survived. Among the extant pieces is a wing armchair, listed in the inventory as an easy-chair supplied *en suite* with commode sofas.

MAHOGANY SECRETARY-BOOKCASE, WORKSHOP OF NATHANIEL GOULD, BOSTON, c.1779 *(left)*

MAHOGANY ARMCHAIR, THOMAS AFFLECK, 1776 *(below)*

This chair with hairy-paw feet belonged to General John Cadwalader. The carving is attributed to Bernard and Jugiez of Philadelphia.

MAHOGANY CHEST-OF-DRAWERS, CONNECTICUT, c.1779 *(above)*

This elegant piece from Connecticut has a serpentine front and bombé sides. The handles and escutcheons are fine pieces of Rococo metalwork.

THE CLASSICAL
REVIVAL

By the middle of the eighteenth century the Rococo style had already reached the climax of its development. Critics in more advanced Parisian circles began to speak out against its extravagant sinuous forms and to demand a return to a noble, more sober Classicism. The inevitable reaction against the Rococo had begun.

This reaction found its focus in a revaluation of the legacy of classical antiquity. In 1738 the first organized excavation of the ruins of Herculaneum started, and in 1755, with the publication of the first volume of the sumptuously illustrated *Antichità d'Ercolano*, reliable archaeological information concerning that city became freely available. Although some ancient furniture was unearthed at Herculaneum, the new breed of designers was more influenced by the large numbers of wall paintings.

The Venetian-born architect Giovanni Battista Piranesi (1720–78), first active in the 1740s, was an important influence on many of these designers. His powerful engravings of Roman ruins revealed a sublime potential in terms of the new Neoclassical style, while his own designs discarded the accepted forms of classical composition to interpret afresh the spirit of the 'antique'.

Rome was now generally accepted as the climax of the Grand Tour for wealthy young aristocrats from England, sent abroad to complete their artistic education and perhaps acquire a collection of ancient sculpture and a few pictures. By the 1750s these young men might, on their return to England, join the Society of Dilettanti in London and subscribe to the ever-increasing number of archaeological publications. From books such as James Dawkin's and Robert Wood's *Ruins of Baalbec* (1752) and *Ruins of Palmyra* (1757) or Robert Adam's *The Palace of The Emperor Diocletian at Spalato in Dalmatia* (1764) a wealthy patron could derive inspiration for grandiose schemes.

THE CORNER ROOM, PAVLOVSK PALACE, *c*.1817

The decoration and furnishings in this room were conceived by Carlo Rossi, architect to the imperial court in 1817. The seat furniture, of smoked birch, carved and picked out with gold, was made in the Bauman workshops to Rossi's designs.

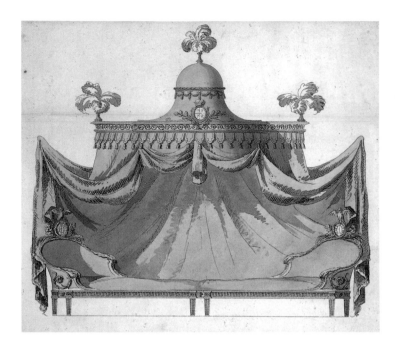

DAY-BED, JOHN VARDY, c.1760 *(above)*

Although essentially a Palladian architect, Vardy designed this early Neoclassical seat furniture.

THE EMPRESS JOSÉPHINE'S BED, JACOB-DESMALTER, c.1810 *(right)*

Part of a scheme for Malmaison designed by Napoleon's decorators, Percier and Fontaine, this is the Empire style at its most opulent, using the imperial connotations of Neoclassicism as an expression of political splendour.

It was at about this time that the first accurate engravings of Greek ornament were beginning to appear. Between 1751 and 1755 the Scots architect James Stuart (1713–88) and his English associate Nicholas Revett (1720–1804) were working on the first volume of their *Antiquities of Athens*. By the time this was published in 1762, it had already been pre-empted by the rather less scholarly *Les ruines des plus beaux monuments de la Grèce* (1758) by the Frenchman Julien-David Le Roy. Through the publication of several authoritative works, Johann Joachim Winckelmann (1717–68), a German working in Rome as Cardinal Albani's librarian, became the leading propagandist of Greek art – even though he himself never visited Greece. His *Geschichte der Kunst des Altertums* was published in Rome in 1764, and two years later English and French translations appeared.

This background of archaeology lay behind the Neoclassical movement of 1760 to 1830. At about the time that enthusiasm for Rococo style was beginning to flag, designers were able to draw upon a whole host of new decorative motifs.

This renewed perception of the ancient world was to become increasingly important as the eighteenth century wore on and as furniture designers strove to create ever-more faithful interpretations of antiquity.

FRANCE

The dominant international style of the second quarter of the eighteenth century, the Rococo, had originated in Paris. Fittingly, this same city provided an important focus for the newly emergent Neoclassical style. As with the Rococo, the Neoclassical style was initially fostered by the web of patronage extended by a few extremely wealthy aristocrats closely connected with the French court. Among them were the marquis de Marigny and the comte de Caylus. The prestige of French fashions ensured that this new style would be adopted throughout Europe over the next thirty years.

With the ascendancy of Madame de Pompadour (1721–64) in Louis XV's affections, her former protector, the financier Le Normant de Tournehem, was appointed *Directeur-Général des Bâtiments du Roi*, the government post which carried responsibility for all official patronage of the arts. The man groomed to be de Tournehem's successor was La Pompadour's younger brother, Abel-François Poisson (1727–81), who later became the marquis de Marigny. In preparation for his future role he had been sent to Italy with his artistic mentor Charles-Nicolas Cochin (1715–90) and the architect Jacques-Germain Soufflot (1713–80), both of whom were known agitators against the Rococo style.

Another influential aristocrat who, like Marigny, was to campaign against the Rococo and argue for a return to the antique was the comte Anne-Claude-Philippe de Caylus (1692–1765). De Caylus had assembled over the years an extensive collection of exceptionally fine antiquities, every item of which he himself drew and described meticulously in the seven volumes of his *Recueil d'antiquités égyptiennes, étrusques, romaines et gauloises* (1752–67).

Men like de Caylus created an environment in which the Neoclassical style could flourish. This new style was already being pioneered far away from Paris by some of the members of the French Academy at Rome. The designs of men such as Jean-Laurent Le

Geay (c.1710–90), Louis-Joseph Le Lorrain (c.1714–59), Nicolas-Henri Jardin (1720–99) and Ennemond-Alexandre Petitot (1727–1801) heralded a radical departure from the abstract organic forms of the Rococo, replacing them with a style which fused architectural elements drawn from the Classicism of Louis XIV's reign.

The first important pieces of furniture to be produced in the new style were designed by one of the members of this circle. Le

PARQUETRY TULIPWOOD WRITING-TABLE, LACROIX, c.1775 *(below left)*

The maker's stamp, R.V.L.C., is that of Roger Vandercruse (called Lacroix) who was received as a master in 1755.

MARQUETRY *ENCOIGNURE*, P. ROUSSEL, c.1770 *(below)*

Although essentially Neoclassical, this piece betrays lingering Rococo influence.

Lorrain, a protégé de Caylus who had trained as an architect, had newly returned from Rome when he received the commission to design a desk (*bureau plat*) and filing cabinet (*cartonnier*) from the wealthy financier Lalive de Jully. This commission exemplified what were to become the key features of much Neoclassical furniture. Straight tapering legs of square section replaced the sinuous curves of the Rococo cabriole leg. The mounts of naturalistically moulded foliage and rocaille which had adorned Rococo furniture were here ossified into architectural swags of laurels. Massive classical motifs, like the Greek key and Vitruvian scroll, were applied in emphatic horizontal bands. The mounts were juxtaposed with the unadorned veneer (in this case ebony) so as to define the

form of the piece in the manner of an order articulating the façade of a building.

In its massive gilt-bronze mounts and ebony veneers, the desk and cabinet consciously acknowledge their debt to Louis XIV furniture rather than to antiquity; indeed, it must be emphasized that Le Lorrain was trying not to recreate ancient furniture, but rather to suggest something of the spirit of the antique. However, these pieces prefigure much of the Neoclassicism of the later eighteenth century.

In 1766 the Baron von Grimm observed that everything in Paris was '*à la grecque*'. The so-called *goût grec* was the first important manifestation of the Neoclassical style, and it built upon what Le Lorrain had accomplished. However, the movement towards

Neoclassical forms was not accomplished overnight. Although it is difficult to assess the progress of the new style, it is clear from paintings that several pieces in it had been created by the early 1760s, and various entries in the Salon exhibition guides of the period describe pieces which are clearly not in the Rococo taste.

As was increasingly the case in the eighteenth century, engraved designs ensured the popularity of this new craze, but it is unclear whether many of these designs were ever executed. The most prolific designer was Flemish-born Jean-François Neufforge (1714–91), whose published designs, *Recueil élémentaire d'Architecture*, eventually comprised nine volumes (the first appeared in 1757). His furniture designs featured the straight legs and heavy architectural decorative forms pioneered by the furniture Le Lorrain had made for Lalive. Another publisher of similar designs in the new style was Jean-Charles Delafosse (1734–91), whose *Nouvelle iconologie historique* (1768) relied greatly upon the heavy Vitruvian scrolls and Greek key motifs originally seen on Lalive's furniture.

Perhaps the most influential pieces produced in the early 1760s were the *secrétaires à abattant* produced in the workshop of the *ébéniste du roi*, Jean-François Oeben (c.1720–63). They interpreted the architectural decorative vocabulary and rectangular forms of the Lalive furniture in a lighter, more elegant manner. Corners were rounded, and in place of ebony veneer Oeben used delicate marquetry patterns. These pieces were designed to stand against walls and complement the lines of the *boiseries* (wooden wainscots) of Parisian hôtels, which were acquiring an increasingly architectural flavour and were commonly rigidly divided into panels by orders of pilasters.

In the early 1760s such pieces seem to have been very much in the avant-garde, but from the middle of the decade the exuberant Rococo forms which during the preceding years had formed the staple of the Paris furniture trade were noticeably being chastened. The pieces which mark the transition between the Rococo and the acceptance of Neoclassicism into mainstream Parisian fur-

niture design often combined rectangular forms and classicizing mounts with floral marquetry, rounded corners and cabriole legs. In place of their *bombé* and serpentine outlines, commodes and *encoignures* were given breakfronts of rectangular or trapezoidal form.

The single most famous piece of furniture from this transitional period was the *bureau du roi*, commissioned from Oeben by Louis XV. Technically, its mechanisms were of a novel complexity and it developed the newly introduced form, the roll-top desk, on an unprecedented scale. To be sure, the legs are cabriole and the carcase is *bombé*, but the extravagant curves of Meissonnier's designs

LOUIS XVI GILTWOOD ARMCHAIR, STAMPED TILLIARD, MID-18TH CENTURY

have largely disappeared. The mounts are moulded naturalistically, rather than as abstract *rocaille*, and form part of a classically inspired iconographic programme symbolic of the monarchical virtues. The gallery which surrounds the top is faced by a regular chain-like pattern derived from classical sources. The body of the desk is draped with heavy

gilt-bronze garlands of bay leaves, a motif reminiscent of the furniture commissioned by Lalive four years earlier. Even the interior is marked by a new restraint: the drawer-fronts are inlaid in rigidly geometric patterns while the pigeonholes are divided by caryatid terms of *goût grec* derivation.

It is not clear who actually designed the piece, but Michel-Ange Slodtz, who had been appointed *Dessinateur des Menus-Plaisirs* in 1758, seems a likely candidate (the *menus-plaisirs* comprised the government department responsible for temporary decorations). The mounts were cast by Étienne Forestier to models provided by one of the Duplessis family. They were then chased by Louis-Barthélémy Hervieu. The carcase and marquetry were, of course, furnished by Oeben's workshop (although it is known that his assistant Wynant Stylen worked upon the marquetry), and it seems likely that it was his responsibility to co-ordinate the project. The *bureau du roi* was completed and delivered in May 1769, six years after Oeben's death, and it bore in its marquetry the signature of the new head of the atelier, Jean-Henri Riesener.

By the middle of the 1770s the Louis XVI style was well established in the works of the Parisian *ébénistes*. Case furniture adapted easily to rectilinear forms, although contours retained a certain suppleness. The high-waisted commodes of the transitional period were now supported on straight legs or – if, as was more usual, they had three deep drawers – on short feet turned like tops. *Secrétaires à abattant* remained popular pieces. *Bureaux plats* assumed the rectangular forms of the new style, becoming more refined. They were often inlaid with marquetry in geometric patterns and applied with bronze mounts of a restrained architectural character, emphasizing their underlying rectangular forms. Console tables were at first supported on volute-like scrolls and then later carried on turned and fluted legs joined by stretchers.

Seat furniture, like the smaller tables, seems to have adapted less quickly to the Neoclassical style, and much of it retained the undulating curves and cabriole legs of the Louis XV period until well into the 1780s. A

PARQUETRY *SECRÉTAIRE À ABATTANT*, J.-H.
RIESENER, *c.*1780 *(below)*

This secrétaire *was designed for Marie-Antoinette's
use at the Trianon and is remarkable for the jewel-
like crispness of its mounts, a characteristic of
Riesener's furniture of this period.*

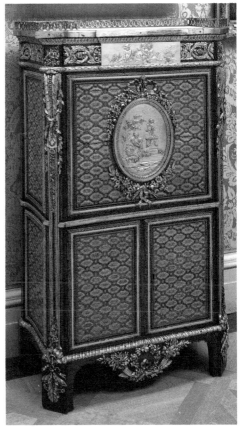

BUREAU DU ROI,
J.-F. OEBEN AND
J.-H. RIESENER,
1760–9 *(left)*

*Designed for the
Cabinet-Intérieur du
Roi, Versailles, this is
arguably the most
important example of
French furniture ever
commissioned.*

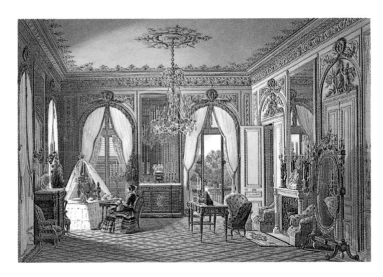

ST CLOUD INTERIOR,
*c.*1852 *(left)*

*Although it dates from
the mid-nineteenth
century, this watercolour
gives a fairly accurate
impression of a Louis
XVI interior. The
marquetry furniture is by
Riesener.*

portrait of Lalive de Jully by Jean-Baptiste
Greuze shows him seated upon a kind of low
bergère, presumably designed by Le Lorrain.

Designs made for chairs in the second half
of the 1760s by Neufforge, the duc
d'Orléans' architect Victor Louis (1731–
1800) and the bronze *sculpteur-ciseleur-doreur*
Jean-Louis Prieur (*fl.*1765–85), show the
emergence of the basic form of the Louis XVI
chair. The pattern-book published in 1772 by
Jacob Roubo (1739–91), *L'Art du Menuisier
en meubles* (1772–5), illustrates many designs

in the new style. Typically they were carried
on straight tapering legs that were usually
turned and often fluted, reeded or spiralled.
Seat-rails were sometimes straight but frequently slightly bowed and carved with
chain and guilloche motifs. The joints in the
chair-frame (for example, at the junction of
the leg and seat-rail) were often punctuated
by rosettes. Chair-backs were increasingly
oval or rectangular in form, and were often
flanked by colonettes. As in the Louis XV
period, seat furniture was painted and gilded.

The Ébénistes

The most important *ébéniste* of the Louis
XVI period was Jean-Henri Riesener (1734–
1806). Having arrived from Westphalia, he
had found employment in Oeben's atelier in
the 1750s. When the master died in 1763, his
widow continued to administer the business
and by 1765 Riesener had become foreman.
In 1767, following a practice common
among cabinet-makers, he married Mme
Oeben and took over the running of the

business. On 23 January 1768 he finally became a *maître-ébéniste* and was entitled to stamp furniture with his own name.

During the early part of the 1770s he supplied only a handful of pieces to the Crown. However, in 1774 he succeeded the octogenarian Gilles Joubert (1689–1775) as *ébéniste du roi*. With his appointment French furniture reached levels of hitherto unparalleled splendour. Between 1774 and 1784 Crown expenditure was more than double that for any previous decade. Riesener's most important work was carried out for the Queen of the newly crowned Louis XVI, Marie-Antoinette. Under her direction the palaces at St Cloud and Compiègne were refurbished in the most sumptuous style, while her apartments at Versailles and Fontainebleau were filled with new furniture of the very highest quality. Riesener's work of the early 1770s was still in many ways transitional in character.

Around 1780 the furniture produced in Riesener's workshop entered a new phase. The forms were much lighter and less dependent on the prototypes established in Oeben's workshop. The bronze mounts acquired a lapidary crispness. Pieces were adorned by exquisitely chased, naturalistically observed garlands of the Queen's favourite flowers and complex lambrequins (valances) of swagged drapery. Gilt-bronze oval medallions in the manner of the sculptor Clodion (1738–1814) and small friezes modelled and chased in the manner of Pierre Gouthière (1732–1812/14), the greatest producer of bronzes of the period, were applied sparingly. Many of these pieces were veneered with a delicate marquetry trellis picked out with black-and-white fillets. Being *ébéniste du roi*, and therefore exempt from guild restrictions, Riesener was able, unlike other cabinet-makers, to manufacture and design his own mounts, and these contribute much to the character of his later pieces.

Many pieces from Riesener's workshop may have been conceived by the *Dessinateur du Mobilier* the innovative Neoclassical

MADAME DE
MAINTENON'S
BEDROOM,
FONTAINEBLEAU

The bed and chairs of this highly sophisticated interior are characteristic of the Louis XVI period.

architect Jacques Gondoin (1737–1818).

Riesener remained the Queen's favourite cabinet-maker even after the retrenchments forced upon the royal household in 1784. However, he was only one of the many *maître-ébénistes* who were working in Paris during the 1770s and 1780s to produce furniture of unsurpassed elegance and sophistication. Outside the court, the catalysts of the Neoclassical style were the *marchands-merciers*, the shopkeepers and traders who commissioned and designed some of the great Parisian *ébénistes'* most luxurious pieces. Men like Simon-Philippe Poirier and Dominique Daguerre possessed a very wealthy and exclusive clientele among whom, as well as Louis XVI and Marie-Antoinette, were members of various European royal families and English aristocrats. Chief among the *marchands-merciers* was Poirier, whose shop, À la Couronne d'Or, lay in the rue St Honoré. He commissioned furniture from Bernard II van Risen Burgh and from Roger Lacroix. These were often small pieces intended for ladies, such as work-tables, *guéridons* or *bonheurs-du-jour*.

The *marchands merciers* constantly tried to develop new furniture types in response to the demands of changing social customs and domestic planning. The increasingly informal arrangement of rooms in the houses of the wealthy generated a need for small yet luxurious pieces. As ceremonial rooms became less important, the furnishing of informal rooms, notably the boudoir, became more opulent. Although many of these pieces featured geometric inlay and architectural mounts or designs, most retained the cabriole legs and soft outlines of Louis XV furniture until well into the 1780s.

From 1766, when he became a master cabinet-maker, it was Martin Carlin (d.1785) who provided some of Poirier's most luxurious pieces. Typically these were mounted with plaques of porcelain supplied by the Royal Sèvres factory, painted with reserves of flowers on brightly coloured grounds.

In 1772 Poirier went into partnership with Dominique Daguerre (1744–94), and in 1777 Daguerre took over the whole business. He continued the search for ever-more luxurious furnishings and began to use Adam

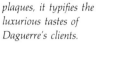

SECRETAIRE-CABINET, ADAM WEISWEILER, c.1780

This cabinet was almost certainly acquired from marchand-mercier Dominique Daguerre by the Grand Duchess Maria Fedorovna during her visit to Paris in 1784. With its Sèvres porcelain plaques, it typifies the luxurious tastes of Daguerre's clients.

GILT-BRONZE MOUNTED CONSOLE TABLE, J.-H. RIESENER, 1781

This table formed part of the furnishings of Marie-Antoinette's Cabinet-intérieur at Versailles during the winter months. In summer it was replaced by a carved giltwood console table.

Weisweiler (c.1750–c.1810) as his cabinet-maker. Panels of the finest-quality Japanese lacquer were cut from antique screens to face commodes and secretaires. Such pieces were veneered with exotic woods like thuya, amboyna and plum-pudding mahogany, and Wedgwood medallions provided even greater adornment. The doors and drawers of the most lavish pieces were fitted with panels of Florentine *pietre dure*. All of these pieces were adorned with gilt-bronze mounts exquisitely chased in the workshops of such men as Pierre Gouthière and Pierre-Philippe Thomire (1751–1843).

The End of an Era

The final phase of the Louis XVI style was heralded by the appointment in 1784 of Thierry de Ville Avray as *dessinateur Garde-meuble du roi*. One of his main objectives was to cut the royal household's massive expenditure on furnishings in the face of a looming economic crisis. Among the first casualties of the new policy was Riesener, who was replaced as *ébéniste du roi* by the German-born Guillaume Beneman (fl.1784–1811). Beneman's own work is often hard to detect, as most of the furniture bearing his stamp seems to have been altered or repaired, rather than made, by him. This was no doubt as a result of royal economies.

It was in this atmosphere of comparative austerity that the fashion began to predominate for restrained furniture, veneered *à l'anglaise* with plain sheets of mahogany, offset by discreet gilt-bronze or brass mounts. Among the most significant pieces of furniture made during this period was the suite of mahogany seat furniture, in the *style étrusque*, supplied by the *menuisier* Georges Jacob (1739–1814) in 1787 for Marie-Antoinette's dairy at the King's château at Rambouillet. The designer of the suite was the painter of classical ruins, Hubert Robert. They were among the first chairs to have over-scrolled backs, in imitation of antique couches and further broke from tradition in that the backs were carved with a pierced lattice pattern, rather than upholstered. The other significant innovation was the use of polished mahogany in the English manner.

INTERIOR AT BAGATELLE, F.-J. BÉLANGER

Conceived as a pleasure pavilion for Louis XVI's brother, the comte d'Artois, the arabesque wall decoration at Bagatelle was among the most influential Neoclassical decorative schemes. The secretaire is by Röentgen.

Directoire and Empire

With the fall of Louis XVI and the turmoil of the French Revolution (1789), the Paris furniture trade entered a fallow period. There was little demand for new pieces and the market was largely swamped by the dispersal of the collections of the Crown and aristocracy. Daguerre fled to England, where he died in 1793. Riesener was employed by the new government to remove the royal cipher from existing furniture. However, men who had produced some of the finest furniture of the *ancien régime*, for example Georges Jacob, Bernard Molitor and Joseph Stöckel (1743–1800), continued to produce pieces, admittedly in an increasingly austere style. As the turmoil which marked the height of the French Revolution began to subside, there came the regime known as the Directoire, which afforded a time of comparative stability. Austerity was still necessary, and the period is characterized by the adaptation of a simplified form of the late-Louis XIV style—*style étrusque*—to bourgeois taste. Publications such as La Mésangère's *Journal des Dames et des Modes*, through their coloured engravings, ensured the widespread adoption of the new styles. Furniture became more angular, and mounts were greatly simplified, often being executed in brass rather than gilt-bronze.

It was not until the accession of Bonaparte as first consul that official patronage can be said to have revived and the French furniture trade to have recovered. The most influential designers of the Consulate and Empire periods were Napoleon's architects Charles Percier (1764–1838) and Pierre-François-Léonard Fontaine (1762–1853). Both men had been trained under the *ancien régime*, and at the end of the 1780s had travelled extensively in Italy, where they studied not only the ruins of antiquity but also the palazzos of the Renaissance. On their return to France they were commissioned by Georges Jacob to design the president's desk and speaker's tribunal for the salle de la Convention at the Tuileries. In 1798 Percier assisted Louis-Martin Berthault (1771–1823) with the designs for the house of the banker Récamier, and here the Empire style can already be seen in its maturity.

However, it was under the patronage of Napoleon's consort, Joséphine de Beauharnais, that Percier and Fontaine were established as the most important decorators in France. The Hôtel de Beauharnais (c.1799) was stylistically one of their most successful projects. It was followed in the early 1800s by the interiors at Malmaison. After 1802 they worked exclusively for Napoleon. When he became Emperor in 1805 they became responsible for the decorative style of the whole Empire. Their engraved designs, *Recueil de décorations intérieures* (1801), ensured that their style was exported over the following years, more or less intact, throughout Europe.

Essentially the Empire style was not particularly revolutionary but rather a development from the *style étrusque* of the late

GILTWOOD ARMCHAIR, c.1810

The rectangular form of this chair and the mask arm-supports are typical of the weighty grandeur of the Empire style.

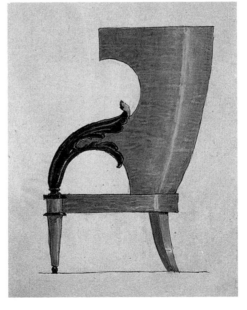

CHAIR DESIGN, c.1790

This design reflects the austere forms pioneered by the Neoclassical avant-garde in the late 1780s. Georges Jacob made similar pieces for the painter David.

ARMCHAIR, PRE-1804

This chair was used by the painter David for some of his preliminary sketches of Napoleon's coronation. It represents the archaeological extreme of Empire taste.

1780s. The tented interiors of Joséphine's château at Malmaison look back to those of the Comte d'Artois' pleasure pavilion at Bagatelle, while the heavy forms of the case furniture recall the commodes supplied by Stöckel to the royal palace at Compiègne. The impact of the style, however, proved to be enormous, and it spread throughout Europe in the wake of Napoleon's conquests. The prestige of Parisian cabinet-makers was at a level unsurpassed by that of the *ébénistes* of the *ancien régime*.

Empire forms tended to be more massive in scale and more emphatically rectangular than those of the Directoire. The fashion continued for mahogany, the value of which was further exaggerated by its scarcity during the Napoleonic blockades. These prevented the wood from being imported from the English colonies and cabinet-makers were therefore forced to use indigenous woods as well. Gilt-bronze mounts remained in use, especially for more expensive pieces. Commonly classical figures, often exquisitely cast and burnished, were applied directly to the veneer in low relief. Grotesque decoration, occasionally filling the whole surface of the piece, was also employed. Other favourite motifs included the lyre, the wreath, arrows, the sphinx, amphorae, palmettes and anthemia.

Seat furniture evolved from the 'Etruscan' forms of the previous decade, but around 1805 the carved scrolled back began to be replaced by a flat rectangular variety which was invariably upholstered. Sometimes the frames were of beech, painted and picked out with gold, but more usually they were of mahogany, occasionally adorned with gilt-bronze mounts. The fine tapered legs of 'Etruscan' furniture became slightly thicker and were now either turned like balusters or of square section. Arm-rests were supported either by uprights following the line of the front legs or by sphinx figures; another solution was to down-scroll the arms towards the seat-rail, and after about 1810 the arm-rest was often supported by a down-scrolled cornucopia.

Case furniture became increasingly rectangular. Typically, a commode and secretaire were made *en suite*, with both of

MEUBLE À HAUTEUR D'APPUI, JACOB FRÈRES *c.1800 (below)*

INLAID MAPLEWOOD DAY-BED, *c.1820* (bottom)

similar form and covered by plain marble tops. Such pieces would usually have a deep frieze drawer which rested upon pilasters or columns at the angles. These columns were headed by plain Tuscan gilt-bronze capitals, often engine-turned. A common alternative to columns were term figures headed by female masks in either classical or Egyptian garb. More expensive pieces would be adorned with a profusion of gilt-bronze mounts by *bronziers* like Thomire.

The console table remained an important piece during the Empire. Most were simply supported on plain columns or term figures, but the grander pieces rested on giant animal

introduced under the Empire and these were given the classicizing names typical of the period. Related to the small *guéridon* table was the *athénienne*. *Athéniennes* were used variously as perfume burners, wash-stands and *jardinières*. Among the most important of these pieces is the Baptismal Font of the King of Rome. The work of the Italian goldsmiths Luigi and Francesco Manfredini, it was a present given to the Empress Marie-Louise by the city of Milan. In almost every detail it closely follows an elaborate tripod excavated from Pompeii and illustrated by Piranesi. Another important *athénienne* stood in the Emperor's apartment at the Tuileries.

demand from an ever-widening bourgeoisie, less wealthy than earlier patrons and less interested in historic adornments. The richly coloured mahogany veneers of the early 1800s were largely replaced by lighter indigenous woods. Patterns of inlaid darker woods showing stylized classical motifs provided decorative accents to the plain surfaces of such furniture.

Although such pieces derived from classical forms, they lacked the Neoclassical conviction of Directoire and Empire furniture and now had to compete against designs which looked back to France's medieval history or to the Rococo.

PLATE 20,
*MEUBLES ET
OBJETS DE GOÛT*,
LA MÉSANGÈRE,
1807–1818

The colour illustrations published by La Mésangère ensured the rapid spread of Empire taste throughout France and Europe.

monopodia (supports in the shape of a beast's head and body, with one leg and foot), often winged, which were either gilded or were painted black to simulate the appearance of patinated bronze.

Empire *guéridons* came in many forms. The tops, usually of marble, were supported upon three or four simple columns or terms on a concave-sided plinth – these were usually of polished wood, mounted with gilt-bronze. Alternatively, large animal monopodia could be used to create a grander effect. *Guéridons* could also be supported on a single pedestal which, in the early years of the century, was of concave triangular section and tapering profile, in the manner of antique altars and candelabra; later pedestals were often turned like balusters. Smaller *guéridons* could rest on fine gilt-bronze supports.

Several new articles of furniture were

Made to the design of Charles Percier by the goldsmith Martin-Guillaume Biennais (1764–1843), it served as a wash-stand, the silver bowl being supported by elegant gilt-bronze swans.

Other new pieces included the *psyché* (a full-length cheval-glass) and the *somno* (a bedside table, usually modelled in the form of a classical plinth). Among the most extravagant furniture to be produced during the Empire period were beds, which took on increasingly massive forms and had high over-scrolled ends.

After the restoration of the Bourbon monarchy, the Neoclassical furniture of the Empire continued to be produced but began to evolve into simpler, softer forms. Gradually gilt-bronze mounts became rarer and the columns and term figures began to disappear. This simplification was due to increased

BRITAIN

English Neoclassicism can be said to have evolved from the Palladian Classicism which preceded it. Although in England the decorative arts had come briefly under the spell of the Rococo, the style had never rooted itself entirely. Moreover, Lord Burlington and his circle had anyway founded their style in archaeology and the study of the antique. Thus some of the best English furniture of the 1760s derives from Palladian furniture designs of twenty years before. As an example, the carved laurel wreaths secured by foliate clasps found on some of the works of the royal cabinet-makers, William Vile and John Cobb, can be seen in some of William Kent's furniture designs of the 1730s.

Arguably the earliest Neoclassical furniture in England was the suite of seat furniture designed from 1758 by James 'Athenian' Stuart for the drawing-room at Spencer House in St James's, London. Stuart, with Nicholas Revett, published *The Antiquities of Athens* and was one of the pioneers of the Greek revival. The seat furniture was not an attempt to create a reproduction of a Greek original but fused the serpentine contours of a Louis XV *canapé* with archaeologically inspired winged-lion terminals and heavy paw feet. The use of paw feet, lion masks, sphinxes and other such motifs had of course been an established practice since the Renaissance, but from the 1760s they were to become increasingly symptomatic of the new Neoclassical style.

GILTWOOD SOFA, JAMES STUART, c.1760

Part of a suite designed by Stuart for the painted room at Spencer House. Stuart took the form of the bold antique griffins from his considerable experience of archaeology.

The Adam Style

By the middle of the decade Stuart's ascendancy as the premier Neoclassical designer in Britain had been undermined by the success of his rivals Robert (1728–42) and James (1732–94) Adam, the former recently returned from Italy. Robert Adam's furniture designs, like Stuart's, drew upon the new archaeology, but they took as their starting-point the ruins of Rome. For a while, Stuart and Adam battled for the same commissions and many of their designs show a striking similarity. Ultimately Adam was to better his rival as both a designer and a businessman.

Adam took the total integration of interior design to a level never before seen in England. Furnishings were made to fit into a succession of contrasting spaces which the architect had planned in the manner of Roman baths. Ceilings were matched to the specially woven carpets beneath them in order to extend and underline the special effects which Adam termed 'movement'.

Every aspect of the interior was submitted to the overall scheme of decoration. Thus the plasterwork filigree grotesques with which Adam lined his interiors were extended into the carving of painted and gilded furniture (chairs, pier-glasses and tables) and echoed in the marquetry of the veneered furniture (cabinets, commodes, etc.) so that the whole interior conformed to a uniform decorative

style. The furniture designed for such interiors often has, therefore, something of the quality of a theatrical prop. For example, the *trompe l'oeil* urns-on-pedestals in the saloon at Kedleston Hall (1759–60), Derbyshire, actually serve only to mask a primitive central-heating system.

Robert Adam introduced to English furniture design a whole new vocabulary of decorative motifs plundered from antiquity. The sphinxes, griffins, caryatids, bucrania (ox-skulls), aegricanes (rams heads), putti, medallions, urns, tripods and candelabra found in antique reliefs and wall-paintings were rendered in paint, plaster, composition, marquetry and carved wood and linked to a decorative ensemble by trailing and coiling acanthus, paterae and husk swags.

In terms of international Neoclassicism in the 1760s, Adam's single most important innovation was the development of the arabesque or grotesque (from the word grotto) motif in the decorative arts. The Adams stretched their webs of classical ornament over relatively simple geometric forms. Although it seems likely that the brothers relied for the motifs of their early furniture on the highly sculptural forms of Neufforge and the *goût grec*, the decorative emphasis of the brothers' designs moved increasingly towards surface rather than

volume. Carved wood was largely replaced by metal and composition ornaments which could be shaped into highly intricate, albeit shallow, forms and then applied to the furniture so as to create a delicate layer of filigree decoration.

Although the Adam brothers designed a considerable amount of furniture to complement their interiors, the bulk of their designs seem to have been for wall furniture or decorative pieces. Their houses were often furnished with case and seat furniture in a conforming style by other prestigious contemporary cabinet-makers. Among these were Thomas Chippendale (1718–1779), the Linnell brothers, John (d.1796) and William (d.1763), and the firm of Ince and Mayhew. It seems likely that Robert Adam often indicated roughly what he wanted with a sketch and then left it to the craftsmen to supply the finishing details themselves.

Indeed, Adam-style furniture is perhaps seen at its best in the work of other craftsmen, notably Chippendale — a point perfectly illustrated by the commode at Harewood House, Yorkshire. The elements of the Adam style are all to be found here, rendered in marquetry and even mounts of gilt-bronze (rare in English furniture), but Chippendale exploited his materials in order to achieve a much more robust effect.

The Adam style took England by storm throughout the 1760s and 1770s. A host of imitators appeared, chief among them being the young James Wyatt (1746–1813). The influence of Adam on English furniture design is testified to by the pattern-books of men such as George Hepplewhite (d.1786), who first published his *Cabinet-Maker and Upholsterer's Guide* in 1788. Pattern-books of this kind ensured that the types of furniture which graced Adam interiors could be imitated on a less grand scale by cabinet-makers throughout the land.

Of the designs published by Hepplewhite, the ones with which he is most readily associated were for the pierced-splat and shield-back chairs which were to prove influential abroad. However, his designs featured also the typical box-like Georgian forms of chest, bureau, press and bookcase established in the early eighteenth century – but now adorned with the typical 'Adam' decorative vocabulary, sometimes executed in marquetry, sometimes painted and, in the case of seat and wall furniture, often carved in low relief. In general, cabinet-makers of this time seem progressively to have adopted lighter forms and more refined proportions in their work.

Robert Adam himself drew heavily upon contemporary Louis XV and XVI styles when designing chairs and the residual influence of the French Rococo was important to the forms of Hepplewhite furniture, too. Chairs could have cabriole legs, while case furniture was often marked by a serpentine outline. However, despite the presence in England of workers in ormolu such as Dominique Jean and, more importantly, Matthew Boulton (1728–1802), mounted furniture seems to have been the exception.

Although English furniture was unable to compete with the luxury furniture of the French *ébénistes* and *menuisiers*, it was prized in many areas of Europe for its unpretentious utilitarian character, and pattern-books such as Hepplewhite's enjoyed a wide circulation both on the Continent and on the other side of the Atlantic in the United States.

Henry Holland

At the beginning of the 1780s, an elegant alternative to the Adam style was beginning to emerge in the form of a series of interiors by the architect Henry Holland (1745–1806). Holland practised a francophile Neo-classicism inspired by the work of architects such as François-Joseph Bélanger. His designs found favour with the Whig circle associated with the Prince of Wales, the future George IV, a fellow francophile whose

COMMODE, ATTRIBUTED TO WILLIAM INCE AND JOHN MAYHEW, 1773 *(above)*

This commode was one of a pair made for Osterley House to a design by Adam. The marquetry medallions are probably by Christopher Furlogh.

KEDLESTON HALL, DERBYSHIRE, *c.1768 (above left)*

Adam's design reveals the importance he assigned to the integration of furnishings and the architectural shell into a single coherent decorative scheme.

PEDESTAL AND URN, THOMAS CHIPPENDALE, *c.1770 (above)*

These pieces were part of a group of furniture designed for the dining room at Harewood House, Yorkshire, in the Adam style.

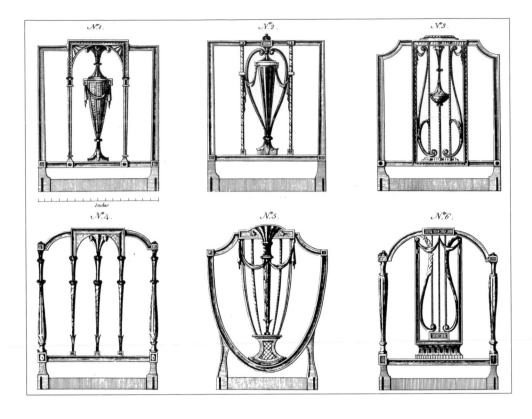

MAHOGANY ARMCHAIR, *c.1785 (below)*

The shield-back design was popularized by Hepplewhite's Cabinet-Maker and Upholsterer's Guide *of 1788 and 1794.*

DESIGNS FOR CHAIR-BACKS, THOMAS SHERATON, 1791–4 *(above)*

In his Cabinet-Maker and Upholsterer's Drawing Book *Sheraton developed the forms of chair-backs illustrated by Hepplewhite, but the influence of Georges Jacob can also be discerned.*

taste was to be enormously influential throughout this period. Holland provided interiors for the Whig palaces of Samuel Whitbread at Southill and the Duke of Bedford at Woburn, but his most important commission came in 1783 when the Prince himself commissioned Holland to remodel his London residence, Carlton House. To furnish the lavish interiors Holland designed furniture which reflected contemporary Louis XVI styles. The *émigré* cabinet-maker François Hervé probably supplied some of the chairs, while the Parisian *marchand-mercier* Dominique Daguerre supplied furniture by Georges Jacob and Adam Weisweiler. The design of many of these pieces was in the new *style étrusque*, the last word in Louis XVI Neoclassicism, and as such anticipated Regency themes. Like Adam before him, Holland made sure that he designed furniture with an eye to the overall decoration of the interior.

Thomas Sheraton

Holland's interiors seem to have had an enormous influence upon the designer Thomas Sheraton (1751–1806). To a certain extent the pattern-books published by Sheraton popularized Holland's francophile style, while the plates of his *Drawing Book* illustrate a room based on the Prince's drawing-room at Carlton House.

Sheraton's *The Cabinet-Maker and Upholsterer's Drawing Book*, published in parts between 1791 and 1794, was the most influential pattern-book of the 1790s, and his designs are representative of much of the furniture produced around the turn of the century and into the Regency period of 1810–20. His books were indicative of the public's ever-growing demand for comfort and its voracious appetite for new fashions – indeed, Sheraton refers cuttingly to the outmoded nature of the designs which Hepplewhite had published only a few years before. New types of furniture, having highly specialized and often mechanical or metamorphic functions, seem constantly to have evolved. Innovative forms such as the sofa-table – an elongated Pembroke table – appeared in this period. Dining-tables supported in the centre on turned pedestals and sabre legs began partly to replace the established models (i.e., those with legs set around the edge); card-tables, too, began to be supported on pedestals. Breakfast-tables – likewise supported on a single pedestal – were scaled-down versions of dining-tables, having hinged tops which could be rectangular, oval or circular; a further variation was the drum- or rent-table, which usually had a circular leather-lined top supported on a single pedestal. One of Sheraton's most popular designs was a D-shaped writing-table with a leather-lined writing surface surrounded by a superstructure of drawers and pigeonholes, supported on tapering legs. The original had been made for the Prince of Wales's Carlton House, from which the piece subsequently derived its name.

The typical Sheraton chair combined increasingly fine lines with a square back, fine splats and thin, turned front legs. Usually these were in carved mahogany but many were japanned or painted – occasionally they had caned seats.

Most of Sheraton's designs were meant to be executed in mahogany, but more expensive pieces from this period often combined satinwood veneers – newly fashionable, albeit costly – with painted decorations of swags, garlands and grisaille medallions in an 'Etruscan'-inspired style, a further refinement of the Adam decorative vocabulary. Again, French influence may have been important to the designs, as Holland employed at Carlton House the decorative painter Louis-Alexandre Delabrière, who had worked with Bélanger at Bagatelle, to execute elaborate arabesque ornament.

Sheraton's designs of the 1790s show a continuing fascination with simple geometric forms but, like Hepplewhite, Sheraton combined them with residual traces of French Rococo influence as evidenced by their gently undulating serpentine contours.

Between 1794 and 1796, to provide a further source for his designs, Holland had employed the architect, Charles Heathcote Tatham (1772–1842), making drawings of antique decoration and furniture in Italy. The furniture executed in response to Tatham's engravings at Southill and Carlton House foreshadows the increasing bulk of Regency furniture. One of the more interesting designs is for a stool, based on an original Roman marble stool, and carved to simulate drapery folds. Painted and marbled beechwood versions of this stool exist, while some of those illustrated in the view by the artist William Henry Pyne of the circular

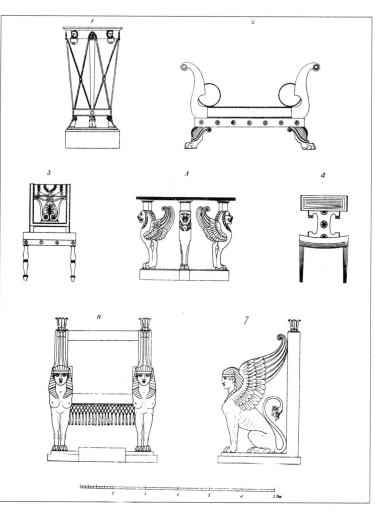

PLATE 19,
HOUSEHOLD FURNITURE AND INTERIOR DECORATION,
THOMAS HOPE,
1807

Like those of Percier and Fontaine, Hope's brittle line engravings underlined the almost abstract simplicity of his designs but gave little impression of the splendour of his lavish interiors.

drawing-room at Carlton House appear to be upholstered. Pyne also illustrates a large gilt-wood throne which was clearly influenced by the massive forms of a classical antique marble original.

The Regency

The work of Tatham ushered in a new era of English furniture design, in which the archaeological references were notably literal-minded. Sheraton's *Encyclopaedia* (1805) introduced some new archaeologically inspired chair designs, which he styled 'Herculaneum' chairs, but the new force in English furniture design was now an amateur called Thomas Hope (1769–1831).

At his house in Duchess Street, Cavendish Square, London, Hope created a series of interiors to frame his collection of antiquities.

These interiors derived their inspiration from the designs of Napoleon's decorators Percier and Fontaine and from the researches into Egyptian antiquity of Baron Dominique Vivant Denon (1747–1825), the director of the Musée Napoléon. This French influence was tempered by Hope's essentially romantic vision of Greek antiquity. He replaced the refined lines of the Sheraton period with massive geometric forms. Console tables or circular centre tables were supported by lion or griffin monopodia, full caryatids or terms headed by Egyptian masks rather than thin, tapering legs. Writing-tables rested on thick trestles shaped like the ends of Roman sarcophagi. Chairs took on the exaggerated proportions of the *klismos* (with its four sabre legs, curving supports and a curved backboard), as represented in Greek red-figure vase-paintings, or reproduced the

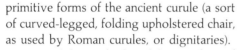

JAPANNED AND
PARCEL-GILT SOFA,
c.1805 (right)

This elegant sofa is in the
mainstream of Regency
taste. English chairs of
this period were
frequently of beech,
japanned or grained to
resemble rosewood.

EBONIZED AND
PARCEL-GILT
ARMCHAIR, c.1805
(below left)

The fanciful snake motif
on the back-rail is
copied from one of
Sheraton's later designs,
while the elegant sabre
legs are derived from
those of the classical
Greek klismos.

primitive forms of the ancient curule (a sort of curved-legged, folding upholstered chair, as used by Roman curules, or dignitaries).

Hope did not look solely to classical antiquity: he produced also Egyptian and Indian rooms. His austere line engravings, in the style of the sculptor John Flaxman, give little impression of the lushness that characterized his interiors. Much of this was derived from the richly coloured fabrics and highly complex upholstery which set off the geometric forms of the furniture. As well as couches, Hope favoured fully upholstered long banquettes and ottomans.

Despite Hope's influence many furniture designs of the Regency period were derived from Sheraton models of the 1790s. The pierced backs and the turned spindle-like front legs typical of Sheraton-style chairs of the 1790s gradually gave way to a *klismos* type, with a yoke back-rail and front legs that were either turned or sabre. Unlike comparable European chairs, the sabre legs at the back and the support for the back-rail were made from a single piece of wood to create a lighter, more elegant effect.

The marquetry and painting characteristic of much Hepplewhite and Sheraton furniture had largely disappeared by the early 1800s. Decorative effects were now created through the use of strongly figured veneers, often of flame-figured mahogany or rosewood, and occasionally of more exotic woods such as sabicu, zebrawood and coromandel, usually outlined by abstract patterns of ebonized stringing or cut-brass inlay. Carved-wood monopodia supports

were painted black or green to simulate patinated bronze and following the French taste, Egyptian masks were widely used.

Hope published his *Household Furniture and Interior Decoration* in 1807, but by 1808 the prolific pattern-book publisher George Smith had produced *Designs for Household Furniture*, his own rather crude interpretations of Hope's designs, including bulkier forms, lions' heads and Egyptian mask monopodia. Smith's much heavier designs testify also to the increasing influence of the French Empire style upon English cabinet-makers, which chiefly manifested itself in progressively heavier forms and more massive proportions.

A further index of Regency style can be

found among the plates of *Repository of Arts*, a London magazine produced from 1809 to 1828 by Rudolf Ackermann (1764–1834). Some of the designs are based closely upon originals by Percier and Fontaine. Ackermann's plates and Smith's pattern-books are notable also for the number of Gothic designs which they included. At this period medieval archaeology was in its infancy and Smith's designs simply applied crocketed finials and lancet-and-ogee panelling to existing Neoclassical forms, a style analogous to the 'Gothick' architecture of James Wyatt and Jeffrey Wyatville (1766–1840). This was to remain the case until Pugin's more serious work of the 1830s. Another alternative to Neoclassicism was provided by a later flowering of chinoiserie, as exemplified by the Prince Regent's Pavilion at Brighton and his Chinese drawing-room at Carlton House.

In the opening decades of the nineteenth century the influence of the contemporary French Empire style upon men like George Smith co-existed with a taste for French eighteenth-century furniture, a taste largely initiated by the Prince Regent who, in his role of patron of the arts, seems to have consciously emulated the Bourbons of the *ancien régime* (some of the carpets at Carlton House were indeed woven with fleur-de-lis). The Prince commissioned the French *émigré* craftsman Louis Le Gaigneur (*fl.*1815–17) to create furniture using the cut-brass-and-tortoiseshell-inlay technique favoured by Louis XIV's *ébéniste du roi* André-Charles Boulle. Although the furniture took the shape of contemporary Regency pieces, such as the drum-table or the sofa-table, the inlay added a touch of Bourbon splendour to the Regent's interiors. The lavishness of such pieces pre-figured the full-blown 'Louis Quatorze' revival of the later 1820s and 1830s. Although some Regency Boulle work used tortoiseshell veneer, such complex cut-brass inlay was more commonly used with rosewood.

Other French *émigré* makers of furniture included S.J. Jamar, who is known to have produced work in the mainstream Regency style as well as pieces in the French style. John McLean (fl.1774–1814) of Leicester Square and, later, Tottenham Court Road and Marylebone Street, London, produced pieces of typically English form, but his use of cast- and chased-metal mounts suggests French influence. Late interpretations of the style pioneered by Holland at Southill, drawing upon French furniture of the Directoire period, such as secretaires and commodes with fluted colonettes at the angles, were still being produced in this period. The French influence was also sustained as a result of the large amount of French eighteenth-century furniture which had found its way into English private collections following the many sales held at the time of the Revolution.

The most innovative cabinet-maker of the later Regency period was George Bullock (d.c.1819). His commissions included the furnishing of Napoleon's quarters on St Helena and of Tew Park for the industrialist Matthew Robinson Boulton, as well as work for the Duke of Atholl and for the Portuguese ambassador, the Duke of Palmella. Many of his designs were published in Ackermann's *Repository of Arts* and he seems to have achieved a reasonable degree of fame. His style was a highly idiosyncratic interpretation of late-Regency forms, drawing upon contemporary Empire designs but almost always with highly original results.

Bullock furniture is often imposing in scale through its bold massing of volumes. For his more elaborate commissions he used gilt-bronze mounts together with borders or panels of intricate cut-brass inlay in floral

SOFA, GEORGE BULLOCK, c.1810 (above)

Made to one of Bullock's designs, this piece shows the increasingly heavy forms of the later Regency period. The decorative cut-brass work is a hallmark of Bullock's work.

ROSEWOOD WRITING-TABLE, c.1810 (below)

The simple yet elegant form of this table is typical of English furniture of the early nineteenth century.

DESIGN FOR A STATE BED, GEORGE SMITH, c.1807 (above)

Resembling a chantry chapel, this design is a testament both to the fantastic opulence of Regency taste and the sophistication of the Gothic revival.

patterns. Sometimes he simply inlaid flat patterns of woods of contrasting tone. Although, like most furniture-manufacturers of the Regency, he employed some exotic imported woods, he also pioneered the use of home-grown varieties such as yew, holly and pollard oak. The tops of cabinets were often covered with slabs of Mona marble dug from Bullock's own quarry in Anglesey.

By the time of Bullock's death contemporary pattern-books were becoming filled with varieties of competing styles, including those of the Gothic, the Elizabethan and the Rococo revivals. Although furniture of recognizably Neoclassical form was being produced into the middle of the century, few new stylistic developments took place in England after 1830.

ITALY

The continuing strength in Italy of the late-Baroque style was for a while at odds with the country's role as the cradle of the nascent Neoclassical style. However, like the rest of Europe, Italy was gradually to succumb to the new movement. Perhaps her single most important designer in this period was the Venetian Giovanni Battista Piranesi (1720–78). Piranesi had come to Rome in the 1740s and had begun to engrave views of the ancient monuments. His works became increasingly archaeological in subject matter and he drew upon his knowlege of antiquity to publish a series of

ological character of later Neoclassicism, but in them can be found many of the ingredients of the later Empire style, notably a certain massiveness of scale combined with the lavish use of monopodia supports. Another way in which Piranesi looked forward to the Empire period was in pioneering the application of Egyptian ornament to interior decorative schemes.

The French-born architect Ennemond-Alexandre Petitot (1727–1801) provided a further early influence on Italian Neoclassicism. In the 1740s, while a student at the French Academy in Rome, Petitot had espoused the new style. In 1753 he was appointed, at the recommendation of the comte de Caylus, *architetto delle fabricche*

Hapsburg governor of Lombardy, and his furniture designs reveal an elegant adaptation of the work of men such as Neufforge. By this time cabriole legs had begun to disappear and straight lines to predominate.

Despite foreign influence, much Italian furniture maintained a strong national identity. Often the tapering legs of Italian pieces of this period have an exaggeratedly triangular profile, frequently headed by recessed necks. The frames of looking-glasses were straightened, but the scrollwork of their crestings and aprons still retained a Baroque exuberance. The comparative scarcity of good timber meant that furniture was often painted, usually with arabesques or grisaille panels in the Neoclassical manner.

YELLOW DRAWING-ROOM, CA' REZZONICA, VENICE *(left)*

The Louis XVI style was given a distinct regional flavour by Venetian craftsmen.

designs for furniture and interiors, *Diverse maniere d'adornare i cammini ed ogni altra parte degli edifici* (1769). Only two known pieces of furniture were created according to Piranesi's designs, the extravagance of which rendered them largely impractical. However, they are important for their use of features borrowed from surviving ancient furniture, notably the monopodia derived from bronze tables. Many of his designs have Venetian exuberance somewhat at odds with the dry, archae-

ducali in the service of the Duke of Palma. Petitot is known to have designed furniture which had a heavy, architectural style, in many ways analogous to that of his compatriot Le Lorrain.

In the ports of Genoa, Naples and Leghorn, the important influence was English, but elsewhere the Italians began to produce an indigenous form of the Louis XVI style. In Milan, Giocondo Albertolli (1742–1839) created a series of interiors for the

PALISANDER WOOD TABLE, PARMA, *c.*1770 *(above)*

The heavy form of this piece suggests the influence of the French architect E.-A. Petitot, one of the pioneers of Neoclassicism and a resident of Parma at this time.

WALNUT CHAIR, *c.*1790 *(opposite)*

Part of a suite, this Italian chair derives from English prototypes and, in particular, the engraved designs of Hepplewhite. English influence was strong in the Italian ports during the late eighteenth century.

The finest cabinet-maker in Lombardy during the last quarter of the eighteenth century was Giuseppe Maggiolini (1738–1814). He specialized in the typical Lombard form of the commode, whose simple rectangular shape was veneered with a combination of inlaid arabesques and pictorial marquetry (often to the designs of Andrea Appiani, 1754–1817.) Maggiolini's fellow Lombard, Gianni Maffezzoli (1776–1818), produced similar pieces of furniture, but often with the addition of Ionic columns at the angles.

However, in the closing years of the eighteenth century it was in the field of sculpted furniture that Italy was without equal. The most important man working in

this field was Giuseppe Maria Bonzanigo (1745–1820). A Piedmontese, born in Asti, Bonzanigo had moved to Turin by 1773 and was already working for the court, where he carved frames for the royal apartments. In 1787 Vittorio Amadeo III appointed him wood-carver to the Crown. Several pier-tables survive to this day which are thought to be from his hand and all feature minutely observed naturalistic detail confined within a Louis XVI framework. In the later years of

his life, Bonzanigo turned increasingly to portrait sculpture.

With the rise of Napoleon and the installation of several of his relatives on the various thrones of Italy, the influence of Paris – and of the Empire style – became paramount. The palaces used by the new Bonaparte monarchs were often furnished by French craftsmen like Jacob-Desmalter. Napoleon's sister Elisa Bonaparte, Princess Baciocchi and Grand Duchess of Tuscany, redecorated the state apartments of the Palazzo Pitti in Florence for her brother in lavish Empire style and set up a furniture workshop where Italians were trained under imported French craftsmen. She also patronized the Florentine cabinet-maker Giovanni Socchi (fl.1809–15), who produced several austerely geometric commodes and an ingenious metamorphic writing-table for the Palazzo Pitti.

Another designer of Empire furniture was the Siennese architect, Agostino Fantastici, who worked in an Egyptian style which owed as much to Piranesi as it did to Dominique Vivant Denon, influential collector and director of the Musée Napoléon, and whose pieces provided an elegant contrast to the prevailing dry style of Jacob-Desmalter.

The influence of the Empire style in Italy proved tenacious; even when the historical revivals of the 1830s had begun to have their impact upon the decorative arts throughout Europe, Pelagio Palagi (1775–1860) was producing Neoclassical seat furniture for the Palazzo Reale in Turin (1836–40).

SPAIN

Charles III, King of Naples, ascended the Spanish throne in 1759. The owner of a vast collection of antiquities excavated from Herculaneum and Pompeii, he seems to have preferred late-Baroque forms to the newly emergent Neoclassical style. His refurbishment of the royal palace in Madrid produced work mainly in an exuberant Iberian version of the Louis XV style.

However, some of the later pieces from this period show the influence of contem-

porary French designs. In the suite of King Francisco de Asis in the royal palace in Madrid there is a roll-top desk, made to the designs of Mathias Gasparini, which clearly derives from the work of Oeben, and in particular from the *bureau du roi*. Gasparini was one of a number of Italians whom Charles had brought to Madrid on succeeding to the throne; his work was in a highly idiosyncratic late-Baroque style.

With the accession of Charles IV, attention was turned again to the refurbishment of the palaces of La Granja, Aranjuez and El Escorial. Italian furniture, with its somewhat exaggerated interpretation of the new style, again appears to have been an important influence on much Spanish Neoclassical furniture. Thus, although tapering legs, straight lines and antique-inspired decoration became the norm, the proportions of the furniture often retained an almost Baroque extravagance. However, elsewhere in Europe, the fashions of Paris exerted a compelling influence. The *dessinateur du Garde-meuble du roi*, Jean-Démosthènes Dugourc (1749–1825), provided designs for furniture and upholstery in the most advanced Parisian taste for the Casita del Príncipe, the pavilion built by Charles for himself in the grounds of El Escorial, and for the Casita del Labrador built during the 1780s for the Duchess of Alba in the park of Aranjuez. The Palacio Real in Madrid was refurbished during the 1790s under the direction of the architect Juan de Villanueva (1739–1811), who designed the Prado Museum. Much furniture from this period is still extant. It is characterized by an exuberant interpretation of Directoire style.

The Empire style arrived in Spain around 1800, when Charles commissioned from Percier and Fontaine the design of a small room for the Casita del Labrador, to be entirely panelled with mahogany mounted with platinum arabesques. The panelling was executed in Paris and then transported to Spain along with a suite of Empire seat furniture by the Jacob brothers.

In 1808 both Charles and his son abdicated and Joseph Napoleon was installed as king. The whole of the Iberian peninsula became embroiled in a bloody war. Never-

theless, the Empire influence upon the deco
rative arts remained strong, even after th
restoration of the Bourbon monarchy. Spa
ish craftsmen were able to reproduce Empi
designs from engravings, often with the a
of imported French bronzes, although mu
of their work during this period retained
authentically Spanish character. The furi
ture of the Fernandino period – that
during the reign of Ferdinand VII, 1814–3:
derived its basic forms from the Empire st
but gradually became heavier and m
rounded, a development analogous to t
Biedermeier style of northern Europe.

PORTUGAL

The Neoclassical style arrived in F
tugal in the 1770s and the Po
guese adapted their traditional fo
to produce an indigenous version of
Louis XVI style. Commodes adopted a
tangular breakfront form, were raised u
square tapering legs and were inlaid
geometric marquetry patterns. A distinc
note was provided by deep, shaped apr
and handles with enamelled medallions.
characteristically tall giltwood pier-gla
and consoles which had developed in
middle of the century were straightened
and carved with classical motifs. Seat f
ture revealed the influence of English
tern-books, most notably those by Sher
By the turn of the century the influence c
Empire style had become widespread.

GERMANY

German Neoclassicism em
gradually during the 1770s
wake of the Seven Years
However, the Baroque and Rococo
were still strong influences in Germar
the progress of the new classical styl
not necessarily automatic.
   The most successful German ca

ECLECTICISM

The revival of the Bourbon dynasty in 1814, when the comte de Provence became King of France, initiated a revival of the classical styles that had been so popular in the court of the count's brother, Louis XVI. When there was a change of fashion in France, the rest of Europe was sure to follow. This classical revival did not depend on a precise rendition of former styles, although exact copies were to become a feature of the 1840s and 1850s. Instead, the general classical outline was retained but lightened with marquetry and porcelain in a similar manner to the court pieces of the late 1770s. The Empire style was a continuation of the classical revival and, until the full impact of the revival styles was felt, Empire forms simply served as a vehicle for bolt-on Gothic or Rococo, or as a basis for Biedermeier. The French political hotbed, which eventually culminated in the July revolution of 1830, the end of the Bourbon line and, in 1848, the final blow to the monarchy, created new design ideals as well as fresh political incentives. This new movement coincided with enormous industrial development, reaping the fruits of the previous century's investments.

In Britain, too, the position of the aristocracy as arbiters of taste was gradually usurped during the nineteenth century by the rapidly growing and increasingly prosperous middle class, whose new wealth and social aspirations provided opportunities for enterprising and inventive furniture-manufacturers. In the United States, as elsewhere, the nineteenth century was a time of great industrial and social advancement. Improved transport and communications between the East and West coasts and across the Atlantic made new ideas, materials and methods of manufacture more accessible to a larger number of people. Mechanization of the furniture industry was more advanced than in Europe and factory

THE DRAWING-ROOM, HIGHCLERE CASTLE

The room was decorated in the French style in the 1890s with silk damask wall-coverings,
the gilded ceiling in Louis XV manner. The furniture, in Louis XV and XVI
styles, was made in England as well as in France.

production quite rapidly replaced the traditional craft-apprenticeship system.

Throughout the second half of the nineteenth century, international exhibitions were a forum for world trade, so that almost for the first time fashion was set on an immediate international footing. These exhibitions invariably had large displays of costly and lavish furniture, often made to show virtuoso craftsmanship rather than for practical use. The first of the major international exhibitions was held in 1851 in the specially erected Crystal Palace in Hyde Park, London. Known as the Great Exhibition, it featured all categories of exhibit, from machinery to sculpture. France, not to be outdone, held an Exposition Universelle in 1855 and, regularly, at eleven-year intervals. The last of these huge exhibitions was the Paris Exhibition of 1900, in which revival styles and the works of François Linke and Emile Gallé were seen under the same roof – reflecting the wide choice that had become available as a result of the inventiveness of nineteenth-century design and marketing.

Other European countries held exhibitions, although not on the grand scale of Britain or France. An almost annual exhibition was held in Munich from 1818, and subsequently Metz, Vienna and Oporto (from 1865) followed suit. Patrons came from all parts of the world, and included royal and noble households. Royal and imperial purchases – by the Russian Tsar, Napoleon III, Queen Victoria and Prince Albert, and by Indian maharajahs – must have helped trade considerably. At the 1855 Paris exhibition Queen Victoria purchased a cabinet for £266.9s.6d. in carved wood by the Parisian Grohé Frères. It had been on exhibition eleven years earlier at the Exposition des Produits de l'Industrie Française, so clearly there was no stigma associated with an old design. This may be a key to understanding of attitudes of wealthy patrons during the middle years of the century: it did not have to be new, but it did have to be of good quality.

A style promoted and admired at any one of these exhibitions would be rapidly disseminated to all parts of the civilized world by way of lavishly illustrated line-engraved exhibition catalogues. Not only was the *idea* of a new style of furniture quickly transported, the furniture itself could with relative ease be sent to international destinations. Minor German states and fringe European countries as well as the Eastern Seaboard towns of the United States made cheap pastiches of each new vogue. At the same time, better-quality furniture was exported directly from Paris to overseas destinations. There is even evidence of parts of furniture being exported – for example, it appears that the fine-quality marquetry of Joseph Cremer (who supplied Louis-Philippe and the King of Holland, among others) was sent, probably in sheet form, to New York firms such as that of Herter Brothers. The meticulous company records of François Linke show that he sold furniture to the great houses on Long Island, to South American countries, to the King of Egypt and to Indian rulers. The Vienna-based firm of Gebrüder Thonet exported bentwood furniture, in kit form, all over the world.

New museums, too, played an important part in the dissemination of ideas and styles. The inauguration of the South Kensington Museum in London in 1857, under the guidance of the Prince Consort, was a remarkable inspiration to both the study and design of the decorative arts. The Victoria and Albert Museum, as it is now known, was the first of its kind in the world. It was followed by the Österreichisches Museum für Kunst und Industrie in Vienna (1863), the Bayerisches Nationalmuseum in Munich (1867) and the Hamburgisches Museum für Kunst und Gewerbe in Hamburg (1877).

GERMANY AND AUSTRIA

The use of the Empire style in the German-speaking states had been confined mainly to the larger courts, such as Gotha and Coburg. A rectangular, classical style had been adapted to incorporate the dominant Biedermeier fashion that was universally accepted from Altona in the north to Vienna in the south. This new 'bourgeois' style dropped the formal use of the lion – favoured in decoration by the Prussians as a sign of power – and adapted it within foliage. In France the design and construction of furniture were generally, but by no means exclusively, restricted to Paris, with one or two important exceptions such as Lyon or, in Belgium, Liège and Malines. Germany, however, was a collection of small states, and thus had no such central source. All of its styles, imported or home-bred, have therefore to be looked at on a regional basis. This makes the detailed study of 'German' nineteenth-century furniture – indeed from any period – far more difficult.

The architect and furniture designer Karl Friedrich Schinkel (1781–1841) was influential during the first half of the nineteenth century, adapting classical forms of furniture to suit the new styles as they emerged from Empire into Gothic. Notably, he worked at Schloss Charlottenburg, Berlin, for Friedrich Wilhelm III of Prussia. Leo von Klenze (1784–1864), who had worked in Paris with Percier and Fontaine, was the most notable classical designer of the southern German states. His 1840s street plans for Munich are classically set out but decorated in a light Gothic style not unlike the French *style Troubadour* (see page 116) of a decade earlier. The influence of his work can be seen as far north as Moscow. His heavier classical designs were at odds with the styles being devoured by the mass market; although distinct in their 'late' application of a style, they were a type of aristocratic Town Hall Classicism and some twenty to thirty years behind the fashion – even the fashion in the still somewhat provincial German states.

LAMINATED WALNUT SIDE-CHAIR, MICHAEL THONET, *c.1840*

This is a rare early experimental design by the German-born innovator who 'invented' bentwood furniture.

OAK ARMCHAIR, KARL FRIEDRICH SCHINKEL, *c.1830*

This Berlin-made chair designed in a vigorous Gothic style was possibly made as a garden chair, with its wide feet and sturdy oak construction.

The new Historic style emerged from a combination of the application of new technology and a romantic look at the past, urged on by a widening commercial market and a plethora of designs from London and Paris. Among the many designers, all little known outside their native areas, Wilhelm Kimbel (1786–1875) of Mainz is represented by some high-quality colour prints. Other makers from this traditional furniture-making area were Knussmann and Bembé. The Germanic period of *Romantischer Historismus* was a hectic, almost frenetic time of design and production, which together resulted in an identifiable national style even before the emergence of Germany as a political and economic unit.

When, under the guidance of Bismarck, a unified German nation appeared in 1870 after the Franco-Prussian War, there was a new look at the roots of German culture, which heralded a Nordic renaissance, spurred on by the 1876 Munich Exhibition of Arts and Crafts. In the south these copies were merely interpretations of early forms; in the north, in Hamburg and Altona, a modernized and improved, but 'dumpy', form was used.

The often eccentric nature of German Rococo form is based on a deep-rooted style evolved during the 1750s and 1760s, notably by J.M. Kambli and others, whose work had a great influence on church decoration. The Berlin designer August Fricke published in 1854 a volume of line-engraved designs for furniture. The plates followed the conventions of contemporary 'mass-production', mainly in the safe, predictable Rococo style that had been popular in London and Paris since the early 1840s. However, the overall form was essentially Germanic, its

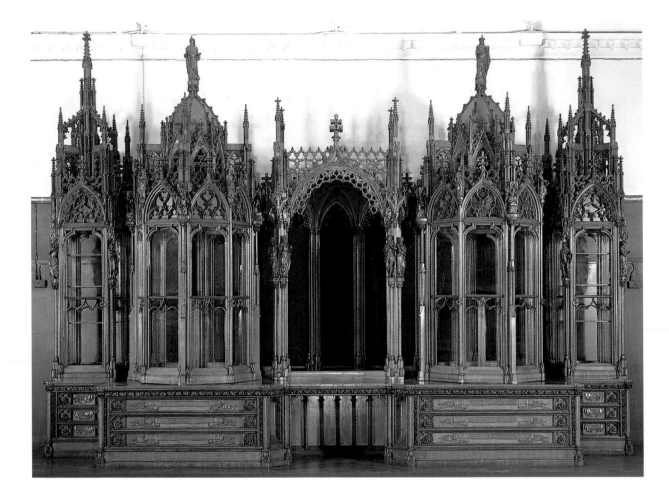

OAK BOOKCASE,
BERNARDO DE
BENARDIS AND
JOSEPH CREMER,
c.1851

*Made for the Great
Exhibition, this
Austrian Gothic
bookcase was purchased
by Prince Albert for his
rooms at Buckingham
Palace and is now in
the Victoria and Albert
Museum.*

somewhat heavy and exaggerated shapes being applied with wild excesses of the plastic Rococo art. The engravings all gave an impression that the designs were for a factory, using machines to cut veneer and to rough out carving. Many of the pieces had plain, thinly veneered doors and seventeenth-century spirals that anticipated the revived Renaissance style normally associated with the 1870s or even the 1880s. Interestingly, in the nineteenth-century revivals or copies these spirals generally run in opposite directions, whereas in the seventeenth century the twist turns (often called 'Salomonic' columns) were turned the same way. In 1854–5 Louis Linke produced similar designs in Berlin, freely adapting the Louis XV style but also designing Renaissance-style furniture, often grafting Rococo decoration onto Renaissance forms, a practice not often seen in finished furniture.

Industrialization

In Berlin, c.1825, Karl Friedrich Schinkel designed a chair which, although in a late Neoclassical form, was intended for production in cast iron. This was some fifteen to twenty years before British manufacturers, notably the firm of Coalbrookdale, produced their sophisticated cast-iron furniture. The lightly designed but enormously heavy Schinkel armchair was made until the 1860s, without any alteration to its highly successful design.

Inventive German design can also be seen in a laminated walnut side-chair created by Michael Thonet (1796–1871) of Boppard-am-Rhine. This chair adhered to a late Empire or Regency form but used the laminated technique that was to become the hallmark of Thonet's work after 1841, when he was granted various international patents.

Thonet moved to Vienna in 1842, working there for the cabinet-making firm of Carl Leistler (1805–57) before, in 1849, establishing his own company. He exhibited bentwood furniture at the Great Exhibition of 1851. Other firms, such as J. & J. Kohn of Vienna, copied Thonet's bentwood forms after his patents had lapsed in 1869. Thonet himself established assembly plants throughout the modern world and by 1900 was employing 6,000 workers producing 4,000 pieces a day – with another 25,000 people employed in Austria alone producing bentwood furniture. This was an exceptional example of industrialization, hardly to be exceeded in the twentieth century, but at the same time these simple forms were of great inspiration to the Modernist movement.

However, comparatively little furniture was mass-produced until factories became more commonplace during the twentieth

CARVED PINE
CUPBOARD, c.1895
(left)

*In the manner of
Richard Riemerschmid
and Georg Hauberrisser,
this cupboard looks
back to fifteenth-century
originals.*

THRONE-CHAIR,
PROBABLY FROM
HANAU, c.1890
(below left)

*One of a pair, this
chair is veneered in
German silver and is
embossed with
Renaissance-style
foliage. It is similar to a
throne of c.1700 by
Sebastian Mylius and
was made possibly for
William II of Prussia.*

turning were made in large numbers (lathes were able to turn several poles at once), but these tended to be for a cheaper market. The archetypal ballroom chair, based on a classic design by Le Bouteiller, from his 1830s collection of designs, *Album de l'Industrie et des Arts Utiles*, is a good example of cheap mass-production. At the close of the century, hooped-iron chairs were made in large numbers for Paris parks and public places.

Cabinet-making

Furniture was still relatively expensive to manufacture, and this limited production. Makers had small, poorly funded workshops and few could afford to make more than a few pieces at any one time, cash flow being as important a factor then as it is now.

Techniques of construction, when examined in detail, varied considerably throughout the different parts of Europe. Each province, principality and country had not only a different access to modern methods of manufacture, but also a widely different traditional background. The access to modern manufacture depended mainly on the geographical relationship of any particular country to Paris – the farther away, the less advanced the techniques tended to be. Only with the advent of an effective trans-European railway system in the middle of the century did communications speed up with the result that established working practices tended to change more frequently than from one generation to the next.

German cabinet-makers, though, were fine technicians and arguably the best masters of their craft. Until the 1870s, a few well-established workshops excepted, there was neither the patronage nor the opportunity to exploit a world market in the German principalities, and many fine craftsmen emigrated to France, usually to Paris.

Woodworking tools varied little from country to country, although each country (and, to a certain extent, each region) had its own stylistic variations. The German *Hobel*, or woodworking plane, was similar to the French *rabot*. Tools were prized articles, often made by the user and handed down from generation to generation until they

century. Nineteenth century machines could adopt only a limited number of dexterous movements. Each section cut or planed by a machine had to be taken out by hand and placed either on another machine or on a workbench to be jointed and finished by hand. Machine-carving, which was becoming widespread by the end of the century, had likewise to be extensively hand-finished. Until the 1920s dovetails were almost without exception hand-cut. Cast-iron furniture lent itself more easily to mass-production – moulds could be used time and time again and reworked when they lost their sharpness – but each section had nevertheless to be hand-finished and -fitted. Apart from Thonet and the bentwood process, there is little evidence that any particular line of furniture was made in more than small numbers or limited editions. Towards the end of the century chairs and other items that relied on wore out or became outmoded. The nine-teenth century, however, saw vast changes in tools and techniques. From about 1830 workshops went from badly lit hovels, where hand-held tools were used, to pur-pose-built efficient establishments. By the end of the century they were factories featuring the latest machinery. During the second quarter of the century the transition was to steam-driven machinery, primarily for planing and cutting veneers. The 1890s witnessed a limited amount of electrical use.

By this time it was possible to do dovetails and carving by machine in the better and more sophisticated workshops of Paris, Munich and Vienna. Machine-made dove-tails, being always evenly spaced, are easy to differentiate from hand-made joints, which nearly always show a scribing or marking-out line. Carving was normally roughed out by the machine and finished off by hand, but in all European countries attention to detail decreased as the century progressed. More-over, as wages began to spiral, quality usually deteriorated, especially after World War I, when more and more machines were used – cutting veneers paper-thin, machining dovetails and kiln-drying cheaper and cheaper timbers.

Outside France, with the exception of Britain, the countries of Europe produced furniture that was generally poorly made (although, especially in the case of palace furniture, there was a lot that was good). German craftsmen, though exceptional, often could not afford the more expensive woods and had to make do with native timbers. Pine, in plentiful supply, was used for the carcase. In wealthy areas the drawer linings might be made in oak, sometimes walnut, so that the visible parts could be of reasonable quality while the back was in cheaper pine. However, the eighteenth-century French practice of finishing the moving and visible parts well and leaving the remainder poorly worked was dying out. Iron was commonly used for locks and hinges, although an increasing use of brass was seen in the third quarter of the century. Brasswork was rarely as good as that in France, although British metalwork always had supremacy.

The Gothic Revival

The Gothic style was the first to be revived during the nineteenth century, first making its appearance in the more sophisticated German states and in France following the accession of Charles X to the French throne in 1820. This elegant, attenuated Gothic style was much lighter than its British counterpart.

An octagonal table by Franz Xavier Fortner (1798–1877), inlaid in the Boulle technique (see page 194), exemplifies Ger-man early-nineteenth-century Gothic style and was possibly influenced by the Schloss Pfaueninsell in Prussia. Fortner was an estab-lished designer in 1826 though this Bavarian table of the 1840s was almost two decades behind the equivalent Parisian style. For the table, Fortner used the light neo-Gothic style popularized in France under Charles X and known as *style Troubadour*. This style relied heavily on cathedral-like form and decora-tion, the form recreating the work of medi-eval stone-carvers. Elegant use was made of crocketed finials and pierced rose 'windows', trefoils, quatrefoils and even the cinquefoil.

PORCELAIN-MOUNTED CABINET, c.1880

Set into an ebony-veneered and ebonized carcase, this cabinet from Dresden is decorated with fine-quality painted porcelain in the Meissen tradition. A similar cabinet was exhibited at the Paris Exposition Universelle of 1878 by William Oppenheim, an agent for the Royal Dresden factory.

A carved-oak bookcase designed by Bernardo de Bernardis (1808–68) and Joseph Cremer (1808–71) was purchased by Prince Albert directly from the Austrian section of the Great Exhibition in 1851 and removed to his rooms at Buckingham Palace. This was a cabinet for a lady's library, and was part of a suite for a dining-room, drawing-room and a state bedroom, all on a massive scale. It was a relatively late piece in the Gothic style.

Rococo Style

German Rococo design was practised throughout the various states, from north to south, but from the second quarter of the eighteenth century was a speciality in Bavaria, surviving through and alongside the rigours of the Neoclassicism of the late eighteenth and early nineteenth centuries. The peculiarly Germanic *Zweites Rokoko* was grafted onto simple Biedermeier forms – so that acanthus could grow out of a gentle curve – and Biedermeier soon gave way to an adapted form of the Parisian Louis XV style, as illustrated in magazines such as the *Journal für Möbelschreiner und Tapezierer*, published by the Mainz cabinet-maker Wilhelm Kimbel. This style found an eager market among the industrious middle class.

German Rococo had been the dominant style in Bavarian churches. Its white and gilt decoration was based on the style that had become popular in the 'Isabellino period' in Spain during the reign of Isabella II. However, during the nineteenth century German Rococo furniture was normally of carved natural woods, especially walnut or limewood. An exceptional example was an *étagère* made for Schloss Linderhof, one of Ludwig II's romantic castles. It was made in the workshops of Anton Pössenbacher, the Munich cabinet-maker who also made Ludwig II's romantic castles. It was made *étagère* anticipated the works of another German cabinet-maker who worked in Paris a decade later, Joseph-Emmanuel Zwiener.

German porcelain cabinets, of Renaissance form but incorporating porcelain painted with copies of seventeenth-century paintings, were made for the international market, and at the Paris International Exhibi-tion of 1878 William Oppenheim exhibited a large cabinet from the royal factory at Dresden. These cabinets were made in some numbers, but the carcases were of poor-quality pine, either veneered with ebony or simply stained black. The porcelain, though, was usually of the finest quality, as one would expect from the Meissen factory. The general acceptance of German Renaissance revival appears to have occurred earlier and to have been more widespread than that in France, where it was prevalent from the 1860s to the 1890s.

Oeben. Montagnat created, probably for the 1855 Paris Exposition Universelle, a spectac-ular marquetry writing-cabinet, some 2.5m (8 ft) high, with swivelling sculpture niches, mechanically operated writing-flaps and, in-credibly, a fully automatic folding prie-dieu.

Records for Paris are reasonably complete and many makers have been documented, notably by Denise Ledoux-Lebard in her *Les Ébénistes du XIXe Siècle*. There was an increase in the volume of production, as the popula-tion rose dramatically and more and more people acquired disposable income, which

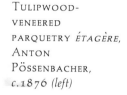

TULIPWOOD-VENEERED PARQUETRY *ÉTAGÈRE*, ANTON PÖSSENBACHER, *c.1876 (left)*

This Munich-made étagère was made for Ludwig of Bavaria for Schloss Linderhof.

BOULLE CENTRE TABLE, M. GRUNWEDEL OF POPPENHEIM, 1843 *(below)*

In the French style Troubadour manner, this table was made by Franz Xavier Fortner.

FRANCE

Paris was indisputably the main centre of European furniture production, in terms of both quality and quantity. Lyon had numerous small workshops, as did almost every other town, but few could be described as furniture-making centres. Tra-ditional crafts, especially chair-making, were practised everywhere. Claude Montagnat was a notable Lyon maker, who took out numerous patents from 1853, one of which was for mechanical devices within furniture, in the eighteenth-century tradition of

ROOM ANTICIPATING
THE *BELLE ÉPOQUE*,
THE MINISTRY OF
FINANCE, PARIS,
COMPLETED 1857

they increasingly spent on furniture and the newly fashionable soft furnishings. By the 1880s there were approximately 17,000 workers in the Paris furniture industry alone, 2,000 of them making the expensive best-quality pieces (*meubles de luxe*), 14,500 making cheaper furniture (*meubles courants*) and another 500 or so *trôleurs*, whose job it was to trundle their finished pieces around to the retail outlets.

The huge Parisian furniture industry serviced almost 1,200 retailers, of which approximately fifty were selling *meubles de luxe*. Makers included Befort, working in the 1830s, Tahan and Jeanselme, flourishing in the 1830s and 1840s, and Millet, working from the 1850s until the end of World War I. Like Millet, the output of the house of Sormani spanned many decades, flourishing

from *c.*1847 to 1934. Its founder, Paul Sormani, died in 1877, but his wife and son continued the prolific family firm.

Traditional values bred complacency and thus discontent in the Paris trade, to the extent that in 1882 there was a strike. The hiccup in production allowed in a flood of foreign goods and French domination of the market would never again be as confident as in the past. However, quality survived whenever there were wealthy people to pay for good workmanship. Wages spiralled as initially rare materials became more readily available and hence less expensive.

The place in history of Parisian furniture-makers was guaranteed by their practice of stamping their furniture. This tradition had grown out of a guild requirement of 1741; later, in the 1790s, the practice was dropped,

only to return with the Restauration, when more and more of the finer makers started to stamp or simply label their work. A practice exclusive to the nineteenth-century makers was that of engraving a signature on brasswork. In the 1840s and 1850s, for example, the houses of Tahan and Diehl engraved a script signature on the main lock of their work, while from the 1870s Henri Dasson (1825–96) engraved a signature, and normally the date, on his gilded metalwork, a device continued by Linke, Millet and Sormani well into the twentieth century.

This practice, although unregulated, had obvious commercial advantages. A good maker could prove that the work was a genuine 'in-house' piece and a retailer could show the signature to buyers. These *marques*, which had been deliberately hidden from the

PORCELAIN-MOUNTED *TABLE AMBULANTE*,
c.1840 *(below)*

*Inspired by eighteenth-century cabinet-makers, this
French table incorporates a Vincennes dish of c.1744
and Sèvres plaques of c.1765. The frieze hides a
spring-operated drawer.*

MARQUETRY CENTRE
TABLE, 1855 *(left)*

*The carcase of this French
table is stamped by
André Lemoine and the
marquetry is signed by
Joseph Cremer, both of
whom supplied furniture
to royalty. It may have
been made for the Paris
Exposition Universelle
of 1855.*

WEDGWOOD-
MOUNTED CENTRE
TABLE, c.1865 *(left)*

*This table, made in Paris,
is identical to one signed
by Charles-Guillaume
Winckelsen whose
business was taken over
by Henry Dasson in
1871.*

view of eighteenth-century buyers who
wished to cut out the retailer, were now, in
the nineteenth century, much more obviously positioned. The engraved signature
was either on the lock, or, more subtly, on the
top right-hand-corner mount.

Materials

France almost exclusively used oak as a base
wood. The timber was always of fine quality
and very well finished. Back panels were
often joined by cross glazing-bars and neatly
panelled, leaving a dry, clean look. French
chair-frames were normally of beech,
although walnut was sometimes used. Both
woods are easy to turn and both make a
sound base for gesso.

Painted furniture and the use of walnut for

chair-frames became less common in France
than it had been in the eighteenth century.
Walnut was a popular medium in the Scandinavian countries, which could not afford to
import large quantities of exotic West
Indian or South American timbers for use
in veneers, let alone in the solid.

Occasionally French drawer linings were
made in walnut with a slightly rounded-off
visible top edge to the drawer, but normally
oak was used. To an extent French craftsmen
kept to the traditional use of the wooden
goujon (peg) that had been used in the
construction of both chair-frames and case
furniture during the eighteenth century.
Where the *goujon* was used it often pierced a
mortise-and-tenon joint. Dovetails were
finer than they had been in the eighteenth
century. Locks had a double throw with an

iron tongue and brass casing. In the 1840s to
1860s hinges and catches were normally
brass and often engraved, especially those by
the Maison Tahan (*fl.*1830–80) and by
Alphonse Giroux et Cie (*fl.*1838–67).

The Revival Styles

Many styles were revived and popularized
during the nineteenth century. Throughout
the Restauration the French used fine beechwood stringing, thereby 'drawing' in a type
of silhouette foliage, and later Gothic outlines of fine-quality light-coloured mahogany or palisander and amaranth were set into
the popular *bois-clair*. The use of *bois-clair*,
ash and maple dominated the 1820s until the
end of the reign of Louis-Philippe.

Although few pieces can now be attributed to him, a formal, late French Gothic was pioneered by Viollet-le-Duc (1814–79). His main work was rebuilding old châteaux and churches. His furniture inspired that of the important British architect William Burges (1827–81). Recent research has brought to light a pair of French neo-Gothic giltwood chairs by Georges Jacob (1739–1814), made between 1803 and 1813 for the comtesse d'Osmond, a friend of the duchesse de Berry. A cotemporary picture of the comtesse shows her in her gallery with her *cabinet gothique* in the background some ten years before the style was thought to have been in fashion.

Alongside this love for Gothic was the perennial French taste for Chinese decoration, or chinoiserie. During the second quarter of the eighteenth century French craftsmen had dominated the world in their imitation of Chinese and Japanese lacquer. Their adaptation of Oriental work included incorporating Eastern panels into Western forms of furniture to the extent that some of them cut up large Oriental lacquer panels, sometimes from screens, and bent them to fit the exaggerated shape of the *bombé* chest-of-drawers or commode. During the late 1820s and the 1830s, imitation Oriental lacquer (japanning) was made, especially in France.

An important French Restauration furniture-maker who made lacquer pieces in the adapted Louis XVI style was Louis-François Bellangé (1759–1827) together with his brother, Pierre-Antoine (1758–1827). Jean-Baptiste Befort, a Belgian by birth, and his son Mathieu worked throughout the Restauration and Second Empire periods, incorporating fine, normally Japanese lacquer in cabinetwork, which was generally of a Louis XVI style.

French japanning at this time was normally restricted to small tables, especially the nest of quartetto tables, a shape popularized by designers such as Thomas Sheraton in late-eighteenth-century Britain. From the 1830s these tables were copied and adapted by the Chinese for export into Europe, so that the French manufacturers were competing against a flood of Eastern imports. Several of these exotic pieces were supplied to palaces such as the Grand Trianon and

Fontainebleau. During the periods of the Second Empire and the Republic, many fine Parisian makers incorporated Oriental panels in their cabinetwork, notably Alfred-Emmanuel-Lewis Beurdeley (1847–1919) and the firms of Krieger and Henry Dasson. The use of Chinese and Japanese lacquer panels was therefore purely a revival of the Louis XV and XVI manners, and is not to be confused with the British Aesthetic movement. This 'Oriental' movement, which ran alongside the traditional popularity of chinoiserie, prompted the individual and

ENAMEL *GUÉRIDON* TABLE, *c*.1860

This French table is in the manner of the Gothicist Viollet-le-Duc.

somewhat eccentric style of Gabriel Viardot. In 1861 Viardot took over his father Charles's Paris firm which sold all kinds of *objets d'art et de fantaisie*. The company's Oriental-style furniture was directly influenced by the French colony of Vietnam. The firm exhibited Oriental-style fantasy furniture in Paris in 1867, 1878 and 1889; it had exhibited Renaissance-style furniture in 1855.

If, during the eighteenth century, France had not been the greatest source of inspiration in the decorative arts, it had certainly been the greatest interpreter. The three French reigns that spanned the eighteenth century followed a particular style: there was

Baroque under Louis XIV; Rococo grew during the Regency of Louis XV and flowered at the middle of the century; and the Neoclassical era, as popularized under Louis XVI, was the first to be revived in nineteenth-century France.

During the nineteenth century these 'Louis Revivals' were adopted one by one, not necessarily in the order in which they had been popular during the previous century, although in each case the revived style continued to be popular and to run alongside the latest reincarnation. To generalize, each revival was first 'improved' by the inquiring, inventive nineteenth-century mind. Although eighteenth-century styles were obviously admired and emulated, it was impossible for the new middle-class designer to resist adapting the purity of that century's forms. In fact, it was this very middle-class 'meddling' that spawned this eclectic period: the new designers did not really understand eighteenth-century principles, while at the same time there was a huge improvement in the living standards of a whole new class of people. Moreover, the scale of furniture had to be reduced to suit the new and generally smaller houses and apartments.

The Survival of Revival

The nineteenth-century phenomenon of reviving styles grew out of a romantic interest in the past which intellectual society had had during the comfortable years of the eighteenth century. As the nineteenth century progressed, the reproduction of the past became more accurate and less eclectic, and exact copies became *de rigueur*.

The work of French and British cabinet-makers of the mid-nineteenth century could often be very similar, which is confusing. Many British makers copied the French style to the letter, especially around the 1850s, when the Louis XVI style was becoming popular. Antique dealers who had taken advantage of the French political and economic upheaval of the Revolution and the Napoleonic Wars had purchased eighteenth-century furniture wholesale and altered it to suit their aristocratic buyers. One known dealer was Edward Holmes Baldock, who supplied George IV and the Duke of Buccleuch with eighteenth-century modern and 'altered' French furniture.

The First Louis XVI Revival, c.1815–40

The last of the great eighteenth-century styles was the first to reappear in the nineteenth century. The overthrow of Napoleon resulted in the restoration of the Bourbon dynasty in the form of the uninspiring Louis XVIII, son of Louis XVI. Furniture styles reverted to a 'modernized' Louis XVI style. In no sense was this a matter of exact copying. The shape and form of some of the less outrageous Empire furniture were simply adapted and encrusted with the Neoclassical ormolu foliage of the 1780s.

Here again the work of Louis-François Bellangé is the most remarkable. It was of the very highest quality, and several pieces were purchased for the Prince Regent to furnish Windsor Castle. Often eighteenth-century 'spare parts' were used – for example, a small table supplied by Bellangé in 1828 for St James's Palace, London (now at Windsor), had Sèvres plaques painted by Dodin in 1774, the first year of Louis XVI's reign.

Charles X, like Louis XVIII, was not inclined to direct fashion (with the exception of Gothic), and so Britain became a revived source of inspiration, as it had in the closing years of the eighteenth century. Recurring political upheaval in the 1830s and 1840s dampened the enthusiasm for this ostentatious, essentially royal style, although it would be rekindled in the 1850s.

The Louis XV Revival, c.1830–1930

In the second quarter of the nineteenth century more households were able to afford the furniture that was being readily adapted to suit modern needs. Formal seating arrangements suitable for palatial eighteenth-century rooms were impossible in smaller dwellings. Well-to-do society wanted above all comfort and luxury, and the ebullient Rococo forms of 1720s to 1750s France were perfect for this 'new' taste. The French word rococo was taken to mean 'antiquated' or 'old-fashioned', and the style the designers

tried to emulate inevitably featured the rocaille of the early Louis XV period.

The revival was well suited to seat furniture, much of it influenced by Théodore Pasquier's Cahier de Dessins d'ameublement of the 1840s, the designs of which perfectly suited the crinoline dress and upright posture of the period. Large numbers of salon suites were made of beechwood and then gilded in the traditional manner of the previous century. In fact, apart from a slight adaptation of form, the whole manufacturing technique was the same as it had been more than a

hundred years earlier, the component parts being made in small, barely mechanized workshops. In the spirit of the new manufacturing age, the suites were much the same whether made in France, Britain or, later, Germany. They were more commonly, but not exclusively, made in sets of seven: a canapé, two fauteuils and four side-chairs.

In the later years of the nineteenth century, the Louis XV- and Louis XVI-style suites generally had slightly smaller chairs and settees and the form was a more exact copy of its eighteenth-century precursor, rather

COMMODE À L'ANGLAISE, HENRY DASSON, 1882 (left)

Made in Paris after a Louis XVI model by Martin Carlin, this commode is set with imitation lacquer or japanned panels.

JAPANNED BUREAU À GRADIN, c.1860 (left)

This bureau was made in Paris and is decorated with lavish gilt-bronze mounts recreating the Louis XV manner to suit the taste of the Napoleon III period.

than a nineteenth-century 'improvement'.

Whatever their nationality, these salon suites almost exclusively used French seat covering. The greatest commercial output was at Aubusson, where small segments of tapestry were pieced together. Less common was tapestry from the National Manufactory of Beauvais or the Gobelins factory.

The Louis XV revival, combined as it was with attractive Rococo forms, dominated the middle years of the century and was still thriving at the century's end, when it was combined with Art Nouveau forms. Advocated as late as 1867 by Victor Quentin in *Le Magasin de Meubles, Journal d'ameublement*, it went on to survive both Art Nouveau and the Modernists, and is still one of the styles most appreciated in the twentieth century.

SILVERED AND GILT-BRONZE CENTRE TABLE WITH MARQUETRY TOP, ÉDOUARD KREISSER, c.1855 *(left)*

This table was made for the Paris Exposition Universelle and was purchased by Queen Victoria for 2,500 francs as a present for Prince Albert.

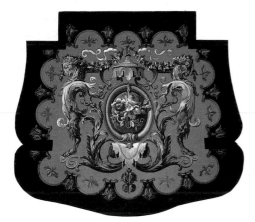

TAPESTRY CHAIR COVER, PIERRE-ADRIEN CHABAL-DUSSURGEY, c.1860 *(above)*

Made at the National Manufactory of Beauvais, the style of this cover is inspired by traditional Louis XV designs.

The Second Louis XVI Revival, c.1850–1900

The second phase of the Louis XVI revival was a popular one, albeit inspired and encouraged by the consort of Napoleon III, the Empress Eugénie. The Empress's bedroom at St Cloud shows original and modern furniture in this Neoclassical style. The *guéridons* of Weisweiler and commodes and writing-desks in the style of Martin Carlin

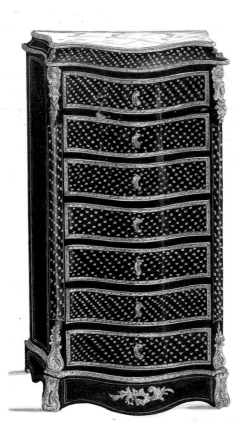

DESIGN FOR A 'BOULLE' *SEMAINIER*, c.1865 *(above)*

Watercolour and encre de Chine *wash with gum arabic. The piece was designed by the Maison Pagny.*

were much admired and copied. The style was made to the very highest standards by the best Parisian makers, but the farther from Paris it was copied, be it in Germany or New York, the poorer the taste generally was. As with Rococo forms, the style lent itself to seat furniture, although all of the basic eighteenth-century forms were copied and theoretically 'improved'.

The Louis XIV Revival

The application of the Baroque style in the nineteenth century is more difficult to assess. It is best seen in the huge commercial output of furniture inspired by the work of the royal cabinet-maker, André-Charles Boulle and the Gobelins factory in the late seventeenth century. His perfection at inlaying cut-brass and pewter into tortoiseshell and ebony was an inspiration to furniture-makers under Louis XVI and again under Louis-Philippe. Boulle's descendants promoted this technique well into the 1840s, and in 1838 Louis-Édouard Lemarchand (1795–1872) supplied a pair of Boulle work tripod stands to the Grand Trianon. 'Boulle' furniture became used more and more in commercial manufacture by the 1840s and 1850s, but in a decreasing spiral of quality. Often the original designs were completely debased.

As in the Louis XVI period, late seventeenth-century furniture shapes, especially *meubles d'appui*, were adopted, either veneered and gilt-bronze mounted or applied with Boulle work. Where the eighteenth century had adapted Boulle's technique to suit its own forms, the commercial designers of the 1850s simply muddled both.

The Renaissance Revival

The earliest evidence of this style in France was a cabinet by Grohé Frères, purchased by Louis-Philippe at the 1839 Produits exhibition in Paris, although designs by Aimé Chenavard (1798–1838) had been published as early as 1835. At about the same time, a large collection of seemingly Renaissance furniture was left to the French nation by

Alexandre du Sommerand. Much of the collection (together with the Soulages collection) was bought mid-century by the new South Kensington Museum. The furniture was destroyed in the 1920s when it was discovered to be assembled from old parts, but not before it had influenced several generations of designers. The most notable French designer in this style was Henri-Auguste Fourdinois (1830–1907). His *tour de force* was a cabinet made for the Paris Exhibition of 1867: it took six years to complete, and had figures designed by the little known Hillaire and Pasti with ornamentation by Neviller. This cabinet was purchased directly from the exhibition by the South Kensington Museum for £2,700. Its style reflects the former glories of the

François I and Henri II periods – those of the latter being often adopted by the revivalists of the 1870s. The Fourdinois firm supplied many pieces, often in this luxurious style, to the Empress Eugénie at St Cloud and to the imperial palaces at Compiègne and Fontainebleau. The architect Maugin designed rooms of ebony furniture for the courtesan, La Païva, in Paris in the 1860s.

The Belle Époque

Baroque architecture had incorporated large sculptural figures as a means of decoration for both the inside and the outside of buildings. It is not surprising that, in a time of historical revivals, nineteenth-century innovators looked to such a medium.

This sculptural style was taken to its often erotic extreme in the Belle Époque by such furniture-makers as Rupert Carabin (1862–1932). A sculptor from Alsace, Carabin anticipated the flowering of Art Nouveau from the 1880s. His exotic furniture incorporating naked female figures carved in full relief and up to 1m (40in) high is among the most Symbolist furniture ever created in France. After his participation in the 1889 Paris Exhibition, he was commissioned to design a magnificent bookcase, his brief being simply 'ce que vous aurez en tête'.

This style was taken a stage further, in gilt bronze, by Linke's sculptor Léon Messagé. However, the work created by Messagé for the Paris Exposition Universelle of 1900 was of a far more traditional and less erotic nature than that of Carabin – Carabin's sculptural excesses obviously had to be watered down for the wider market of an international exhibition with all its commercial applications.

Linke and Zwiener

The cabinet-maker François Linke (1855–1945) stands out from the Paris houses. His reputation has become so great that it has eclipsed those of other fine makers – in some cases unfairly. His most important pieces were clearly signed, so his name became well known and promoted by dealers to the extent that the signature has been added to pieces he did not make. An irony is that, by

CARVED FRUITWOOD AND EBONY SIDE CABINET, DESIGNED BY HILLAIRE AND PASTI, c.1867

This cabinet was made by Henri-Auguste Fourdinois and was purchased for £2,700 from the Paris Exposition Universelle by the South Kensington Museum.

A SHOWROOM OF FRANÇOIS LINKE, PARIS,
c.1904 (below)

*This illustration shows a massive sculptural vitrine
and a copy of the celebrated* bureau du roi.

WALNUT
BIBLIOTHÈQUE,
RUPERT CARABIN,
c.1890 (right)

the law of chance, the signature has on occasion been added to pieces that were indeed made by the house of Linke, although left unsigned at the time of manufacture.

Linke's furniture was exported all over the world, mainly to the Americas, but comparatively little appears to have reached Britain – possibly its ornate and overtly French Louis XV style was too heavy for the British taste.

The Linke firm was prolific in later years, closing in 1940. The magnificent work Linke made for the Paris Exposition Universelle in *1900* was a *tour de force* – he staked his reputation and slender fortune on achieving success there. The style mixed Louis XV and Art Nouveau – the hallmark of Linke's work. Like many gifted cabinet-makers, he had emigrated from his native Austria to France.

Possibly the finest cabinet workshops in Paris in the years immediately preceding

1900 were those established in 1880 by Joseph-Emmanuel Zwiener (b.1849), a German *émigré*. Very little is known about his life. His work, produced only between 1880 and 1895, is rare and always of the finest quality. It is not often signed, although, like Linke's, his *bronze doré* mounts are easily distinguished. Linke and Zwiener appear to have worked together during the former's early years in Paris. Interestingly, a Julius Zwiener is recorded as working in Berlin around 1898, when he supplied a bedroom suite to the King of Prussia. The style of this Zwiener is identical to that of Joseph-Emmanuel. There are no known records to prove whether or not these two makers were related – or even the same person. The Paris Zwiener mysteriously disappeared from his establishment at 12 rue de la Roquette in 1895 – so did Joseph-Emmanuel return to his native country to become Julius?

OTHER EUROPEAN COUNTRIES

Revival styles dominated the whole of Europe. Led by French fashions and fed by the production machine of a newly united Germany, an international style prevailed. The dissemination of style through the huge quantity of printed fashion-plates and, later, through photographic catalogues led to a universal adaptation of, notably, the three main Louis styles. Each country adapted the French and Renaissance styles with its own sense of flair, but often the only clue to the origins of a piece was in the use of local techniques of craftsmanship and the use of cheaper indigenous woods.

Materials

During the nineteenth century virtually every European country used different materials for the manufacture of its furniture. The furniture industry was essentially localized and it looked to local suppliers for its basic materials, especially for the hidden woods of the carcase. Marquetry furniture of the second half of the century was superficially very similar all over Europe, being based on Louis XV or Louis XVI principles, but the wood underneath was different in almost every country. (The actual drawing and cutting of the marquetry foliage or other decoration varied, too, but this variation is not immediately noticeable.)

Oak was in plentiful supply and hence widely used in Holland. Holland still had colonial connections and imported exotic woods from the East Indies, whereas the rest of Europe generally imported from the Caribbean area. Dutch Neoclassical satinwood-veneered furniture was copied at the end of the nineteenth century using East Indian satinwood. Late-Georgian and early-Victorian Britain used West Indian satinwood until supplies became scarce in the middle of the century, after which it was imported from the Dutch colonies. Scandinavian countries used and exported huge quantities of their plentiful pine, as did rural areas in Alpine regions. Italy and Spain used what were generally poor woods, although some Italian carvers, especially in Florence, used walnut. Even olivewood was used for case-work. Fittings, with the exception of external mounts, varied in quality but were rarely fine.

The type of castor used can often be the only means of identifying the nationality of a chair. Generally speaking, the British suites had white or brown ceramic castors, occasionally of brass in the late-eighteenth-century manner. In most continental countries, though, floors were (and often still are) of wood parquet and not close-carpeted, and thus rather crude wood castors were used so as not to scratch the floor.

As industrialization spread, the watering down of local variations became noticeable and led to a cheapening of the finished article

TULIPWOOD AND SIMULATED IVORY CABINET, BOHEMIA, c.1880

in terms of both style and quality of production. During the second half of the century this led to a reaction alongside the French styles as each country looked to its own cultural roots for inspiration. In one sense this coincided with a re-emergence of national pride, but it was a convenient return to proved designs at a time when inspiration was often sadly lacking.

Italy, still a group of small states in 1844, began to sense the seeds of nationhood in the Esposizione dei Produtti Dell'Industria Francesca at Perugia. Italy and Spain produced furniture, often exotically inlaid in ivory in a Moorish style inlaid in the sixteenth-century style with *alla certosina*. By the time unification of Italy had been achieved in 1870, designers were looking back to the magnificent, luxuriously inlaid cabinets-on-stands of the Renaissance. Sculptural furniture, especially in Venice, was accurately

WALNUT PIER-TABLE AND MIRROR, ANGELO BARBETTI, ITALY, c.1845

recreated and blackamoor figures were reproduced well into the twentieth century. Confusingly, before widespread industrialization in the early years of the twentieth century, the techniques of craftsmanship were often exactly the same as those used three hundred years earlier. The Florentine carver/cabinet-makers Andrea Baccetti produced remarkable 'naturalistic' recreations of the Renaissance. The Renaissance style lent itself particularly well to machine production, and it became the staple of a large number of European manufacturers between the 1880s and about 1900. Italian woodcarvers, especially the Sienese Angelo Barbetti, emulated Renaissance carving from the third quarter of the century to around its end. In the 1860s and 1870s Italian craftsmen such as Ferdinando Pogliani of Milan and Giovanni Battista Gatti produced elaborate, finely made cabinets, frequently set with ivory and semi-precious stones, in an imposing mixture of Renaissance and Mannerist styles. This recreation of past forms reflects the latter-day Grand Tourists' yearning for souvenirs of 'old' Italy, and it was only in the work of Carlo Bugatti from around 1880 that we see any sense of a new style.

The countries of the Iberian peninsula copied and interpreted the French style while at the same time continuing production of traditional seventeenth-century furniture, notably of the 'Churrigueresque' style and cabinets of the type exported from Antwerp. At home, as well as in the colonies, this 'Isabellino style' dominated under Queen Isabella II (1833–68).

The neo-Gothic appeared particularly in Spain, where the style was typically Spanish, with white-painted parcel-gilt furniture. The 1832 work by Angel Maeso, now in the Escorial palace, Madrid, is a good example. Gothic furniture on a more massive scale was produced in the 1840s and 1850s, these later pieces being more closely aligned with British work, notably that of Pugin.

Belgium and Holland were able to produce large quantities of furniture, mainly of oak or walnut, much of it in a modernized seventeenth-century style, but made smaller for the new, smaller dwellings. Until the Art Nouveau period, few names are remarkable. Antwerp and Malines were important centres, the Antwerp-based firm of M. Roulé exhibiting at the Crystal Palace in 1851. One of the finest Antwerp cabinet-makers, Frans Franck made exceptional red tortoiseshell-veneered case furniture but in what was in effect an early-twentieth-century adaptation of Baroque magnificence. The Horrix firm at The Hague was a large factory producing furniture in the International Style made largely by machine and with little originality. Dutch marquetry was an ever-popular theme; as well as new pieces of furniture, many old and formerly plain walnut and mahogany pieces were subjected to the knife of the *marqueteur*. There was also a growing export market, especially to England.

Russia's limited production has always included fascinating, highly individual pieces. Peter Gambs made furniture very much in the International Style and kingwood-

PIETRE DURE AND WALNUT CENTRE TABLE, PASQUALE ORLANDINI, 1873 *(left)*

This Florentine table adopts an eclectic Renaissance style and is enriched with gilding. The heads are inspired by those on Ghiberti's doors to the Baptistry in Florence.

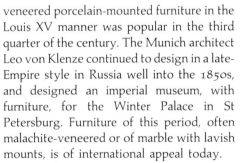

IVORY-INLAID ROSEWOOD CENTRE TABLE, PIETRO BERTINETTI, 1838 *(left)*

Made in Milan, probably for the exhibition there in 1838, this piece is in a late-classical manner.

veneered porcelain-mounted furniture in the Louis XV manner was popular in the third quarter of the century. The Munich architect Leo von Klenze continued to design in a late-Empire style in Russia well into the 1850s, and designed an imperial museum, with furniture, for the Winter Palace in St Petersburg. Furniture of this period, often malachite-veneered or of marble with lavish mounts, is of international appeal today.

Once the uniquely suitable mantle of the Biedermeier and the Neoclassical styles had been thrown off by the third quarter of the nineteenth century, the Scandinavian countries of Finland, Sweden and Denmark developed separately from the rest of Europe.

Salon suites, usually consisting of a settee, four side-chairs and occasionally two armchairs, were produced in huge quantities, at first in the Empire style and subsequently in the French revival styles. These revival styles, with local variations, dominated until the early twentieth century. Parcel-gilt and painted furniture, together with *bois-clair*, were used for all types of case-work, and especially for chairs. The new century saw a return to Viking roots and a *Fornodisk* movement inspired by runic and Celtic cultures. One of the most remarkable of these pieces is a painted polychrome chair by Carl Gustave Christensen in the Victoria and Albert Museum, London.

The House as a Showplace

By the 1880s furniture showrooms throughout Europe were advertising certain types of furniture for specific rooms. The ponderous Renaissance style lent itself to the dining-room, whereas more sophisticated, ebonized furniture, emulating the Henri II style of the 1580s, was fashionable for gentlemen's smoking-rooms. A lady's boudoir would be furnished with luxurious Louis XV-style furniture, while the more formal receiving rooms would have the Neoclassical style of Louis XVI.

Although houses might start off furnished in these 'complete packages', the Victorians and Edwardians – and their European counterparts – soon cluttered rooms with a mixture of styles, old and new.

BRITAIN

The Industrial Revolution had far-reaching effects on all aspects of society and, inevitably, led to a greater concentration of population in towns and cities. House-building boomed and, as a result, new and fashionable furnishings were in great demand. 'Good taste' and respectability became almost an obsession for the middle class, particularly women, whose role in the household suddenly became more dominant. The new breed of middle-class women generally had little experience of fashionable society and, therefore, a large number of books and periodicals was published to advise them on both social etiquette and interior decoration.

Furniture-makers benefited enormously from increased demand. London remained the centre of the furnishing trade, not only housing some of the best craftsmen but, more importantly, being a source of fashionable design ideas for makers elsewhere. At the beginning of Victoria's reign highly skilled cabinet-makers could be found in most large towns and cities, but only a few places had any sizeable concentration of

BOUDOIR OF MARIA ALEKSON, DROUNA, ST PETERSBURG, c.1890 (above)

TORTOISESHELL-VENEERED BUREAU, FRANS FRANCK, c.1910 (above left)

The red tortoiseshell veneers, imported from China, and the ivory inlay are in the tradition of seventeenth-century Antwerp, but the shape is distinctly eighteenth century.

firms – Edinburgh, Glasgow, Bath, Bristol, Norwich, Manchester, Leeds, Liverpool and Newcastle were among them. By the end of the century business everywhere had expanded. Birmingham had become famous for its metal bedsteads, Nottingham and Leicester for their cane and wicker furniture, and High Wycombe for its Windsor and other traditional country chairs.

London trade was effectively divided into two parts: the West End, where the best-quality firms were situated, and the East End, where cheaper goods were produced. A number of firms of middle-range quality were concentrated in the Tottenham Court Road area.

Both sectors of the trade employed specialist designers, many of them French. West End firms tended mainly to produce individual commissions and much of the work was done by hand, although they did buy in a certain amount of stock from the more reputable East End manufacturers. The latter companies mass-produced extensive ranges of furniture, much of which involved employing a number of different craftsmen in its making. By the 1880s many firms had achieved some degree of mechanization, mostly in the form of saws and other cutting equipment, but the majority of pieces still had to be hand-finished.

The larger firms had substantial show-rooms, sometimes on the same premises as their cabinet works and most companies of any size produced extensive catalogues. During the last quarter of the century furniture was increasingly sold through independent house furnishers like Hampton's of Pall Mall and Whiteley's, and through the more diverse department stores such as Harrods and the Army & Navy Stores, where the contents of entire rooms could be viewed. A popular method of advertising was to rent a stand at one of the many trade exhibitions held in the major cities, particularly towards the end of the century. The major international exhibitions, of which the Great Exhibition held at the Crystal Palace in 1851 is the most famous, attracted mainly the high-quality West End makers, as considerable expense was involved.

While many people wanted to prove to others their awareness of up-to-date taste, few had the courage or the inclination to purchase furnishings which were outrageously modern. The majority were content to buy the pastiches of historic styles which characterized the majority of Victorian 'commercial' furniture. For the middle class, whose experience of fashionable interior decoration was presumably rather limited, the familiarity of traditional styles was reassuring and gave the superficial appear-

RECONSTRUCTION OF A VICTORIAN PARLOUR, c.1870.

The presence of a piano, the claret-coloured upholstery, the balloon-back chairs, the marquetry loo table, the display cabinet and the draped overmantel are typical of the period.

ance of a 'respectable' background which they did not actually possess.

By the third quarter of the century customers could choose from a wide range of differing styles. Their choice of furnishings was aided to some extent by a tendency, as in France, to allocate an individual style to a particular room according to its function: the Renaissance was favoured for the dining-room, Rococo for the drawing-room, Elizabethan for the hall, Moorish furnishings for the billiard-room and so on. Manufacturers and house furnishers encouraged this trend by selling long suites of furniture of complementary design, although in reality most houses were furnished as they are today, with a gradual accumulation of favoured objects of varying dates and styles. Antiques were widely used in Victorian interiors and good English furniture was avidly collected.

By 1880 eclecticism had become a prominent feature of domestic interiors, particularly in the drawing-room, where it was joined by an almost overpowering clutter of small decorative objects and pictures. Furniture had by now entirely moved away from its formal eighteenth-century position against the walls. Now a variety of upholstered seating – adorned with cushions, shawls and lace-edged antimacassars – jostled for floor space with potted plants and numerous occasional tables laden with trinkets and oddities, against a background of various desks, whatnots, cabinets and bookcases. Rather sombre wallpapers, dark-coloured paintwork and elaborate drapes over windows, doors and fireplaces combined with poor lighting and heavy lace curtains and blinds to create an impression of quiet gloom. It is hardly surprising that the white paintwork and sparse furnishings advocated by progressive designers of the 1890s caught the public imagination so quickly. After several decades of gloomy respectability, their freshness and light must have had great appeal.

Although historic styles dominated furniture design throughout the entire period, a desire for novelty encouraged the popularity of other styles, particularly after 1870. In addition, many aesthetes and designers strongly disliked historicism and considered

the general state of the decorative arts to be unacceptably low. Their efforts to reform public taste by returning to craftsmanship and straightforward design uninhibited by historic precedents are well known. Now collectively referred to as Arts and Crafts, the work of these various individuals and groups is invariably considered outside the development of mainstream commercial furniture design (see pages 145–152).

Fashionable Styles, c.1830–65

When Victoria came to the throne in 1837 there were already four fashionable styles to choose from. In his *Encyclopaedia of Cottage, Farm and Villa Architecture and Furniture* (1833), John Claudius Loudon (1783–1843) noted: 'The principal Styles of Design in Furniture at present executed may be reduced to four: the Grecian or modern style which is by far the most prevalent; the Gothic or perpendicular style which imitates the lines and angles of Tudor architecture; the Elizabethan style which combines Gothic with the Roman or Italian manner; and the style of Louis XIV or the florid Italian which is characterised by curved lines and an excess of curvilinear ornament.'

No real alternatives were offered until well after 1860 and cabinet-makers continued to use the same pattern-books for several decades. Loudon's *Encyclopaedia* was reissued many times virtually unaltered between 1833 and 1867. Likewise, Thomas King's pattern-book, *The Modern Style of Cabinet Work Exemplified*, first published in 1829, was reissued as late as 1862, although an updated version had been published in 1835. Other influential designers of the period, who like King aimed specifically at the upper- and middle-class market, were Henry Wood and Henry Lawford. Henry Whitaker, who had published the late-classical *Designs of Cabinet and Upholstered Furniture in the Most Modern Style* in 1825, produced in 1847 the *Practical Cabinet Maker and Upholsterer's Treasury of Designs*, in which he, too, included designs for Grecian, Gothic, Elizabethan and Louis Quatorze furniture.

At the time Loudon's *Encyclopaedia* was first published the rather heavy Grecian or

ELIZABETHAN-STYLE BED, ANTHONY SALVIN, c.1840 *(above)*

GILT BEECHWOOD GOTHIC CHAIR WITH EMBROIDERED UPHOLSTERY, c.1830 *(top)*

late-classical style was nearing the end of its popularity for domestic furniture, but was still widely used in architecture for gentlemen's clubs and public buildings. It was chiefly represented by the application of classical ornament to the type of very simple classical and Empire domestic furniture made between the 1780s and the late 1820s. Commercial manufacturers represented the Gothic style in a similar way through the application of decorative motifs derived from Gothic stonework. The style was destined to appear in other forms as well over the next fifty years.

The popularity of the Elizabethan style has largely been attributed to its romantic associations with the past. The vastly popular novels of Sir Walter Scott and the choice of the Gothic or Elizabethan style for the rebuilding of the Palace of Westminster reinforced its position as representative of Britain's national heritage. Large numbers of substantial houses were built or refurbished in Elizabethan style and appropriately adorned with carved-oak furniture against a background of plaster ceilings, Gothic-patterned carpets and wallpapers as well as collections of arms and armour and other more decorative relics of the past. Notable among these houses is Scott's own home at Abbotsford, Scotland which was altered from 1819.

Books such as Henry Shaw's *Specimens of Ancient Furniture* (1836), which showed drawings of genuine early pieces, and Richard Bridgens's *Furniture with Candelabra and Interior Decoration* (1838) provided an important design source for furniture manufacturers. Bridgens's book showed how carved ornament such as Renaissance or Tudor strapwork could satisfactorily be applied to standard pieces of furniture. He fell into what was evidently a common trap at the time of confusing the tall-backed turned chairs of the Restoration period (c.1660–1700) with those of the earlier part of the century. Indeed, many 'Elizabethan' chairs were actually late-Stuart in form – hence the modern description 'Jacobethan'. Both strapwork and spiral turnings were greatly favoured by many of the commercial makers, who soon found them admirable for the

labour-saving machinery increasingly used in the early stages of the carving process.

A number of makers reconstructed reasonably convincing Elizabethan and Gothic cupboards, coffers, tables and chairs by piecing together old panels and other elements of architectural woodwork. Loudon implied that these were freely available. Attempts were also made to reproduce direct copies of earlier pieces, such as the Glastonbury chair illustrated in Shaw's *Specimens*, of which several examples exist.

In very large houses the antiquarian effect was extended to all rooms, but in middle-class homes Gothic and Elizabethan furniture was largely confined to halls and dining-rooms and, where present, libraries. The most noticeable exception to this rule was the tall-backed, low-seated devotional or

'vesper' chair, the prie-dieu, which, most fashionably made in Elizabethan style, became a universal feature of Victorian drawing-rooms. Its popularity was partly due to its suitability as a vehicle for Berlin woolwork, a type of embroidery indulged in by all fashionable leisured women between about 1830 and 1860. Thousands of designs for Berlin woolwork were imported from Germany and many were adapted for use on chairs and various kinds of firescreens. A number of pieces specifically designed to incorporate Berlin woolwork were published between 1840 and 1850 by Henry Wood.

For drawing-rooms and boudoirs – rooms where feminine influence prevailed – furniture based on early-eighteenth-century styles was preferred. The terminology surrounding this type of furniture can be confusing. At the time it was generally referred to as 'Louis Quatorze', or simply 'Old French', but much of it was closer in feel to Louis XV Rococo and as such has more recently been given the name Rococo revival. In fact, with the exception of upholstered furniture — which undoubtedly shows close affinities with the Rococo style — most 'Old French' pieces contained elements of both styles, combining the opulence and basic solidity of Louis XIV Baroque with the lighter and more frivolous scrolls of Rococo,

BRITISH FURNITURE DISPLAYS AT THE GREAT EXHIBITION, 1851 *(right)*

THE DINING-ROOM, HUGHENDEN MANOR, MID-19TH CENTURY *(opposite)*

The combination of Gothic architecture and decoration with 'Elizabethan' (actually late-Stuart) chairs, seen here in Benjamin Disraeli's home, was a common error.

yet at the same time remaining unmistakably British. Thomas King's *The Modern Style of Cabinet Work Exemplified* (1829), for example, showed a number of pieces of this type, which were described by King himself as in the 'English style . . . carefully blended with Parisian taste' and which displayed a number of elements from several different French styles.

Although at first 'French' pieces were fashionably enriched with gilded scrolls, rosettes and other ornament, they were soon universally executed in polished wood. Figured and burr walnut was favoured for drawing-rooms from the late 1840s onwards, but generally mahogany was used elsewhere. Both woods were French-polished to produce a highly glossy finish, particularly fashionable during this period.

Upholstered Furniture

Rococo was most successfully adapted for seat furniture, the shape of whose upholstery had been revolutionized by the introduction of the coiled spring in the late 1820s. Now upholstery had to become much deeper than before. Not only did the springs themselves necessitate an increase in depth, but the padding, too, had to be thicker to prevent the springs from poking through the top cover. Although designed to allow some movement and therefore greater comfort in the upholstery, both springs and stuffing had to be held in place with deeply set buttons. The buttons and the resulting pleating of the material became a decorative feature in themselves. The deep and rounded effect was complemented by similarly rounded edges to both seats and backs and was, of course, particularly well suited to the continuous curves of Rococo-style seat-frames.

From about 1850 onwards upholstered furniture was fashionably sold in suites usually consisting of a sofa or *chaise-longue*, a pair of spoon-back easy-chairs (a large 'grandfather' chair with open arms and padded arm-rests, and a smaller, armless 'grandmother' chair) and a number of occasional balloon-backs. These latter, obviously derived from the Louis XV *fauteuil* but

without arms and with an open rather than a padded back, were rather delicate little chairs, with their thin cabriole legs. They were made in very large numbers — indeed, they and their complementary spoon-backs are probably to the modern eye the most distinctive of all Victorian chairs. Although originally intended for the salon they are now popularly used as dining-chairs. Astonishingly, these chairs were still on sale in the 1880s, even though by then they had become very unfashionable. By now most upholstery had a more rectilinear look. The majority of pieces were fully stuffed over the frame, the only wood visible being the straight legs and arm-supports, which were often turned with simple ring mouldings.

Sofas and upholstered chairs in the Rococo style had polished wooden frames with short legs ending in castors. A curving apron ran along the front and the centre of the back and the knees of the legs displayed a limited amount of foliate carving. The arm-supports were deeply scrolled. In later chairs, turned, tapering legs ousted the cabriole.

Upholstered seat furniture in the 'French' fashion became much more diverse during the first half of the century and various ottomans, sofas and conversation- and love-seats evolved which allowed their occupants to sit at a variety of angles. On all pieces comfort was a prime consideration, so great attention was paid to textiles and trimmings.

Until about 1850, light-coloured patterned fabrics, often with a stripe interspersed with floral designs, were generally preferred to the dark red and green cut velvets and silk damasks which are more closely associated with the term 'Victorian'. The legs of chairs and sofas were often covered by heavy floor-length fringes with deep latticework headings, but these were replaced around the middle of the century by narrow, machine-made gimp (woven braid trimming). Tassels and twisted cord, often made in two or more contrasting colours, provided additional decorative effects.

The use of floral-chintz loose covers was widespread throughout Victoria's reign in drawing-rooms and women's bedrooms. These seem to have had several advantages. They protected the more expensive fixed upholstery from daily wear and tear, and could quickly be removed for important social functions as well as giving the room a lighter appearance. Perhaps most usefully, they provided a cheap method of disguising old-fashioned and worn upholstery.

The Naturalistic Style

Other types of furniture showed a general rounding-off of corners accompanied by a much bolder use of curves and a tendency towards rather heavy and often over-ornate carving. Opulent scrolls were combined with naturalistic carving, mostly of foliate form.

Seen in retrospect as typically Victorian, this rather robust Baroque/Rococo-inspired style was appropriately named the 'naturalistic style'. It was used for a wide variety of furniture between the 1840s and early 1860s and in some cases even later.

In the bedroom, wardrobes and chests-of-drawers were relatively simple and were mostly decorated with applied scroll mouldings and cornices, but bedsteads, dressing-tables and wash-stands (the latter usually with white marble tops) were very curvaceous in outline as well as in decoration. For the dining-room, sideboards and serving-tables were designed along similar lines, with scrolling volute supports and elaborately curved splash-backs. In the drawing-room, particularly popular pieces in this style were loo tables, small davenport desks and music canterburies, which slid under the piano when not in use. While all three had been features of Regency interiors, they gained considerably in popularity by the middle of the century and were much more varied in design – particularly music canterburies, which were often given an extra upper shelf to form a sort of whatnot for the display of ornaments.

On some pieces naturalistic carving was taken to its extremes. Fantastic arrangements

THE DRAWING-ROOM, LINLEY SAMBOURNE'S LONDON HOUSE, 1880s *(right)*

These curvaceous button-back Rococo chairs were present in houses at all social levels during the 1850s and 1860s, and were still fashionable in the 1880s.

WALNUT DRESSING-TABLE, *c.*1850 *(far right)*

London East and West End makers combined French Rococo scrolls and curving outlines with naturalistic carving to produce a peculiarly British style.

of animals, birds, dead game, flowers, fruit and foliage – sometimes interspersed with allegorical figures – almost totally engulfed the basic structure of the piece. The Cookes of Warwick and Morant of London are the best-known names associated with this type of excessive naturalism.

This tendency towards over-ornamentation and the lack of understanding of historic styles were obvious features of the Great Exhibition of 1851. The generally high standards of workmanship could not hide the low standards of design and Richard Redgrave RA, in his *Report on the Present State* of Design as Applied to Manufactures (1857), attacked the whole principle of exhibitions: '... each manufacturer is striving his utmost to attain notice and reward ... by an endeavour to catch the consumers by startling novelty or meretricious decoration, leading, in most cases, to an extreme redundancy of ornament.' Apart from encouraging the work of reformist designers including William Morris and other founders of the Arts and Crafts Movement, public criticism also encouraged the better makers to review their design policies and the furniture displayed at the 1862 International Exhibition, also held in London, was generally of a higher standard.

New Materials

The search for novelty brought to the public's notice the potential of new materials for furniture-making.

Papier mâché was used for only a few pieces, being obviously unsuitable on structural grounds as it had to be superimposed on a metal or wooden frame. The use of papier mâché as a decorative medium, however, has a long history. It is most closely associated with the early-Victorian period. Jennens & Bettridge of Birmingham was both the largest and the most successful

nineteenth-century manufacturer, largely because of its 1825 patent for mother-of-pearl inlay on papier mâché, which was then overpainted with gilding and coloured varnishes. The range of items produced was immense. Furniture included small occasional tables, gaming- and work-tables, chairs, beds, settees, pole screens, music canterburies and even – according to the 1851 Exhibition catalogue, at which Jennens & Bettridge won the highest award in the papier mâché category – 'the entire casings of pianos'.

Some makers produced furniture which, by virtue of its decoration, gave every appearance of being papier mâché but was

made entirely of wood and simply japanned or painted in the same way. Other firms used papier mâché only for the least vulnerable parts. In line with other furniture of their date, most pieces were in the Neo-Rococo or naturalistic style. Its popularity came to a rather abrupt end in about 1870.

Cast iron was another new material used for furniture, mainly for use in gardens, conservatories, pubs and cafés. Most of the early makers were established stove and grate manufacturers in areas such as Birmingham, Sheffield and Coalbrookdale, Shropshire. At first designs were based on eighteenth-century rustic furniture, but soon

A POLE SCREEN, MUSIC CANTERBURY AND SETTEE, c.1860 (left)

These pieces are basically constructed of wood, but decorated and combined with papier mâché. Victorian papier mâché can be recognized by its brightly coloured painted and gilded decoration often combined with mother-of-pearl inlay.

WALNUT DAVENPORT, c.1860 (far left)

Davenport writing-desks were a late-Georgian invention but were particularly popular with Victorian women as bedroom furniture.

more complicated floral and leaf motifs appeared. Garden seats and benches, particularly those made for public parks, usually had cast-iron ends joined by wooden slats which formed the seat and back and tables frequently had marble or wooden tops. Some of the most attractive pieces, including the famous 'fern' seats (one of which was actually produced in bronze), were made by the Coalbrookdale Company. *Jardinières* and hall and umbrella stands were other popular items. All pieces were painted in imitation of wood, expensive bronze, stone or marble.

Between about 1845 and 1855 Coalbrookdale attempted to manufacture a range of upholstered cast-iron drawing-room furniture, but the venture was not a commercial success. Iron 'pompadour' frames, though, were still occasionally used for the upholstered parts of easy-chairs.

Cast iron was used also for bed-frames, although at first the metal was hidden by

DETAIL OF CAST-IRON 'DEERHOUND' TABLE, MADE BY COALBROOKDALE, c.1855

traditional cloth hangings. Half-tester beds (where the curtains hung only over the head-end of the bed) remained popular for some time, but by about 1870 curtains and other hangings were largely dispensed with, leaving the bed-ends totally exposed. Tubular brass commonly replaced black-painted iron, although sometimes the two were decoratively combined and iron was still used for the entire frame of cheaper models. Brass and iron beds were produced in enormous numbers during the last quarter of the century, mostly in Birmingham; many of them were extremely elaborate, with complicated arrangements of vertical and horizontal bars ending in large brass or even ceramic knobs.

A number of manufacturers experimented with furniture constructed from twisted lengths of wire. While various designs for these can be seen in nineteenth-century trade catalogues and advertisements, very few pieces, apart from *jardinières*, have survived.

Experiments were also made with other metals. Loudon described attempts by the R.W. Winfield brass foundry in Birmingham to make chairs out of gas tubing in the 1830s and a tubular-brass rocking-chair received a lot of attention at the Great Exhibition. More successful was the use of strip metal.

A small amount of mostly rustic furniture was made from organic materials. Although usually thought of as German, some rather grotesque furniture constructed from deer antlers incongruously combined with elaborate deep-buttoned upholstery found a limited market in Britain too. A suite of German antler seat furniture formed part of the furnishings at Osborne House on the Isle of Wight. Stools and some chairs were made from the horns of Scottish Highland cattle.

More popular was garden and conservatory furniture made of wicker. Victorian wicker furniture was strongly influenced not by the indigenous rural craft tradition but by the products of contemporary American manufacturers. Following the display of a wicker chair by a New York maker, a Mr Topf, at the Great Exhibition, increasing numbers of firms, based mostly in the Midlands, began advertising ranges of partly upholstered chairs and sofas, small tables and workboxes and a variety of plant-stands and

other small items, under the various names 'cane', 'willow' and 'rattan'. Many of these pieces were of rather bizarre design — increasingly so during the 1880s and 1890s, when wicker reached the height of its popularity. A substantial amount was exported for 'colonial' use and it was very popular with hotels. The largest manufacturers were Morris & Wilkinson in Nottingham and W.T. Ellmore in Leicestershire.

A small amount of experimental furniture was made from totally unsuitable materials such as gutta percha, leather stamped to look like wood, slate and even coal. Victorian coal furniture was made mostly for advertising purposes, or for presentation to visitors.

Fashionable Styles, c.1865–1915

The second part of Victoria's reign saw a wider and more eclectic range of fashionable styles, many of them still historic revivals but some of them more original and exotic. From the 1860s onwards both French and English styles were favoured by the better makers, first Louis Seize and Adam, followed in the 1870s by Renaissance and in the 1880s by Chippendale, Sheraton and Hepplewhite. Elizabethan, Jacobean and an updated version of Gothic continued to be in favour and Carolean furniture increased in popularity. (It should be emphasized that all these Victorian styles were imaginative pastiches of their predecessors, not exact replicas.) Attempts were made to revive an interest in French Empire furniture and its English equivalent, the Regency, but with little success. After 1900 reproductions of Louis Quinze and to a larger extent genuine Queen Anne were adopted (the latter not to be confused with the architectural Queen Anne style associated with the Art Furniture of the 1880s, which bore little relation to the real thing). Most of these styles were still popular at the beginning of World War I, despite the fact that the products of more progressive modern designers were by then widely available. More original styles, fashionable mostly during the 1880s, were Japanesque and Moorish furnishings and Art Furniture, a type derived from a number of other contemporary sources (see page 139).

From the 1860s onwards the demand for French-style furnishings encouraged the better West End firms to produce furniture with the straight lines and refined decoration of Louis Seize and British Neoclassical furniture (often mistakenly called 'Adams' furniture). Marquetry and inlay, inset panels of porcelain, ormolu mounts and pale-coloured figured woods were all features of this decorative, yet formal furniture.

The revival of more ornate Louis Seize furniture stimulated a general interest in the decorative techniques of wood marquetry and buhl work (the French technique popularized by André-Charles Boulle). Buhl was largely confined to the grander drawing-room cabinets and commodes designed for large and luxurious houses. Often of severe form, with ornate ormolu mounts, these slightly ostentatious pieces were produced for the top end of the market. A large number of designs for marquetry and buhl, a style

KINGWOOD SIDE-CABINET, STAMPED BY EDWARD HOLMES BALDOCK, c.1840

OAK MUSIC CABINET, CHARLES BEVAN, 1865 (below)

SIDE-CABINET WITH MARQUETRY DECORATION AND METAL MOUNTS, c.1875 (above)

This piece is of a type commonly produced by London West End firms during the 1870s. The curved sides are reminiscent of earlier naturalistic pieces.

SIDE-CABINET WITH BUHL WORK OF BRASS SET INTO EBONIZED WOOD; 1860s (right)

These cabinets were largely confined to the drawing-rooms of very grand houses.

DESIGN FOR A 'CHIPPENDALE' LIBRARY FROM A CATALOGUE, 1904 (*below*)

This design shows a typical lack of elegance and proportion.

A SIMILAR FURNISHING SCHEME FOR A 'RENAISSANCE' DINING-ROOM, 1904 (*left*)

Overmantels and plain leather upholstery were common features of 'Renaissance' style.

EBONIZED SIDEBOARD WITH SILVER-PLATED FITTINGS, E.W. GODWIN, MADE BY WILLIAM WATT, *c.*1867 (*opposite left*)

first revived in the Regency period, were published by Henry Lawford in 1856 and reissued about fifteen years later in his *Cabinet of Marquetry, Buhl and Inlaid Woods*. Marquetry (and inlay) had a far wider application. After about 1860 it was frequently seen on the tops of loo tables but also appeared on other drawing-room pieces of furniture.

Throughout the 1860s and 1870s, and well into the 1880s, the revivalist Gothic style of A.W.N. Pugin (1812–52) continued to be in favour. Although many architects and designers produced their own individual interpretations of Gothic, they shared the same basic approach to quality construction and decoration. Many reformist designers were employed by cabinet-making firms such as Gillows, Holland & Sons, Marsh & Jones of Leeds, Howard of Berners Street and J.G. Crace (for whom Pugin had worked and who actually reproduced many of his designs). Not all makers shared the reformist ideals; more commercial firms, such as C. & R. Light and J. Shoolbred & Co., produced ranges of 'Mediaeval' furniture of less convincing appearance and lower-quality construction. An important influence on commercial production was *Gothic Forms*

Applied to Furniture, Metal Work and Decoration for Domestic Purposes (1867) by Bruce J. Talbert (1838–81), in which he advocated framed construction, the use of inlay, low-relief carved decoration and large flat metal hinges. In practice Talbert's work (several superb examples of which were displayed at various international exhibitions) was often very detailed. Bold geometric and other inlaid patterns, low-relief metal panels, squares of intricately carved boxwood, rows of small turned spindles and the occasional inclusion of 'improving' verses were characteristic. Many of these features were adopted by manufacturers of the mostly ebonized Art Furniture (see below) for which Talbert also designed stencilled decoration.

Another great proponent of the Gothic style, although never admired for his design capabilities, was Charles Lock Eastlake (1836–1906), whose *Hints on Household Taste* (1868; first published as a series of articles in 1865) was widely read. In it Eastlake castigated the use of excessive ornamentation on much contemporary furniture and advocated a return to medieval methods of construction, in which nothing was concealed by false means. He was never employed as a commercial designer, but Jackson & Graham made a

number of pieces to his designs and less prestigious makers evidently used them as a design source.

The success with which makers interpreted English eighteenth-century styles obviously varied considerably. Chippendale suffered some of the worst bastardization – a mean use of materials, coarse shallow carving, rather spindly legs and uprights, a general lack of generous proportion and a thick, treacly, dark brown stain. Chair-seats tended to be too narrow and table-tops too thin. Metal handles were of poor quality, often of thin stamped metal, and construction was generally shoddy, with poorly made joints and low-quality timber. 'Sheraton', 'Hepplewhite' and 'Adams' designs were generally handled better, ranging from the more precise copies of Gillows and Wright & Mansfield to the cheaper imitations made in the East End. Drawing-room and bedroom furniture were the most popular subjects for these styles. Sheraton pieces were usually executed in light mahogany and decorated with simple inlaid stringing lines and shell and fan shapes, while Adam bedroom furniture was often painted white, a suitable 'hygienic' colour.

Renaissance furniture, too, underwent a

'PET' SIDEBOARD, B.J. TALBERT, MADE BY GILLOWS AND SHOWN AT
THE INTERNATIONAL EXHIBITION IN 1873. *(right)*

revival during the last thirty years or so of the century and was particularly popular in the dining-room. In the average firm's repertoire, elaborate overmantels joined tables, chairs and vast sideboard-cabinets and serving-tables. Both cabinets and overmantels were designed in architectural form and were composed of various arrangements of shelves, brackets, niches and cupboards. Needless to say, cheaper manufacturers relied more heavily on brackets and shelves than on actual Renaissance ornament.

Then there was reproduction furniture. The top end of the trade made a few true reproductions as well as many pastiches of earlier styles. Great care and expense were lavished on the manufacture of these. In London Sir Richard Wallace (1818–90) did not hesitate to commission copies of eighteenth-century French furniture that he could not purchase outright. One notable example of this is a copy of a *bureau à cylindre*. The original, owned by the French nation, was in the custody of Napoleon III; it had always stood in the King's study at Versailles, and had survived the Revolution. The Emperor, who was personally acquainted with Sir Richard, allowed Wallace's cabinet-makers, Webb of Bond Street, London, to commis-

sion Henry Dasson of Paris to take exhaustive and elaborate measurements. The cost of this copy was extraordinary – 90,000 francs, at least £250,000 at today's prices.

Hindley & Wilkinson, whose reproduction business thrived during the Edwardian period, claimed to base their designs for 'French' furniture on pieces in French museums and collections, and commissioned special tapestry seat-covers from Aubusson. Gillows established their own factory in Paris. On the whole great pride was taken in these very good reproductions and no attempt was made to deceive. Undoubtedly a limited amount of faking did go on in the early part of the twentieth century.

From the late 1870s onwards an increasing number of firms called themselves Art Furniture Manufacturers. Aestheticism, in which an appreciation of beauty overrode practical considerations, soon became the basis of an artistic movement which, unlike all other fashionable decorative styles, remained peculiarly British.

The principal source of inspiration for the Aesthetic movement of the 1870s and 1880s was Japanese art, examples of which were first publicly displayed in Britain at the 1862 International Exhibition. The very simple

furnishings – with their sparse ornament set in pale-coloured and uncluttered interiors – provided a complete contrast to the dark and crowded rooms which had become the norm. The more avant-garde proponents of the movement took Japanese ideas to their extreme when furnishing their homes, but for the majority of people Aestheticism was represented by rather spindly commercial Art Furniture set among Japanese pots and fans, embroidered shawls and elegant arrangements of peacock feathers.

The most important furniture designer of the movement was Edward William Godwin (1833–86), who worked for many commercial firms and founded his own Art Furniture Company. Godwin's work was strongly influenced by Japanese principles of design in its careful balance of vertical and horizontal members, the inclusion on some pieces of embossed 'leather' paper and other Japanese materials, and its often ebonized finish. Another designer in the Japanese style was Thomas Jekyll (1827–81), who was responsible for the woodwork in the Japanese Peacock Room designed by James Abbott McNeill Whistler for F.R. Leyland in 1877.

The designer Christopher Dresser (1834–1904) was an important influence on the popularization of the Japanese style. In 1880 he became the editor of *The Furniture Gazette*, a journal which gave a comprehensive view of contemporary styles, and through it he was able to promote his own ideas.

Manufacturers of cheaper furniture attempted to work in the Japanese style, the chief characteristic of which involved various arrangements of Japanese fretwork applied to otherwise standard forms. Bedroom furniture was a popular vehicle for this style of decoration. On better pieces, panels of embossed 'leather' paper and imported panels of carved boxwood and geometric marquetry were incorporated in the design. Designers confused Oriental influences and Chinese decoration was often inadvertently incorporated into Aesthetic furniture, particularly by Robert Edis (1839–1927).

Far more popular as an example of Japanese taste was bamboo furniture, for which virtually all the materials – lacquer panels, 'leather' paper, marquetry, grass matting and the bamboo itself – were imported and made up in Britain in a vast number of inventive and sometimes grotesque designs. The largest manufacturers were W.F. Needham of Birmingham, who patented the only really satisfactory method of construction, which used brass joints and feet. The most popular items were small tables and plant-stands.

Moorish furnishings were popular during the 1880s and 1890s. Near Eastern decoration had been used in interiors earlier in the century, but had had little effect on furniture design. Much of the Moorish furniture available later in the century was in fact imported from Cairo, although some was manufactured in Britain, using sections of imported Musharabyeh panelling, and sold as 'Moorish', 'Arab', 'Saracenic' or 'Turkish'. The most common articles were chairs, folding screens, occasional tables and Koran stands. Because of its obvious associations with illicit smoking and the harem, Moorish furniture was confined to the smoking- and billiard-rooms of large houses, Turkish bathrooms, and other all-male preserves. Divans draped with Turkish carpets and other Eastern textiles (or their European imitations) and piled high with cushions were another popular feature of Moorish interiors.

INTERPRETATION OF THE QUEEN ANNE STYLE, *c.*1895 *(above)*

MOORISH INTERIOR SHOWING ELABORATE WOODWORK, EXOTIC EASTERN TEXTILES AND POTTED PALMS, *c.*1895 *(top)*

Art Furniture

The term 'Art Furniture' is used today to describe a type of decorative ebonized furniture produced by a large number of commercial manufacturers during the 1870s and 1880s. Generally credited as the first piece of furniture of this type was an ebonized cabinet designed by T.E. Collcutt (1840–1924) for Collinson & Lock and displayed by them at the 1871 London International Exhibition. Easily identifiable, Art Furniture actually shows a fusion of elements taken from a number of other contemporary sources. These included the bracket-and-overmantel construction of Renaissance pieces, the numerous small panels favoured by Talbert, the 'Gothic' coved cornices of the Middle Ages, the gilt panels of birds and flowers inspired by Japanese art, the painted panels of classical figures as favoured by Pre-Raphaelite artists, and the ebonized finish popularized partly by Japanese lacquer and partly by the furniture of the leading French *ébénistes*. Other features of this very distinctive style were slender turned uprights, spindled galleries, panels of bevelled glass, simple incised decoration picked out in gold and numerous small shelves and niches. Seat furniture, too, was ebonized, with incised decoration on its wooden frame. Rows of small turned spindles were often combined with upholstery on sofas, *chaises-longues* and easy-chairs.

Sometimes confused with Art Furniture, but quite distinct from it, was the furniture made during the 1880s and 1890s in the architectural Queen Anne style. Its manufacturers made no attempt to reproduce furniture of the Queen Anne period, but rather created a new style. This furniture, of bracket-and-overmantel type, was constructed using early-eighteenth-century classical architectural elements, such as columns, broken pediments, dentil cornices and urns.

The type of British 'New Art' furniture designed by Charles Rennie Mackintosh, C.F.A. Voysey and other progressive designers was widely imitated by the commercial trade. Beaten copper hinges, friezes containing 'improving' verses and panels of stained glass were frequently incorporated into what were otherwise generally simple pieces of furniture. Liberty's, which had opened in London's Regent Street in 1875, sold a rather clumsy range of Art Nouveau furniture under the name 'Quaint'.

DESIGNS FOR 'QUAINT' FURNITURE PUBLISHED IN *THE CABINET MAKER*, 1897 *(above)*

EBONIZED CHERRYWOOD CABINET WITH GILT DECORATION, KIMBEL & CABUS, NEW YORK, *c.1876 (top)*

THE UNITED STATES

In the United States, the establishment of more and better methods of transportation and communication during the nineteenth century meant that there was a greater flow of ideas between the East and West coasts and across the Atlantic. A much greater interest was shown in new technology and the use of new materials — especially, from the 1860s onwards, in the manufacture of mechanical furniture.

With the opening up and development of

HANGER HOUSE,
LITTLE ROCK,
ARKANSAS, 1889.

*By 1880 eclecticism was
common in America too
and the diverse mixture
of furniture styles in
this room do not look
out of place in the
'classical' setting.*

the West, the traditional Eastern centres of the furniture trade – Boston, Philadelphia, Newport, Baltimore and New York – were overtaken in importance by Grand Rapids in Michigan and Cincinnati in Ohio, both of which were from the late 1860s able to supply furnishings to all parts of the country with greater ease, thanks to the railroads. Towards the end of the century, however, New York recovered its position as the principal source of fashionable styles.

Middle-class Americans showed the same conservatism and preference for traditional styles as their European counterparts. Fashionable houses had the same air of gloomy respectability. Heavy drapes and overstuffed upholstery (often with much fussier trimmings than elsewhere), over-ornamented furniture, dark and sombre colours, and a profusion of different patterns and textiles were all common features.

Responsibility for interior design passed increasingly from the hands of architects to those of specialist decorators and house furnishers and later to the department stores in large towns and cities. Trade catalogues and journals provided a popular form of advertising, particularly in less accessible areas. Publications such as *Decorator and Furnisher*, which were aimed particularly at women, gave advice on home furnishing. British and European design publications continued to be an important source of ideas, but pattern-books and trade manuals were published by American designers, as well; the first was *The Cabinet Maker's Assistant* (1840) by John Hall of Baltimore.

Fashionable Styles, c.1830–65

The simple, veneered pillar-and-scroll furniture in the late-classical style, which had evolved during the late 1820s, continued to be fashionable throughout the 1830s and 1840s – and was still widely employed after 1850. The influential publication, *The Architecture of Country Houses*, by Andrew Jackson Downing (1815–52), published several times between 1850 and 1866, illustrated a wide selection of currently available furniture, the classical style being the most popular. This popularity has been attributed in part to its suitability for machine production. The large thin sheets of figured veneer and the single and double scrolls characteristic of this type of furniture could be cut by the new steam-driven machinery, thereby reducing costs.

By 1840, however, other revival styles, most notably Rococo, but also Gothic and Elizabethan, were beginning to challenge late classical's supremacy. The Gothic style, principally favoured for architecture, does not seem to have been widely popular for furniture at this date, although designs for this type of furniture were published in Robert Conner's *Cabinet Maker's Assistant* (1842). Also popular between about 1830 and 1860, though to a limited extent, was furniture in the 'Elizabethan style'. Like many of its British counterparts, this furniture contained elements taken from the fifteenth, sixteenth and seventeenth centuries, and was actually closest to furniture of the Carolean period. Complicated spiral turnings on tables, chairs and cabinets were the most prominent features and the prie-dieu chair, with spiral uprights, was popular.

A similar and cheaper version of the style, advocated by Downing because of its 'picturesque charm' as suitable for cottages and farmhouses, consisted of very straightforward furniture made from painted softwood decorated with various floral motifs. Simpler bobbin and ball turnings were used for uprights and stretchers on chairs and tables and split spindles were applied to the fronts of carcase furniture.

While 'Elizabethan' cottage furniture was especially popular in rural houses, around the middle of the century sophisticated urban homes were generally furnished in the more elaborate and curvaceous Rococo revival style. Rococo was interpreted in a far more flamboyant manner in the United States than elsewhere. Referred to at the time as either 'Antique' or 'Modern French', the style was chiefly characterized by the use of cabriole legs, by outlines composed of various arrangements of 'C' and 'S' scrolls, and by very ornate naturalistic carving, combining various flowers and foliage with human figures, birds and fruit. *Étagères* for the display of ornaments, formed of a series of stepped shelves above a table or cabinet, were particularly popular in this style and their superstructures often had mirrored backing. Many were designed to fit in a corner.

Deeply buttoned and sprung upholstered furniture was widely produced in the Rococo style, and balloon-back chairs, 'sociables' (three-seater sofas), *tête-à-têtes* and love-seats all became popular. Although in general shape these were not dissimilar to equivalent pieces made in Britain and Europe, sections of very ornate pierced carving were attached to the top of chair- and sofa-backs, giving them a rather top-heavy look.

Upholstery was often extremely lavish, with fancy and colourful trimmings. Narrow borders of gathered fabric, edged with twisted cord or welting, were a popular feature on chairs and sofas. French patterned silks and velvets appeared on the most expensive pieces; on cheaper versions cotton took their place. Needlework was popular for 'Elizabethan' chairs. Printed cotton chintzes and cretonnes were used for fixed upholstery as well as for loose slip-covers.

Rococo-style furniture was mass-produced in all parts of the country by well-known makers such as Joseph Meeks & Sons and Leon Marcotte (fl.1848–80) in New York, John Jelliff (1813–90) in Newark, Daniel Pabst in Philadelphia, S.S. Johns in Cincinnati and Prudent Mallard in New Orleans. One of the most famous makers in the Rococo style was the German-born New Yorker John Henry Belter (1804–63), who took out a successful patent for steam-bending and moulding laminated wood so that it could subsequently be carved. Belter is known to have worked in New York from 1844 onwards and he became one of that city's most fashionable cabinet-makers, producing furniture of marvellous quality in a variety of the prevailing styles. Other furniture makers who likewise worked with imported European woods were Charles A.

COL. ROBERT J. MILLIGAN HOUSE, SARATOGA SPRINGS, NEW YORK, 1853 *(above)*

An impression of opulent comfort is given to this room by the Rococo furniture, deep-buttoned upholstery, elaborate window drapes and the lush floral-patterned carpet.

ROSEWOOD BED, JOHN HENRY BELTER, c.1855 *(right)*

Belter used his own patent for laminated wood to provide a suitably robust material for his intricate Rococo and naturalistic carving.

EBONIZED AND
VENEERED CABINET,
NEW YORK, *c.1865*
(left)

*The eclectic neo-Grec
and Neoclassical
decoration is of inset
porcelain and marble.*

ROSEWOOD AND
MAHOGANY
CABINET, *c.1870*
(right)

*This is a more robustly
Renaissance-style
cabinet with inlays of
kingwood, tulipwood
and ebony.*

Baudouine (1808–95) in New York and George Henkels (*fl.*1850–70) in Philadelphia.

Fashionable Styles, c.1865–1900

Rococo remained fashionable until about 1860, when it was replaced by a variety of other styles. One of the most enduring of these, which remained popular from the mid-1860s until the end of the century, was the Louis Seize revival. Although it displayed many elements of original Louis XVI design – most notably straight tapering and fluted legs, oval and square chair-backs, straight arms and rectangular outlines on tables and cabinets – most pieces were heavier and squatter than previously. Polished mahogany or ebonized woods, with incised decoration picked out in gold, were used in place of painting and gilding. Ormolu mounts, metal beading, porcelain or bronze plaques and inlays of mother-of-pearl, ebony and other woods were features of this rather stately and often substantial furniture.

The popularity of French styles was reinforced by the large number of cabinet-makers of French origin working in the United States. The Louis XVI style was adopted by most of those who had previously favoured the Rococo style – Henkels in Philadelphia, Marcotte in New York,

and John Jelliff in Newark.

During the 1860s and early 1870s Renaissance motifs based on a French framework were enthusiastically adopted by makers, particularly in the Midwest, by firms such as the Berkey & Gay Co. of Grand Rapids, who mass-produced large suites of rather ponderous but highly distinctive furniture in this style. Often of massive size, carcase pieces were generally of rectangular construction on a solid plinth and had large panels of mostly burr-walnut veneer set within a lighter-coloured plain framework. Huge columns, broken pediments, scrolling brackets, urns, acorn turnings, bosses and medallions were incongruously grouped together. On chairs, heavy trumpet-turned legs were introduced. Renaissance revival furniture played a prominent role at the 1876 Centennial Exhibition held in Philadelphia.

This exhibition, which commemorated 100 years of independence, encouraged the already growing trend for collecting antiques or, for those who could not afford authentic pieces, reproductions of early American 'Colonial' furniture. General awareness of and interest in antiques and antique collecting was stimulated by travel to Europe. In 1884 the *Journal of Cabinet Making and Upholstery* stated that 'the making of antiques has become a modern indus-

try'. Style and quality varied considerably, the better firms producing pieces closer to the original examples.

The 1870s also saw an interest in modern Gothic furniture, stimulated by the publication in Boston of Eastlake's *Hints on Household Taste* (1872) and Talbert's *Gothic Forms Applied to Furniture* (1873). Never very widely popular, this basically reformist Gothic style was characterized by straight lines, chamfered edges on uprights, incised Gothic decoration, large metal strap hinges, cornices carved with a limited amount of Gothic architectural ornament and rather heavily panelled doors that often enclosed grooved boards. Although Eastlake's book advocated simple, sparsely decorated, functional furniture, the style came to be seen as the type of ebonized Art Furniture newly fashionable in Britain and ironically his name quickly became associated with the mass-produced commercial furniture which he himself despised. The 'Eastlake style' was typified by ebonized furniture with shallow incised lines and geometric decoration, turned uprights and spindled galleries.

The better makers were more impressed by the Anglo-Japanese furniture of E.W. Godwin than by the type of Art Furniture shown at the Centennial Exhibition. The firm of Horner made a great deal of Japanese-style

BEECHWOOD JAPANESE-STYLE BAMBOO SIDE-CHAIR, c. 1880

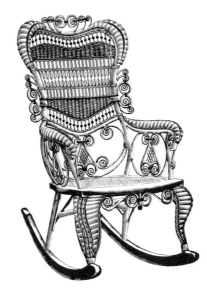

WICKER ROCKING-CHAIR FROM TRADE CATALOGUE, 1860S

CAST-IRON ADJUSTABLE-BACK SPRUNG CHAIR, 1850

furniture, some of it incorporating mother-of-pearl inlay and imported Japanese materials. Elaborate fretwork was a popular feature on chairs, tables and cabinets. A certain amount of bamboo furniture was designed, similar to that in Britain. Imitation bamboo was made, mostly in bird's-eye maple and with turned ring mouldings representing the nodes of the cane.

Exotic Moorish interiors were fashionable also, particularly in large and wealthy houses, and were characterized chiefly by the use of lavish Near Eastern textiles and upholstery. Divans and 'Turkish corners', piled high with pillows and partly covered above by drapery suspended from a canopy, were accompanied by imported brassware, potted palms and small tables and screens inlaid with mother-of-pearl. 'Turkish' chairs, which had a metal frame completely covered by deeply stuffed upholstery and long fringes, were likewise popular; subsequently this type of frame was used for other forms of upholstery as well.

New Materials

Throughout the century American manufacturers experimented with new materials. Some pieces were very close in style and type to their British counterparts, particu-

larly those made using papier mâché, although this material was not as widely popular as in Britain and France. Cast-iron furniture, made principally for outdoor use, tended to be more elaborate, with fanciful arrangements of fruit, flowers and foliage. Delicate twisted-wire furniture – mostly chairs, small tables and *jardinières* – with lacy scrolling patterns of a vaguely Rococo type, was especially popular around 1870. As in Britain, experiments were made with hollow metal tubing and strip metal, both of which were used for rocking-chairs.

Rustic furniture made from the roots and branches of trees found a limited market, mostly in the grounds of large country houses. Particularly in the West, furniture was constructed from various horns and antlers; it was much like its counterparts in Britain and Germany.

Popular on the East coast, from about 1850 onwards (a little earlier than elsewhere), was garden and verandah furniture made from wicker and imported rattan. This was especially elaborate, with very curvaceous outlines and panels filled with openwork designs of scrolls and lattice patterns. Most wicker chairs had an inner frame of wood disguised by the woven cane.

Bentwood furniture made by the Thonet factories in Europe was enormously popular

in the United States. It was cheap, light and easily portable, and its curvilinear designs had a great appeal. Numerous bentwood chairs, tables, rockers and hat- and coat-stands appeared in cafés and restaurants as well as in middle-class homes.

Mechanical Furniture

One of the most distinctive developments was the invention of various types of 'patent' or mechanical furniture. This came about partly because of the demand for space-saving furniture for small apartments and also for railroad sleeping-cars. The first sleeping-cars appeared in 1857 and various forms of seating were devised which could be converted into beds.

A variety of sofa-beds and beds which could be converted to form wardrobes or be disguised as pianos during the day were invented for domestic use. Particular interest was shown in adjustable chairs of various kinds comprising a complicated arrangement of levers, ratchets and springs. Many of them were supported on cast-iron bases. A rotating sprung chair, in which the angle of the back could be altered simply by pressure applied by the sitter, was first invented in the middle of the century. It provided the prototype for the adjustable typing chair.

CRAFT
AND DESIGN

In terms of mainstream furniture production, the bulk of the nineteenth century was a hotch-potch period of historicization, of looking back – styles, forms and materials largely echoed Elizabethan, Rococo and earlier times – and novelty was generally eschewed, although increasingly makers employed new mass-production methods.

In spite of many cabinet-makers' and consumers' insistence on clinging to the past, there nevertheless emerged throughout Europe and North America from mid-century a rich variety of bold, exciting and (unfortunately) high-priced furniture. Some of the craftsmen responsible were, admittedly, drawing on traditional styles, although uniquely restating them. Others, those who were more multi-media designers than solely cabinet-makers, were forging brave new paths and, by the *fin de siècle*, were resolutely looking to the future – indeed, shaping the modern age. Among these innovative furniture creations were hand-crafted or hand-finished variations on the relics of bygone eras and handsome pieces with exotic overtones. Then there were the startlingly new design confections dating from the 1880s onwards, including Art Nouveau furniture in particular and the proto-modern geometric shapes of the Secessionist designers.

The 1800s witnessed, too, the rise of the architect and craftsman as furniture designer. Both types of furniture-maker contributed to an expanded definition of furniture and its relation to both its environment and its users. Just as the *ébénistes* and *menuisiers* in eighteenth-century France had been held in lofty artistic esteem, many multi-talented far-seeing furniture designers in nineteenth-century Europe and North America were elevated to take their places alongside fine-artists, architects, writers and other taste-makers in helping to define a style, be it Gothic revival, Arts and Crafts, the Glasgow School, Art Nouveau or the Vienna Secession.

MAIN STAIRCASE OF THE MAISON HORTA, BRUSSELS, VICTOR HORTA, BEGUN 1898

Horta made abundant use of the whiplash curve, as can be seen in both the woodwork and metalwork of his own house, today the Musée Horta.

BRITAIN

The Craft revival of the nineteenth century was to an extent the result of a misconception – or, at least, of an ambiguity of viewpoint.

The eighteenth and early nineteenth centuries had enjoyed a wealth of great designers whose furniture had been executed by highly skilled craftsmen. As an ever-greater proportion of the population became comparatively affluent, cabinet-makers tried to supply them with furniture which at least *looked* as good as the best. There emerged a style and a technology of cabinet-making to suit the taste and pocket of the new rich. The earlier excellence – achieved by a combination of good design, carefully selected materials and the finest craftsmanship – was superseded by a mediocrity which depended for its effect on elaborate ostentation achieved by mechanical processes.

In Europe and North America – at different times in different countries, according to how endemic the malaise had become – a body of opinion emerged which regarded most of the contemporary furniture as contemptible. A cry for reform went up. And it was at this point that ambiguities crept in and dilemmas arose. If design were to be reformed and meretricious ornament eliminated, the furniture produced would be regarded as plain and unattractive by most people, who would consequently decline to buy it. The whole point of mass-production would therefore be negated. Conversely, if the aim was to revive the traditional crafts of the cabinet-maker, the resulting furniture would cost so much that only the wealthiest would be able to afford it. Only rarely could the would-be reformers balance these two conflicting factors.

Pugin and the Neo-Gothic Style

The architect Augustus Welby Northmore Pugin (1812–52) was the first to try to reform the style and manufacture of the furniture being made in Britain. All three of the prevailing styles – Rococo, Elizabethan and naturalistic – gave ample scope for coarse carved ornament. In 1835 he published his first book, *Gothic Furniture in the Style of the Fifteenth Century*, in which he illustrated the kind of furniture he would design during the remainder of his short life; he died insane when only forty. Much of this furniture was decorated with carving, and Pugin always supervised his craftsmen to ensure that this ornamentation was competently executed; moreover, the carving was never allowed to hide the structure clearly stated in the design. Sometimes, indeed, the structure was emphasized – for instance, an extended tenon might be secured by an exposed peg. (This feature, derived from medieval joinery and commonly used by provincial craftsmen until the middle of the eighteenth century, was employed by many designers associated with the revival of the crafts in both Britain and North America). The use of oak, a wood that had, except by country carpenters, been rarely used for furniture since the Restoration, became common among the cabinet-makers of the Arts and Crafts Movement. The Gothic reformers often polished their wood to a light brown-yellow not the dark brown associated with medieval and Jacobean furniture.

For the three decades after Pugin's death, in 1852, those manufacturers who had made furniture to his designs continued to do so, but frequently not to the high standards of craftsmanship that he had demanded; other firms plagiarized his work, producing, in the name of 'Gothic', furniture which was exactly the sort of 'vile trash' that Pugin had hoped to see eliminated. However, a handful of architects was inspired by his example to design furniture in a medieval style which was notable for its construction as well as its decoration. Two of them, George Edmund Street (1824–81) and John Pollard Seddon (1827–1906), had links with leading firms of cabinet-makers: Street's first wife was a close friend of Jessie Holland, the daughter of a director of the famous firm of Holland & Sons, and two years after his first wife's death Street married Jessie herself. Seddon was the son of Thomas Seddon, another important London cabinet-maker. Street and Seddon designed furniture for the buildings of which they were the architects, and both employed a neo-Gothic style inspired by Pugin's work. The structure of their furniture was always clearly stated. Each exploited his familial connections with skilled cabinet-makers to ensure that a high level of craftsmanship was used in the furniture's manufacture. The example of Pugin and the teaching of John Ruskin (1819–1900) lay behind their work. In his *Seven Lamps of Architecture* (1849) and *Stones of Venice* (1851–3), Ruskin had not only established the worthiness of the Gothic style but had also urged the importance of structural frankness and a fundamental truth to materials.

The Medieval Court

It was because this reformed furniture was in the Gothic style that examples by various designers, including Seddon, were exhibited in the Medieval Court at the International Exhibition held in 1862 at South Kensington.

Some pieces of furniture exhibited in the Medieval Court were elaborately decorated. Seddon himself showed an oak roll-top desk ornamented with marquetry and a cabinet painted by Pre-Raphaelite artists with scenes from King René's honeymoon. There was a large bookcase designed by the architect Richard Norman Shaw (1831–1912) and carved and painted by James Forsyth. The architect and antiquarian William Burges (1827–81), who had been entrusted with the organization of the Court, showed several pieces of furniture painted with elaborate figurative subjects by artists of the calibre of Edward Poynter (1836–1919), Simeon Solomon (1840–1905), Albert Moore (1841–93) and Edward Burne-Jones (1833–98). The notion of decorating furniture with paintings was inspired in some instances by French thirteenth-century cupboards at Noyon and Bayeux and in others, probably, by Renaissance *cassoni*. Another feature of early French furniture adopted by several of the designers showing in the Medieval Court was an extensive use of metalwork, particularly for drawer- and door-handles and strap hinges. These last, often in wrought iron or steel, became almost a badge to be worn by Arts and Crafts cupboards and cabinets well into the twentieth

OAK CABINET, JOHN POLLARD SEDDON,
c.1862 (above)

This cabinet, which was exhibited at the 1862 International Exhibition in London, was decorated with panels depicting King René's honeymoon painted by the Pre-Raphaelite artists Dante Gabriel Rossetti, Edward Burne Jones and Ford Madox Brown.

OAK TABLE AND CHAIRS, A.W.N. PUGIN
c.1850 (above right)

This room in the Palace of Westminster shows Pugin's neo-Gothic treatment of interior decoration. The construction of the furniture is clearly expressed and the carved ornament is restrained.

MAHOGANY BED, CABINET AND WASH-
STAND, WILLIAM BURGES, 1862–1867
(right)

Despite the elaborate painted, carved and stencilled decoration, the furniture has an underlying architectural strength and simplicity.

OAK DRESSER, PHILIP WEBB, c.1860 (left)

This simple, functional piece of furniture was made for the Red House, William Morris's home in Bexleyheath, Kent. Elaborate metal fittings were a common feature of Arts and Crafts furniture.

RUSH-SEATED CHAIRS, MORRIS & CO., LATE 19TH CENTURY (below)

Among the chairs shown on the right-hand page (from a Morris & Co. catalogue) are examples designed by Dante Gabriel Rossetti (top left) and Ford Madox Brown (bottom left and right).

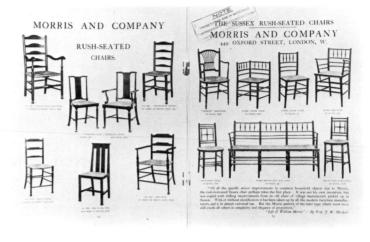

century. Sometimes they were constructionally redundant, being applied to, say, cupboard doors made from boards rather than from smaller, separate planks, which needed to be held together.

The drawback of furniture decorated by talented painters and sculptors was that it had to be expensive, and the practice was soon abandoned by the reformers. Commercial cabinet-makers, however, adopted the idea, but in their hands it was debased and emasculated. The task of painting panels for furniture became hack-work for impecunious artists. Not until the end of the century was painting used again by Arts and Crafts designers as a means of decorating furniture, and then only on a limited scale. Just over fifty years after the display in Burges's Medieval Court, however, furniture painted by leading avant-garde artists was offered by the Omega Workshops, founded by Roger Fry (1866–1934) in 1913.

The most famous exhibitor in the Medieval Court of 1862 was the firm of Morris, Marshall, Faulkner & Co. (soon to be renamed Morris & Co.). This company showed furniture designed by the architect Philip Webb (1831–1915), who, like Shaw and William Morris (1834–96) himself, had worked in Street's office. For Morris's home, the Red House at Bexleyheath, Kent, Webb had designed several pieces of furniture which had been painted by Dante Gabriel Rossetti (1828–82), Burne-Jones and others. Webb developed a very distinctive style for his furniture, influenced at first by Gothic design and subsequently responding to a wide variety of sources, including Queen Anne and Japanese. But he was never a slavish follower of fashion. His designs are distinguished for their poise and vitality, achieved by an idiosyncratic arrangement of masses and a sensitive judgement of angles and curves. He made a further contribution

to the Arts and Crafts Movement in the example which he set of a designer's close attention to the details of manufacture.

Country Furniture

Morris & Co. introduced a new dimension to the reform of furniture design and decoration. William Morris and his associates explored the forms and techniques of traditional country furniture. It was not only the debased quality of contemporary furniture that alarmed them but also the decline of ancient skills.

'Of all the specific minor improvements in common household objects due to Morris,' wrote J.W. Mackail in his *Life of William Morris* (1899), 'the rush-bottomed Sussex chair perhaps takes the first place'. Morris & Co. made several versions of this traditional country chair. Ford Madox Brown (1821–93) and Rossetti both designed variants, and the basic form was produced as an armchair, a corner chair and a settee. Although a conscious excursion into vernacular furniture design, the Sussex chair was usually sold with an ebonized finish, presumably with the intention of easing the chair's entry into the London sitting-room, where the art furniture of the Aesthetic Movement was often similarly finished. Certainly the chairs would have had a plainer appearance to suit a cottage parlour.

If the ebonized Sussex chair presents something of a contradiction within a single item of furniture, a similar dichotomy is shown by the contrast in character of the alternative kinds of furniture made by Morris & Co. In *The Lesser Arts of Life* (1882) Morris pointed out the difference between 'the necessary work-a-day furniture' and 'state furniture'. He described the latter as 'sideboards, cabinets and the like, which we have quite as much for beauty's sake as for use'. Such pieces, he asserted, may be made 'as elegant and as elaborate as we can with carving, inlaying or painting'. Here is the nub of the problem facing those who wanted to revive the crafts of cabinet-making. Only a very limited clientele could comprehend what was being attempted and appreciate the artistic intentions of the reformers. Many important patrons of the Arts and Crafts Movement were wealthy landowners, bankers, merchants and industrialists; they understood the aesthetic ideas underlying the reform of design but did not necessarily sympathize with the ethical views.

Richly Decorated Furniture

Alongside the chairs based on country originals and the simple bedroom furniture in stained oak designed by Ford Madox Brown, Morris & Co. began to make much more richly decorated pieces. Two factors expedited this development. Firstly, in 1887 the firm purchased from Holland & Sons a workshop in Pimlico, London, where the necessary facilities and staff were available. Secondly, at about the same time, George Jack (1855–1932) was appointed chief designer. Born in the United States on Long Island, New York, Jack had worked for

architects in Glasgow and London before being taken on by Philip Webb as an assistant. As well as having considerable design skills, he was also an accomplished craftsman with a great talent for wood-carving; many of the pieces he designed for Morris & Co. incorporated carving or marquetry, and often both.

The same duality that characterized the furniture produced by Morris & Co. is evident in the work of Arthur Heygate Mackmurdo (1851–1942), an architect who in 1882 founded the Century Guild. At one end of the spectrum, he designed an oak desk which was severely rectilinear in form, and which was probably built for him by a jobbing carpenter; at the other, when the Century Guild was commissioned in 1886 to furnish and decorate Pownhall Hall, Cheshire, for the wealthy brewer Henry Boddington, he designed much more ornate furniture which was manufactured by the Manchester cabinet-makers E. Goodall & Co.

Woods richer than oak were often used for the grander furniture of the Arts and Crafts Movement. Morris & Co. pieces designed by Jack were often made of mahogany — sometimes of walnut, if there was carved decoration. Furniture produced for the Century Guild's more prestigious clients was usually made of mahogany or satinwood — the latter being by the second half of the nineteenth century mostly imported from the East Indies and having a grain distinctive from that of its Western counterpart.

The Craftsman-Designer

Several architects tried to achieve, if not actual mastery of manual skills, at least a close collaboration with the cabinet-maker. In 1888 Ernest Gimson (1864–1919), a young architect working in an office next door to Morris & Co.'s showroom in London's Oxford Street, visited the Herefordshire village of Bosbury to work with Philip Clissett, a chair-maker who still used a pole-lathe to make rush-seated ladder-back chairs. Two years later Gimson, W.R. Lethaby (1857–1931), the brothers Edward (1863–1926) and Sidney (1865–1926) Barnsley and two other architects founded

the firm of Kenton & Co. to manufacture the furniture they designed, renting their own workshop and hiring a team of craftsmen. Unhappily the scheme was under-funded and lasted little more than a year. Nevertheless, in that short space of time the company produced furniture which amply demonstrated the advantage of close co-operation between designer and craftsman. The materials and crafts of cabinet-making were allowed to determine the form and decoration, the designer's role being restricted to creating the concept and overall style.

In 1893, Gimson and the Barnsley brothers left London and settled in the Cotswolds, at Ewen, Gloucestershire, where they set up their own workshops. Later, they moved to Sapperton, also in Gloucestershire, where the furniture Gimson designed was made by a team of skilled carpenters. Oak, walnut and black and brown ebony were the principal woods used. Although some pieces were quite plain, many were decorated with sometimes elaborate inlays of holly, fruitwood, ivory, abalone shell and silver – another example of the Arts and Crafts Movement's dichotomy between luxury and austerity. Sidney Barnsley by temperament leaned towards the latter. He mastered the skills of carpentry and became an accomplished cabinet-maker, building himself the furniture that he designed. He nearly always used oak and left most of his pieces plain, except for some chamfering and simple gouged ornament or, occasionally, a small amount of inlay. The furniture designed by his brother Edward was similar, but made by professional carpenters.

Innovative Designers

In the work of the Cotswold school, style was almost submerged in an aesthetic of traditional techniques and materials. Elsewhere in Britain, however, furniture was being created that relied for its effect mainly on the originality – even the eccentricity – of its design. The architect Charles Francis

Annesley Voysey (1857–1941) had been for a short time a pupil of Mackmurdo, and there are sometimes suggestions of the latter's influence on his furniture designs, which are otherwise entirely innovative. Voysey had a keen awareness of the visual qualities of oak, the wood which he generally used, and was equally sensitive to standards of craftsmanship. He usually selected with care the cabinet-makers to whom he entrusted his designs. Charles Robert Ashbee (1863–

MAHOGANY HALL TABLE, KENTON & CO., c.1890 *(above)*

This table, with inlaid decoration and brass feet, was designed by W.R. Lethaby and made for Avon Tyrrell, a house that he built in Hampshire.

WATERCOLOUR SKETCH OF A CABINET, C.R. ASHBEE, 1906 *(above right)*

Furniture designed by Ashbee was made by the craftsmen of the Guild of Handicraft.

OAK CHAIR, C.F.A. VOYSEY, c.1902 *(right)*

The plain design and elongated tapering uprights are characteristic of Voysey's style. He always demanded the highest standard of craftsmanship in the manufacture of the furniture he designed.

1942), who founded his Guild and School of Handicraft in 1888, designed furniture which was made by craftsmen recruited from the workshops of London's East End cabinet-makers. The visual impact of his work, however, relied less on craftsmanship than on stylish decoration and a distinct mannerism of form and proportion.

The Scottish designer George Walton (1867–1933) created furniture which seems sometimes to be almost a deliberate caricature of Arts and Crafts principles and prac-

OAK CHAIR AND PINE WARDROBES, CHARLES RENNIE MACKINTOSH, 1903 (below)

These fitted wardrobes in the main bedroom of Hill House in Helensburgh are decorated with coloured glass inserts. The chair and its pair were ebonized, creating a stark contrast to the rest of the room's furniture which was nearly all painted white.

tice. For the Buchanan Street Tea Rooms, Glasgow, he adapted a traditional Scottish rush-seated chair. But this was unlike the spindle- or ladder-back chairs produced by Morris & Co. or Gimson; Walton's model was a much more bizarre design, its arms, springing from a narrow, solid back, sweeping forwards in a wide curve. At the turn of the century Walton designed a desk which was again a flamboyant gesture in the face of Arts and Crafts reticence. The exaggerated horizontals of the top and shelves echo Mackmurdo's oak desk of nearly twenty years before; however, whereas that had been an exercise in simplicity and plainness, Walton made his desk into an elaborate – almost lavish – piece.

Another Glasgow designer, the architect Charles Rennie Mackintosh (1868–1928), created some of the most outstanding furniture to have been made during the last hundred years, but generally Mackintosh paid even less lip-service to the principles of the Arts and Crafts Movement than did

Walton. His furniture was usually made of stained or painted oak or pine, and neither the materials nor the construction play much part in its dramatic impact. Yet Mackintosh's roots in the tradition of Pugin and Morris are clearly revealed in a few examples of his work. An 1897 dining chair in untreated oak, on which a hand-grip pierced in the top-rail is deftly exploited as practically the sole decorative feature, is close in feeling to contemporary work by Voysey and the Cotswold school; while some of Mackintosh's ladder-back chairs could almost be confused with similar pieces designed by Gimson. However, Mackintosh's design should really be considered in the context of Modernism rather than the Arts and Crafts revival.

Around 1900 the style and quality of Arts and Crafts furniture began to be introduced into commercial cabinet-making by a handful of firms, including J.P. White (who made pieces designed by Mackay Hugh Baillie Scott [1865–1945]), J.S. Henry & Co. and the Bath Cabinet-Makers' Company. But the

OAK CHAIR, M.H. BAILLIE SCOTT, c.1900 (above)

The mother-of-pearl inlay in the back of this chair is typical of Baillie Scott's decorative style.

most successful furniture-manufacturing firm to reflect the efforts and aspirations of the reformers over the previous sixty years was Heal & Son. Situated ironically in London's Tottenham Court Road, a heartland of the sort of furniture-manufacturers which Pugin and Morris had so abhorred, Heal & Son made oak furniture designed by Ambrose Heal in a distinctive style that combined elements of sophistication and provincialism, virtuoso craftsmanship and sturdy construction. In short, the company made furniture in the English taste.

THE UNITED STATES

In the early nineteenth century immigrants arrived in America from France who, trained in the academic tradition, now became the furniture designers and stylists. From the forests of Germany and Austria came carpenters and wood-carvers who were among the most skilled craftsmen of Europe. British immigrants provided various accomplishments, manual or cerebral, but most importantly they brought progressive artistic philosophies and the novel ideas of Pugin, Ruskin and Morris. Out of all these ingredients there evolved, towards the end of the century, furniture that was essentially North American.

Pugin's ideas seem first to have been assimilated in America by Andrew Jackson Downing (1815–52), an architect and landscape designer, who recommended neo-Gothic furniture to his clients. He particularly favoured the work of the New York firm of cabinet-makers Burns & Trainque, who in his estimation made 'the most correct Gothic furniture . . . executed in this country'. He sometimes collaborated with Alexander Jackson Davis (1803–92) who designed neo-Gothic furniture for, among other houses, Lyndhurst, a mansion built about 1840 on the Hudson River. Although some of the pieces of furniture emanating from Downing's circle displayed

the Puginian principles of clearly expressed structure and restrained ornament, others – 'Gothick' rather than Gothic in style – should be seen as merely a subdivision of the prevailing Rococo revival.

Perhaps the biggest impact that Downing had on North American furniture design was through his pupil Clarence Cook (1828–1900). A Harvard graduate, Cook became an influential writer on the architecture and design of the United States. His criticism consistently expressed the Puginian principles which he had imbibed from his mentor, Downing. The articles he wrote for the *New York Daily Tribune* and *Scribner's Monthly* during the 1860s and 1870s, and his book *The House Beautiful* (1878), played a considerable part in creating a demand for well-designed furniture.

A more direct and more practical link between Pugin and North American furniture was provided by Henry Lindley Fry (1807–95), an English wood-carver who emigrated to the United States in about 1850. In England Fry had worked on the decoration of the Houses of Parliament, designed by Pugin, and on a screen in Westminster Abbey designed by George Gilbert Scott (1811–78). He had acquired an extensive knowledge of Gothic ornament and design, which he used in decorating several churches and private houses in Cincinnati, Ohio, where he settled in 1851 with his son William Henry Fry (1830–1929), also a wood-carver. During the late 1850s the Frys worked on the home of a successful Cincinnati merchant, Joseph Longworth, and in 1868 Longworth commissioned them to decorate a house that he had built for his daughter, Maria (founder of the famed Rookwood Pottery), and her husband, George Ward Nichols. Many of the young women of Cincinnati were invited to inspect the Frys' work at the Nichols's home; their enthusiasm was fuelled by reports of a fashion for amateur wood-carving in Britain, and in due course the Frys were persuaded to give them instruction in the skill. In 1873 more formal classes in wood-carving were instituted at the University of Cincinnati School of Design, where the instructor was Benn Pitman (1822–1910), another English

emigrant. Like the two Frys, Benn Pitman was an avid reader of John Ruskin's books.

The Eastlake Style

In 1872 the first American edition of *Hints on Household Taste* by Charles Lock Eastlake (1836–1906) appeared. The book presented an easily accessible résumé of advanced British views on furnishing and decoration and drew the reader's attention to the merits of the neo-Gothic style: following the precepts of Pugin, furniture should have a clearly expressed structure that was directly related to its function, and decoration should never be allowed to interfere with either. Furniture made in what became known in North America as the 'Eastlake style' was produced in large quantities, being carved by the amateurs in Cincinnati and many other cities. In 1877 the New York Society of Decorative Art was founded by Candace Wheeler (1827–1923); wood-carving was one of the activities encouraged and taught there and at the many similar institutions.

Isaac Elwood Scott (1845–1920), a self-taught wood-carver, made furniture in the Eastlake style for the home of J.J. Glessner in Chicago. Glessner, a manufacturer of agricultural machinery, commissioned further furniture from Scott for the Chicago offices of his company and for his summer home in New Hampshire. While Scott was engaged on this work, during the early 1880s, he was also teaching wood-carving at the Chicago Society of Decorative Arts. Another cabinet-maker, Daniel Pabst (1827–1910) of Philadelphia, made furniture in the Eastlake style, some pieces to designs by the architect Frank Furness (1839–1912). Such furniture was produced at a more commercial level by the Cincinnati firm of Mitchell & Rammelsberg and in New York by the partnership of A. Kimbel & J. Cabus. In the hands of the latter firm, the style became rather debased.

Furniture in the Eastlake style was much in evidence at the Philadelphia Centennial Exposition of 1876. However, among the furniture displayed there were hints of alternatives to the neo-Gothic style. To celebrate 100 years of independence there was on show a reconstruction of a late-eighteenth-century New England kitchen. At this time little of what we might call 'rural' furniture had entered the homes of fashionable Americans. In Britain the homespun effect had been created a decade earlier by the Sussex chairs introduced by Morris & Co.; examples of these had been imported by the Boston firm of Bumstead, agents for Morris & Co., and imitations had been produced by local manufacturers. In one of the articles Clarence Cook contributed to *Scribner's Monthly* in 1876 (two years later his pieces were to be collected to form a book, *The House Beautiful*), he claimed that the furniture 'in use in this country in the time of our grandfathers' was simply but excellently designed and made. The Colonial revival extended far beyond the recovery and restoration of Chippendale-style chairs and tables to embrace also widespread admiration for simple farmhouse furniture.

There were other indications that design-

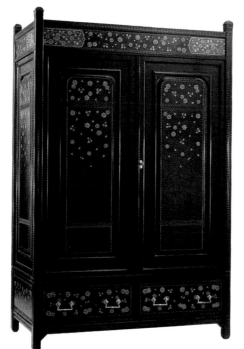

ers and consumers alike were finding the principles of the Eastlake style to be something of a straitjacket. Eastlake himself, writing in the preface to the 1878 edition of *Household Hints,* disclaimed responsibility for much that had been perpetrated in the United States in his name. This edition was, moreover, illustrated with several examples of the Queen Anne revival, by that time well under way in Britain. Similarly, in the illustrations to *The House Beautiful* Cook showed furniture in other styles besides neo-Gothic. Some of the pieces illustrated bore distinct affinities with the 'Anglo-Japanesque' furniture designed by the British architect E.W. Godwin (1833–86).

Other plates showing furniture in a style derived from Japanese art were drawn for Cook's volume by Alexandre Sandier (1843–1916), a Frenchman who worked during the 1870s for Herter Brothers, a New York firm of cabinet-makers. Herter Brothers had already won critical approval for their neo-Gothic furniture. The firm had gained a reputation for good design and fine craftsmanship, and these qualities were apparent in their Japanese-style furniture. The wood was usually ebonized cherry and the elaborate marquetry decoration was often of flowers rendered in a Japanese manner.

Such exquisite pieces were made only for wealthy clients — Herters supplied furniture to William H. Vanderbilt and several other millionaires — but the company produced furniture in a wide variety of styles. Several pieces were revivals of classical, Renaissance or French eighteenth-century furniture, decorated with much gilding and carving. Although these were always made to the firm's high standards of craftsmanship, their design hardly looked forward to the future.

Associated Artists, which existed from 1879 to 1883, and the various other decorating companies formed subsequently by Louis Comfort Tiffany (1848–1933) made furniture for clients as wealthy as those who patronized Herter Brothers. The 1880s were the years when New York was developing into a city of international prestige, and its wealthiest citizens were among the richest people in the world. Tiffany provided them with furniture of the finest craftsmanship and

CHERRYWOOD WARDROBE, HERTER BROTHERS, 1880–85 *(above right)*

Japanese art was one of several exotic influences that inspired the American furniture designers of the 1880s. Furniture made by Herter Brothers was always of high quality.

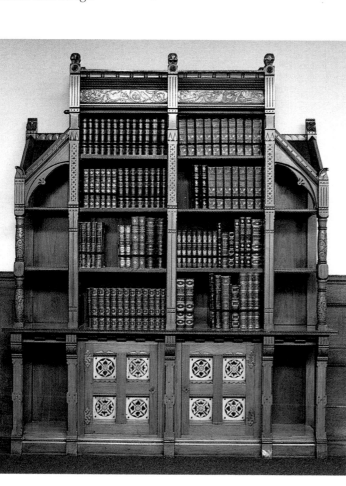

WALNUT BOOKCASE, ISAAC E. SCOTT, 1875 *(right).*

The style of this bookcase was derived from the Gothic revival furniture that had been produced in Britain from the middle of the nineteenth century.

OAK SIDE CHAIR, HENRY HOBHOUSE
RICHARDSON, 1882 *(left)*

*Made for the Converse Memorial Library in Malden,
Massachusetts, the design of this piece was based on
the traditional Windsor chair.*

OAK SIDE CHAIR, TIFFANY STUDIOS, *c*.1905
(far left)

*The natural beauty of the wood and the basic skills of
the carpenter are well displayed in this piece. The
stencilled velvet upholstery is contemporary.*

OAK SIDE CHAIR, FRANK LLOYD WRIGHT,
c.1905 *(opposite left)*

*Wright was a populist at heart and he wanted his
furniture to be machine-made, with the result that he
designed it using only simple, straight-edged parts.*

materials, sometimes in the Moorish taste, sometimes with a Japanese flavour, but always lavish and often exotic.

In an article entitled 'Decorative Art and its Dogmas', which appeared in the February-March 1880 issue of *Lippincott's Magazine*, Marianna Griswold Van Rensselaer discounted the rigid principles taught by Eastlake and Cook and argued instead for a more eclectic approach to the styles of the past. The following year she published *Henry Hobson Richardson and his Work*. In the furniture designed by Richardson (1838–86) can be found stylistic elements from many different sources. For instance, the chairs which he designed in 1882 for the Converse Memorial Library in Malden, Massachusetts, were based on the traditional Windsor chair and are a reflection of the architect's visit to William Morris's workshops at Merton Abbey. The much grander chairs he created two years later for the Court of Appeals of the State of New York in Albany bear traces of Byzantine and Romanesque influence, a testimony to his travels in Europe and the Near East. Despite their different sources,

Richardson's furniture designs have a unifying freshness and rugged vigour.

At his death in 1886, Richardson was working on a new house for J.J. Glessner, the Chicago magnate who had earlier commissioned furniture from Isaac Scott. The building was completed by the firm of Shepley, Rutan & Coolidge. A set of chairs designed by Charles Allerton Coolidge (1858–1936) for Glessner was manufactured by a company which had made much of the furniture designed by Richardson, A.H. Davenport & Co. of Boston and East Cambridge, Massachusetts; the firm's chief designer, Francis H. Bacon (1856–1940), had worked for Herter Brothers and for Richardson before joining Davenport's. The chairs Coolidge designed for Glessner were in a style closely related to Richardson's – a style to which Bacon may well have contributed. Its main elements were the use of motifs from various traditions and closely spaced rows of narrow spindles. This latter feature is very distinctive, and is found also in many of the pieces of furniture created by Tiffany. Elements of the design, although sometimes unnecessary

to the structural cohesion of the piece, were derived from the traditional carpentry of the cabinet-maker – in other words, designers were beginning to use the vocabulary of the craftsman, rather than merely a dictionary of historical styles, in order to make their own statements.

The Chicago School

In 1887, the year the chairs designed by Coolidge were installed in the Glessner house in Chicago, a youth called Frank Lloyd Wright (1869–1959) entered the architectural office of Joseph L. Silsbee in the same city. There he met two other young trainees, George W. Maher (1864–1926) and George Grant Elmslie (1871–1952). All three regarded Richardson as the greatest of all American architects – an admiration they did not forswear even when, later, they all worked in the office of Louis Sullivan.

In the early furniture of Wright and Maher, particularly, we can recognize Richardson's influence. For the John Farson house in Oak Park, Illinois, built in 1897,

MAHOGANY
FURNITURE, CHARLES
S. AND HENRY M.
GREENE, c.1908 (left)

*The furniture designed by
the Greenes was made
from superb materials and
to a high standard of
craftsmanship by the
Peter Hall Manufacturing
Company of Pasadena.*

Maher designed furniture which had all the eclecticism that had characterized Richardson's work – although, again like Richardson, Maher created from disparate influences an original style of his own. We can see from the furniture that Wright designed for his own house at Oak Park, when he modified and expanded some rooms in 1895, that he had assimilated the new aesthetic ideas implicit in the designs of Richardson, Bacon and Coolidge. The forms expressed both the crafts of the cabinet-maker and the qualities of the material. A chair which has a simple rectilinear frame with a back-rest consisting of a row of closely spaced, narrow twisted spindles clearly looks back to Richardson's work, and yet also – just as clearly – looks forward to the more mechanistic style that Wright was to develop at the turn of the century.

In 1901 Wright gave a talk to the Chicago Society of Arts and Crafts entitled 'The Art and Craft of the Machine'. He declared that the furniture which he designed was suitable for machine production, and that the machine was to be abhorred only when it was set non-mechanical tasks, such as the carving of ornament.

Wright's intention – that his furniture should be machine-made and therefore affordable by a greater number of people – reflects his assimilation of William Morris's ideas. Recalling the 1890s some sixty years later, Wright wrote that 'good William Morris and John Ruskin were much in evidence in Chicago intellectual circles at the time'. Indeed, all over the United States the theories of the British Arts and Crafts Movement were being disseminated through books and magazines. Particularly influential was *The Studio*, a monthly magazine published in London from 1893. In its pages were to be found illustrations of furniture designed by Mackmurdo, Voysey, Baillie Scott and others, most of which tended towards a severe simplicity of structure and finish.

The American response to these exemplars was enthusiastic, swift and widespread. At Grand Rapids, Michigan, the centre of the country's furniture industry, David Wolcott Kendall (1851–1910), chief designer with the Phoenix Furniture Co., created in about 1894 an armchair made of oak which had a cane seat and back-rest, arms made of simple planks supported by square-sectioned struts and with, as the only decorative details, aprons below the arms and a seat-rail cut into shallow arches or curves. The model was to prove popular for the next thirty years, and could be said to have answered Wright's plea for cheap mass-produced furniture seven years before he actually presented it. In 1887 one commentator noted that the Phoenix Furniture Co. had 'the most improved modern machinery of any factory of its kind in America'. These machines were used to make not only simple pieces like the armchair but also a wide range of ornate furniture in historical styles which had likewise been designed by Kendall.

Mission Furniture

Around the time that Kendall was designing his armchair the New York retailer and designer Joseph P. McHugh (1854–1918), who sold metalwork and furniture by Liberty's and Morris chintzes at the Popular Shop, (his store on West 42nd Street), was offering chairs based on an original from an old Spanish mission in California. These were quickly bought, and McHugh started manufacturing a range of furniture in the same simple style. Made of stained oak or ash, his furniture was very plain, with little more than whittled leg-ends for decoration. This seems to have been the first example of what was to become known as 'Mission furniture'. In 1896 McHugh was joined by Walter J.H. Dudley, who designed furniture in a slightly more sophisticated Arts and Crafts idiom.

Mission furniture was made also at Elbert Hubbard's (1856–1915) Roycroft community and Gustav Stickley's Craftsman Workshops. Furniture produced from 1897 by the Roycrofters, in East Aurora, New York, featured copper fittings and prominent mortise-and-tenon joints. Most of it was made of oak (given a special finish that was a secret) and waxed. Several designers collectively achieved a consistent 'Roycroft style', which often featured canted legs or sides and rounded bun feet. The Mission furniture made by Gustav Stickley at the Craftsman Workshops, Eastwood, near Syracuse, New York, has the appearance of having been more solidly and more professionally manufactured than most of the Roycroft pieces. Gustav Stickley (1857–1942) was one of five brothers who had as boys all worked at their uncle's chair factory. Stickley initially manufactured conventional Victorian furniture, including reproduction Chippendale, but in 1898 he travelled to England and the Continent and on his return began making furniture which combined the floral forms of Art Nouveau with the materials and methods of the British Arts and Crafts Movement. In Buffalo, New York, Charles Rohlfs (1853–1936) was mixing these ingredients to produce rather different furniture.

Rohlfs persisted in this vein until well into the twentieth century, making only a few simple, unadorned pieces towards the end of his career, but Stickley almost immediately abandoned the hybrid style and started to make pure Mission furniture. His designs were rigidly rectilinear, relieved only by gently and subtly curved aprons and brackets or by slightly swelling legs. The carpen-

OAK ARMCHAIR, GUSTAV STICKLEY, c.1905

The closely spaced spindles are typical of American Arts and Crafts furniture.

try of his furniture was generally less obtrusive than that of Roycroft, although the ends of dowel pins, cut off flush with the surface, and the commonly used butterfly joints were often made into decorative features through the use of different stains. Some pieces of Stickley's furniture were designed by the architect Harvey Ellis (1852–1904); these were usually inlaid with stylized floral motifs in variously coloured woods, which are reminiscent of Baillie Scott's decorative designs. At its best, Stickley's simple unadorned furniture is as much a statement about the beauty of handcrafted wood as Wright's is an expression of the power and precision of the machine.

Among many firms of cabinet-makers which produced a range of Mission furniture were two founded by the brothers of Gustav Stickley – L. & J.G. Stickley of Fayetteville, New York, and Stickley Brothers of Grand Rapids, Michigan.

The furniture designed by the brothers Charles S. (1868–1957) and Henry M. (1870–1954) Greene from 1907 for houses

OAK DESK AND CHAIR, CHARLES ROHLFS, c.1900

The swirling motifs of the carved decoration on Rohlfs' furniture blends well with the figure of the grain in the wood.

which they built in Pasadena, California, can be seen as the culmination of developments in American cabinet-making over the previous fifty years. The structure is clearly stated, the craftsmanship is superb and the decoration is rich but restrained. We can perceive Oriental influence on forms and decoration, but it is always made subsidiary to the expression of the craftsman's skills. While the structural honesty is reminiscent of Eastlake-style furniture, the aesthetic of craftsmanship is related more to the work of Stickley. The assimilation and control of exotic influences suggest the designs of Richardson, and the quality of the inlays – of ebony, fruitwoods, silver and gemstones – recall the luxurious marquetry on pieces by Herter Brothers. So, in many respects, the Greenes' furniture was a culmination but at the same time also a *cul-de-sac*. Such sophisticated design and craftsmanship led nowhere. The future story of American furniture would follow quite different lines.

FRANCE

Progressive furniture produced in Europe from approximately 1880 to 1910 is usually referred to as Art Nouveau, a term derived from the name of the influential Paris shop of German-born Siegfried Bing (1838–1905). Purists prefer to apply the term only to the largely nature-inspired, curvilinear French pieces that were being made in Paris and Nancy, but furniture of great significance and beauty – and often of impeccable craftsmanship – was originating in other European cities too, including Brussels, Munich, Milan, Barcelona, Vienna and Glasgow.

In France the Art Nouveau period – the apex of which was Paris's 1900 Exposition Universelle – was a highly fertile one. Indeed, 'fecund' is an appropriately organic adjective to describe an era whose designers took much of their inspiration from the forms of nature. Sometimes these were faithfully maintained and replicated, as in some of the botanical motifs adorning the furniture and

glass of Emile Gallé; at other times stylized and exaggerated, as in the startlingly undulating cabinets of Hector Guimard. These two hugely talented men, arguably the premier creators of Art Nouveau furniture, represented the two design centres of the time – first, Paris, which in effect comprised several distinct divisions, Guimard and other individuals going off on their own separate tangents and Bing's designers (Colonna, de Feure, Gaillard *et al.*) maintaining a somewhat controlled *status quo*; and, second, the École de Nancy, whose foremost exponents were Gallé and Louis Majorelle. The Art Nouveau period was significant, too, for the emphatic use of the *ensemblier*, who saw to it that all the design aspects of a room, from its furniture and its floor- and wall-coverings to its curtains and its fireplace accessories, were coordinated – a technique first used during the French Rococo period.

The Paris Designers

Hector Guimard (1867–1942) was, in the eyes of many experts, the paragon of Parisian Art Nouveau – and an *ensemblier extraordinaire*. An architect and designer trained at the École des Beaux-Arts, Paris, Guimard was encouraged by his Rationalist teachers, who had themselves been nurtured on the principles of the illustrious Eugène Viollet-le-Duc (1814–79) to study the past – not to imitate it but to utilize it, redefine it, with the aim of developing a fresh new style.

Guimard's own resultant style was remarkably revolutionary, bearing the stamp of the present yet drawing upon elements – especially decorative ones – of the past. His best-known designs – the cast-iron entrances to Paris's Métro (installed 1900–13) – are neither architectural nor for furniture, but they can be related to many of his buildings and pieces of furniture, all of which proudly manifest the 'abstract naturalism' that charac-

CARVED-WOOD AND STAMPED-LEATHER *BANQUETTE*, HECTOR GUIMARD, 1897–98

This handsome piece was made for the Maison Coilliot, Lille, after a similar example in the Castel Béranger, Paris.

terized this flamboyant designer's *oeuvre*. After the flair of the 1900 Exposition, Guimard toned down his style for commercial purposes, making it more symmetrical but no less energetic. Some of his earliest pieces of furniture – such as the lovely desk of olive wood with ash panels which he designed for his own house c.1899 (remodelled in 1904), today in the Museum of Modern Art, New York – show his predilection for natural ornamentation. The panels were carved in high relief and featured the wavy, quasi-organic designs seen on so much of Guimard's furniture: so realistic are they, and so seemingly incongruous with their medium, that they appear to give the wood an elastic, almost breathing, quality. Interestingly, Guimard based his design repertoire on the lower parts of trees and flowers – in other words, on the stems, branches and roots rather than the blossoms and leaves.

For the Castel Béranger, a block of flats which Guimard worked on for Mme Fournier between 1894 and 1898, he created massive built-in furniture which, despite its size, possesses a rhythm and flow as soft and delicate as that of rustling silk. A cabinet of pear and ash from that Paris apartment house, today in the Virginia Museum of Fine Arts, defies both tradition and gravity with its bold asymmetry and carved projections.

Three major furniture designers in Paris at the turn of the century were associated with Siegfried Bing's retail shop, La Maison de l'Art Nouveau, from which the style received its name: Georges de Feure, German-born Edward Colonna and Eugène Gaillard. Furniture pieces sold by Bing and designed by these three (and others, including Charles Plumet and Tony Selmersheim) were much more restrained and refined examples of the Art Nouveau style. Bing was after all first and foremost a businessman, and the furniture and other objects he marketed were designed to appeal to and be bought by the wealthy *demi-monde* – people whose tastes did not necessarily lean towards the avant-garde but who wanted something different and contemporary, but not *too* outrageous. The bulk of Bing's furniture – exhibition pieces apart – therefore sported subtle curves and organic flourishes on its practical, almost traditional, frames and upholstery. Most of the pieces of furniture sold in his shop was much quieter and less (literally) florid than other examples of French and Belgian Art Nouveau.

A quintessential example of this branch of Paris Art Nouveau is a table made *c.*1899 by Edward Colonna (1862–1948). As a young man, Colonna had worked in the United States as a designer; he came to France in 1893 and was employed by Bing between 1893 and 1903. The table could be ordered in purple wood, palisander and other types of wood. Its form was essentially quite simple: a rectangular top, slightly upward-curving sides and rather thin legs which flared out gently. The decorative elements were quite minimal, being restricted to carved curving and scrolling designs that rose up from the bottom of the legs to just under the top. A settee and chair designed by Colonna from the same period, made of carved maple, have subtly curving silhouettes and interlacing bow designs carved at the tops of their backs

and in the centre of the settee's apron.

The furniture of Georges de Feure (1868–1943) was characterized in its time as being much more graceful, indeed more feminine, than that of his colleagues. As one critic aptly put it, he 'cultivated flower ornaments with an effeminate feeling for their tenderness'. Although their basic shapes were roughly similar to those of most of the other pieces from Bing's workshop, the designs of the de Feure chairs, settees, tables, cabinets and screens were often more highly ornamented and their upholsteries more florid; sometimes their carved surfaces were even gilded. Delicate, opulent and refined, they on occasion harked back to the type of Neoclassical eighteenth-century French furniture which Marie-Antoinette might have used.

By contrast, the designs of Eugène Gaillard (1862–1933) – the first designer hired by Bing for his atelier – seem to occupy

MAHOGANY AND LEATHER SIDE CHAIR, EUGÈNE GAILLARD, *c.*1900

Gaillard was one of the designers associated with Siegfried Bing, the German-born entrepreneur whose Paris shop, La Maison de l'Art Nouveau, gave the French style its name.

more space and to proclaim their function loudly. Gaillard's pieces were usually made of the darker and/or generally more substantial woods, such as mahogany, palisander, oak and walnut. They were also more dramatic and dynamic than either Colonna's or de Feure's creations, sometimes approaching (although never equalling) the verve of Guimard's work. Unlike the eclectic Colonna and de Feure, Gaillard concentrated on furniture-making, in 1906 even writing a treatise on the subject, *À Propos du Mobilier*. Gaillard's talents were used extensively by Bing at the 1900 Exposition: he designed the vestibule, the dining-room and a bedroom for Bing's pavilion.

The École de Nancy

At the same time that Guimard's whiplash curves were captivating Paris and Bing's Maison de l'Art Nouveau was making its influential mark, a design school of great significance was creating perhaps the most exuberant, joyful, Symbolist and nature-ridden Art Nouveau furniture of all. This was the École de Nancy, in the province of Lorraine, which was spearheaded by its founder Emile Gallé (1846–1904), a furniture and glass designer of great repute, and shaped by Louis Majorelle (1859–1926), a cabinet-maker by trade.

Emile Gallé concentrated on creating earthenware pottery during the 1870s – his father owned both a pottery and a glassworks – but he quickly turned to stoneware, porcelain, glass and, from the 1880s, furniture. Most of the basic designs of his furniture echoed traditional Louis XV forms, but the decoration, whether carved or inlaid, was unabashedly and extravagantly organic in style.

The École de Nancy, which Gallé founded in 1901, was a decorative-arts centre profoundly influenced by the Symbolist movement in art and literature and it took much of its inspiration from nature – not surprisingly, since the young Gallé had studied both philosophy and botany (he wrote scholarly articles on horticulture). The expression of his multi-faceted training can be said to have reached its peak in his outstanding one-off

CARVED AND INLAID 'DRAGONFLY TABLE',
EMILE GALLÉ, c.1900 (left)

*This guéridon is a superb example of the École de
Nancy's love of nature. Designs of water-lilies in
inlaid fruitwoods feature on its top and bottom
shelves, and a trio of carved dragonflies acts as legs.*

WALNUT, FRUIT-
WOOD, BRONZE AND
MOTHER-OF-PEARL
ÉTAGÈRE, EMILE
GALLÉ, c.1900 (left)

*This étagère features both
carved and marquetry
cow-parsley designs, as
well as cut-out metalwork
blossoms. Inlaid on the
top right is part of a
verse by Paul Verlaine:
'L'instant est si beau de
lumière au fond de
nous dans notre coeur'.*

glass and furniture pieces which included, respectively, engraved or inlaid verses from Symbolist poetry. Gallé contributed furniture and glass to Bing's Maison de l'Art Nouveau, but his largely delicate and precious wood forms – unlike the 'house pieces' designed by Colonna, de Feure and Gaillard – were embellished with strongly asymmetrical flower- and leaf-laden motifs, be they firescreens, *coffrets*, chairs, headboards, buffets or tables. Despite the traditional shapes and carcases, Gallé's furniture was dominated by its decoration. To choose just a few examples: the exquisitely realistic inlaid iris on an armoire displayed at the 1900 Paris Exposition; the carved snails, moths and bats on a hall *étagère*; a table with a round top showing a droll scene of courtship among frogs; the cornice of a vitrine comprising a swarm of overlapping dragonflies; a rectangular wall mirror with a spray of cut-out umbel-flower clusters at the top; and a number of side-tables and other furniture pieces with massive, almost monstrous dragonflies serving as legs and side supports.

Insects likewise dominated the head- and foot-board of the spectacular *Aube et Crépuscule* ('Dawn and Dusk') double bed commissioned from Gallé by the magistrate Henri

MAHOGANY AND GILT-BRONZE LADY'S DESK CHAIR, LOUIS MAJORELLE, c.1900 (left)

This cabinet-maker from Nancy was renowned for his use of gilt-bronze mounts, especially those taking the form of the nénuphar, *or water-lily.*

MAHOGANY, GILT-BRONZE AND EMBOSSED-LEATHER 'ORCHID DESK', LOUIS MAJORELLE, c.1905 (left)

The most daring ornaments on this elegant desk are the massive orchid mounts capping the front corners, running down the legs and terminating in sabots.

Hirsch and displayed at the Exposition de l'Art Décoratif Lorrain in Nancy in 1904 (the year of Gallé's death). This painterly master-piece, through the media of inlaid woods and mother-of-pearl, bas-relief wood sculpture and carved glass, represents the beginning and end of the day in the guise of fantastic moths. The footboard shows two moths with nacreous wings hovering over an opalescent egg of crystal (daybreak or birth) and the headboard features a wooden landscape at day's end, revealed between the curtain-wings of a darkly striated moth. The sensitive decoration of the bed as a whole is richly poetic and melancholic, an essay on life and death.

The furniture of Louis Majorelle, on the other hand, although richly ornamented lacks the symbolic elements and unified organic design of Gallé's works, while making much richer use of gilt bronze and wrought iron for its mounts. Majorelle studied painting in Paris, but he became head of the cabinet-making workshop owned by his father, Auguste, on the elder Majorelle's death in 1879. From 1860 this had produced reproduction eighteenth-century furniture. Around 1890, under the influence of Gallé, Majorelle changed the backward-looking tendency of the family firm and instead strongly embraced the new, nature-inspired style. At the same time, however, Majorelle

did not abandon the principles of fine French craftsmanship – even though his designs were made up using some machine-made parts. He thus emphasized massive, sculptural mounts, while both domestic and exotic woods, carefully chosen to harmonize with the types of furniture of which they formed a part, were expertly inlaid, veneered or carved. The *nénuphar*, or water-lily, design is perhaps his best-known motif for mounts, with the orchid a close second.

From around 1898 to 1908, Majorelle's furniture designing was at its zenith. The so-called 'Orchid Desk' of c.1905 – one example of the design is in the Musée d'Orsay, Paris – is a typical, outstanding piece by Majorelle in his guise as master cabinet-maker. Other desk designs boast a pair of lamps, one affixed to each side, their floriform glass shades emerging from serpentine stem mounts. In fact, ignoring the mounts, the forms of Majorelle's furniture were – unlike those of Gallé – somewhat fluid and abstract, regular but almost sculptural.

Majorelle specialized in sets of whole suites of furniture rather than in one-off exhibition pieces. One such bedroom ensemble, now in the Virginia Museum, comprises a bed, two nightstands, two side chairs, two armchairs and a cupboard. The set is a quintessential example of the excellent-quality furniture this master was able to produce.

All but the chairs are embellished with *nénuphar* mounts, and the large, vertically patterned panels of veneered rosewood which dominate the headboard and cupboard doors present a strong decorative statement. Again the furniture's lines are gently curving, the gilt-bronze mounts strongly organic and emphatic.

Although Majorelle's furniture generally featured less marquetry and inlaid panels than that of Gallé, some pieces are jigsaw-puzzle-like *tours de force* of wood veneers and marquetry – sometimes carving as well. Another piece by Majorelle, *La Mer*, is a mahogany cabinet with, in marquetry on its upper, quasi-half-moon section, a scene of underwater life – appropriately enough, the wrought-iron mounts and carved-wood designs at the base depict seaweed.

Majorelle continued to make furniture into the Art Deco period (after his death, in 1926, his firm kept up production until World War II), but the undisputed peak of his career was in the last years of the nineteenth century and the first decade of the twentieth.

Several other furniture designers of note were connected with the Nancy school. Among these were Eugène Vallin (1856–1922), Jacques Gruber (1870–1936) and Victor Prouvé (1858–1943).

Elsewhere other French furniture designers were at work during the Art Nouveau period who did not have a close alliance with either the École de Nancy or the Parisian designs of Guimard and the Bing atelier. One such designer was Alexandre Charpentier (1856–1909), who often depicted voluptuous female nudes in bas-relief on his clockcases, cabinets and other massive and broadly curvilinear pieces. His hefty *Meuble Quatuor à Cordes* ('Cabinet for a String Quartet'), now in the Paris Musée des Arts Décoratifs, is a huge, blocky piece, distinguished not so much for its subtle curves as for its bronze panels depicting nude women (two *danseuses* and two musicians, *Le Violon* and *La Contrebasse*). Displayed alongside this piece at the 1901 Société Nationale des Beaux-Arts exhibition was a pair of lovely revolving music stands designed to match it. Of carved hornbeam, the stands' massive supports undulated sinuously, more akin to the movement of rippling fabric than to wood.

BELGIUM

The country whose furniture was most closely allied to that of the French Art Nouveau period was, not surprisingly, its north-eastern neighbour Belgium. Not only was there an active interchange between the Belgians and French at the *fin de siècle*, but Belgium's star designer, Antwerp-born Henri van de Velde (1863–1957), was well represented in Paris, his creations being sold at Bing's shop and at La Maison Moderne, which was owned by Julius Meier-Graefe. A spate of commissions from Germany led van de Velde to settle in that country in 1898 and he worked in many parts of Europe, but he is still thought of as primarily a Belgian designer.

Like Guimard in Paris and Mackintosh in Scotland, van de Velde was first and foremost concerned with the idea of the totally harmonious, organic environment. Along with several of his colleagues, he was during the 1890s part of the trendsetting La Libre Esthétique group in Brussels, which was in part devoted to the *Gesamtkunstwerk* concept. Indeed, he took this belief so far as to

design not only furniture, carpeting, embroidery, windows and interior wall-coverings, but even complementary dresses (his wife wore his fashion designs). His furniture, usually made of light native woods such as beech and oak, sometimes featured homely rush seating, although elaborate batik upholstery was on occasion used to cover his chairs. (One splendid armchair of 1896 had just such a batik covering, designed by Jan Thorn Prikker, the Dutch painter.)

Perhaps van de Velde's most widely known project, executed in 1896–8, was the design of his own home, Bloemenwerf, in Uccle (near Brussels). Immediately apparent when one looks at the house's rooms in

general (one was shown in the 1896 Salon de La Libre Esthétique in Brussels) as well as at individual pieces of furniture is van de Velde's firm control of line. Unlike some of his designs for jewellery, graphics and fabrics, his desks, tables, cabinets and chairs were simply and rationally constructed; their decoration was spare, and function was foremost. The several rush-seated, carved padoukwood chairs he designed for Bloemenwerf – including a child's high chair – recall the sturdy, straightforward Arts and Crafts seating of Morris & Co., or even of peasant furniture, yet their subtle but energetic curves definitely belong to the Art Nouveau style.

OAK AND BRONZE DESK AND CHAIR, HENRI VAN DE VELDE, *c.*1898 *(above)*

PAIR OF PADOUK-WOOD ARMCHAIRS, HENRI VAN DE VELDE, 1896 *(left)*

The cool symmetry and subtle curves of these pieces are typical of van de Velde.

DINING-ROOM IN
THE MAISON
HORTA, BRUSSELS,
VICTOR HORTA,
BEGUN 1898

*Horta's overall design
schemes often featured
dizzy exercises in
curvilinearity. Here, in
his own home, the line
is rather restrained,
although subtly present
in such elements as the
floor tiling, carved
doorway and unusual
metalwork.*

A pioneering Brussels designer of some-what more forceful Art Nouveau furniture was Victor Horta (1861–1947), a cobbler's son who at first studied music, then drawing and architecture. Unlike van de Velde, Horta spent most of his working life in Belgium, designing furniture only for his own buildings. Not surprisingly, his unabashedly energetic, whiplashed and scrolling style had a great impact on many Parisian designers such as Guimard.

A creator of a total, harmonious environ-ment, inside and out, Horta's first major design was a house in Brussels for the engineer Emile Tassel. Dating from 1892–3, this house – considered by many scholars to be the first full-fledged Art Nouveau struc-ture – was designed as two separate sections, with floors of differing heights connected by upper galleries. The *leitmotiv* was the inces-sant, aggressive, whiplash curve, which united the various elements of the house – from the bronze door-handles to the mosaic-tiled floors to the marvellous ironwork of the staircase. Unlike Guimard's more restrained curves, Horta's exuberant ribbon-like loops almost vibrate with life; indeed they can seem to go out of control and take over their setting, literally from floor to ceiling. How-ever, the furniture for the Tassel house and for other major commissions, such as Brus-sels' Hôtel Solvay (1895–1900), does not display the verve and abandon of the permanent fittings or of smaller, nearly totally abstract objects, such as inkwells and photograph stands. The whiplash curve was there, certainly, but it was more controlled, perhaps more in keeping with the actual functions of the pieces. Horta favoured mahogany, maple and soft fruitwoods for his furniture, and the upholstery was usually rich and luxurious – made using such lavish fabrics as velvet and silk.

The other Belgian furniture designer of international acclaim, and the most commercially successful of the three, was Gustave Serrurier-Bovy (1858–1910). From a family of cabinet-makers, Liège-born Serrurier-Bovy (the 'Bovy' was adopted when he married Maria Bovy) incorporated many typical Art Nouveau elements in his furniture – floral designs, flowing curves, ornate metal mounts – but he is significant also in that he adapted English Arts and Crafts furniture forms and materials and other design components to fit in with the essentially Continental decoration of Art Nouveau. Among all woods he preferred oak, an Arts and Crafts staple. His metal mounts tended to be of simple brass and pewter rather than the lavish *bronze doré* of his Gallic contemporaries.

AUSTRIA

At the same time as Guimard was making his undulating furniture statements in Paris and Gallé was creating his poetic marquetry confections in Nancy, Otto Wagner and members of the Vienna Secession – including Josef Hoffmann, Koloman Moser, Adolf Loos and Joseph Maria Olbrich – were designing truly classic furniture for the new century – furniture which has become timeless. They were the immediate predecessors of Art Deco and the Bauhaus, and can even be considered as precursors of the post-modern. The Secession was founded in 1897 and consisted of a group of progressive architects, painters and designers who were disgruntled with conservative academies and teachers and who wished to break away from mouldy historicism and make bold, new statements in all the artistic media.

Otto Wagner (1841–1918), who joined the movement in 1899, was the *éminence grise* of the Secessionists, most of whom had earlier been his students. In 1895 he had published an influential book, *Moderne Architektur*, which had played a part in the establishment of the Secession. Essentially a 'no-frills' functionalist, Wagner designed chairs, tables and other items of furniture which were simple yet bold (some might say 'cold') economic exercises. His best known structure, the Austrian Postal Savings Bank in Vienna (1904–6), featured bent beechwood, plywood and aluminium armchairs manufactured by Gebrüder Thonet of Vienna. Besides being made of revolutionary new materials – some of which had been subjected to relatively new production techniques – these chairs were a paragon of 'Good Design', a beacon of Modernism.

Another architect-designer whose forms were spare and functional was Adolf Loos (1870–1933). Loos trained in Dresden and in the United States, settling in Vienna in 1896. He is famous for the aphorism that 'Ornament = Crime' (the title of an 1908 article). His admiration of English and American Arts and Crafts designers is evident in the three-legged Egyptian-style black-polished beech-

BEECH, PLYWOOD AND ALUMINIUM ARMCHAIR, OTTO WAGNER, 1902–4 *(above)*

Made by Gebrüder Thonet, this chair was created for the Austrian Savings Bank in Vienna, a building Wagner also designed.

wood stools he designed for one of his buildings, the Villa Karma, near Montreux, Switzerland (1904–6). These curved-leg, saddle-seat stools are an obvious homage to Liberty's famous Thebes stool of 1884.

The two most distinctive furniture designers of Secession Vienna were Josef Hoffmann (1870–1956) and Koloman Moser (1868–1918), who in 1903 were co-founders of the Wiener Werkstätte ('Vienna Workshops'), a craftsmen's society modelled after C.R. Ashbee's Guild of Handicraft. The society's object was to apply artistic design to an extensive range of products, from glass, ceramics and textiles to metalwork, furniture and even buildings. Hoffmann designed for the group until 1931, although Moser left it as early as 1907.

Hoffmann was born in Moravia. He studied painting in Munich and architecture in Vienna, where he was taught by and then worked for Otto Wagner. His first major design was the *Ver Sacrum* room at the first Secession exhibition in 1898 (*Ver Sacrum* was the name of the Secession's journal). The next year he was appointed Professor of Architecture at the School of Applied Arts, Vienna, a position he held until 1941.

In the last years of the 1890s Hoffmann's furniture designs leaned towards curvilinearity, but, almost as if alerted by the approach of the new century, his style had metamorphosed by 1900 into a kind of protracted abstraction, partly due to the influence of Charles Rennie Mackintosh, whose work was widely admired in Vienna. One of Hoffmann's best-known commissions, the Pürkersdorf Sanatorium (1903–6), provided him with the opportunity to design not only a building but also its furnishings. A bentwood and leather-upholstered chair (about eighty were made by the firm of Jacob & Joseph Kohn, who were keen competitors of Thonet) for the sanatorium is a simple yet singular design. The back legs and back comprise one inverted U-shaped piece of wood, while the two front legs are separately attached to the seat. There is minimal but striking decoration, consisting of variations on the theme of the circle and sphere and present in the fifteen pairs of cut-out holes on the back splat, the upholstery's rounded studs and the wooden globes affixed to the corners where the seat and legs meet.

For the Palais Stoclet, Brussels, (1905–11; done in collaboration with the Wiener Werkstätte), Hoffmann's *chef d'oeuvre* of architecture and interior design, the furniture is much more opulent, and hence a direct forerunner of much French Art Deco furniture of a decade or so later. The noble proportions, rich materials and quiet dignity of the fittings and furniture were an apt setting for the house's masterwork: a romantic, glittering mosaic of glass, marble, metal, maiolica, enamel and semi-precious stones designed by Gustav Klimt, executed by Leopold Forstner and covering the bulk of the walls in the Palais's dining-room. In contrast, Hoffmann's chairs for the room were simple and square-backed, covered in dark leather and embellished with gilded studs and an ornate roundel on the back.

A multi-talented architect and designer, Koloman Moser was a Professor at the

MAPLE, GLASS AND MIRROR TRIPARTITE SCREEN, ADOLF LOOS, c.1900–2

The subtle striations of inlaid wood are the only decorative elements on this minimalist piece.

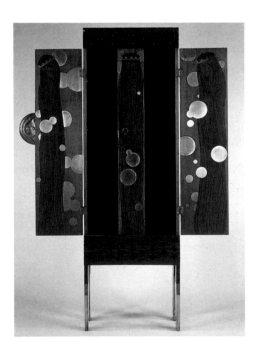

PALISANDER, GLASS, WOOD AND SILVERED-METAL CABINET, KOLOMAN MOSER, 1900

BEECH ARMCHAIR, JOSEF HOFFMAN, c.1905

This bentwood armchair was called 'Sitzmachine' in Germany and made by J. & J. Kohn.

School of Applied Arts from 1899 until his early death less than twenty years later. His furniture from the 1890s and early 1900s was largely geometric and rectilinear, but on the whole more colourful and decorated than other Viennese pieces. The ornamentation tended to be stylized and this nicely complemented the right angles of the pieces. A dining-room armchair from 1904 is richly decorated, although its shape is squared off and rectilinear. The form gives way to the ornament, however, with the luxuriant rosewood and maple veneer, the frieze of circles-within-squares at the top and bottom of the chair's back (which extends down below the seat to halfway between it and the floor), and the smaller rectangle at the back, inlaid with a stylized dove bearing an olive branch, executed in mother-of-pearl and exotic dark woods.

Far removed from these opulent, veneered pieces is the 1902 armchair which Moser designed for the Pürkersdorf Sanatorium. In keeping with its subdued surroundings, the boxy white-painted chair features vertical struts all around the sides, back and bottom and a chequer-board pattern on the dyed-fibre webbing. As austere as the Pürkersdorf chair are many of the large built-in or case pieces which Moser designed; which were often painted white (as were many such works by Mackintosh), but the white was nicely offset with colourful chequer-board patterns, dark painted outlines or, in the case of a sideboard and fireplace for Moser's own guest-room, ceramic tiles.

Architect and designer Joseph Maria Olbrich (1867–1908), Silesian by birth, was a founding member of the Vienna Secession; in 1897–8 he designed its dramatic exhibition building. Also of note were the architectural and other designs which he executed at the Mathildenhöhe artists' colony in Darmstadt, to which he was summoned in 1899 by its founder, the Grand Duke of Hesse, Ernst Ludwig II. Olbrich's furniture designs were few when compared with the prolificness of his architecture, graphics and metalwork. Most pieces were distinctively fluid yet ornamental examples of Jugendstil.

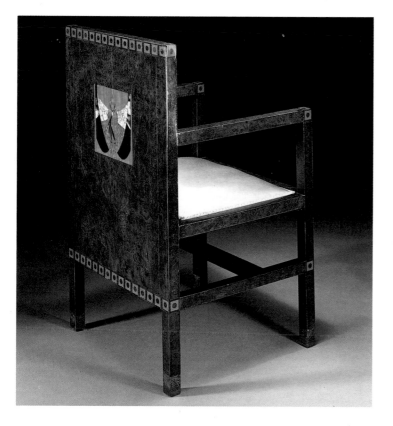

ROSEWOOD, MAPLE AND MOTHER-OF-PEARL ARMCHAIR, KOLOMAN MOSER, 1904

With its veneered back reaching well below the seat, this severely rectilinear dining-room chair by the Wiener Werkstätte co-founder is at the same time luxurious and handsome.

GERMANY

Jugendstil took root in the mid-1890s in Munich, which proved to be Germany's centre of 'new art'. The term 'Jugendstil' means 'young style' and this movement was the German contemporary of Art Nouveau. Among the furniture designers with early ties to Munich were Peter Behrens (1868–1940), August Endell (1871–1943), Richard Riemerschmid (1868–1957) and Bernhard Pankok (1872–1943), all of whom, like so many of the Franco-Flemish Art Nouveau designers, created works in a variety of media. The above four, working also with Otto Eckmann (1865–1902), Hermann Obrist (1863–1927) and Bruno Paul (1874–1968), formed a progressive group in search of a new style. Many of these designers had trained as painters but, disillusioned with the fine arts, were now turning their talents to the decorative arts. On the whole their furniture deliberately lacked the florid embellishments of their French and Belgian counterparts, so that it was more closely allied with the Austrian (and some British) furniture of this period.

Hamburg-born Peter Behrens, an architect and designer as well as a painter and teacher – whose many talented students at one time or another included those stalwarts of the Bauhaus, Mies van der Rohe and Walter Gropius – was one of those who founded the Munich Vereinigte Werkstätten für Kunst im Handwerk ('United Workshops for Art in Handiwork') in 1897. He was called to the Grand Duke's artists' colony at Darmstadt, where he designed the Haus Peter Behrens and he was responsible for the design of the German entrance hall at the Turin Exposition of 1902. From 1903 to 1907 he was director of the Düsseldorf School of Applied Arts and went on to teach at both the Vienna and the Berlin Academies.

His dining-room at Darmstadt (1901) manifested a harmony of design, with its moulded swirling pattern on the ceiling, its handsome cabinet with curved-frame glass doors and its table and chairs, the latter gently curving. All were painted white, giving the room a lightness and airiness akin

DESIGN FOR A
YOUNG GIRL'S
LIVING-ROOM, OTTO
STRUCK, 1908

*The clean, straight lines,
light-coloured furniture
(both built-in and
movable) and simple
decorative motifs marking
this Jugendstil interior
give it a northern
European sensibility, with
more than a reference to
the Vienna Secession.*

to that of a space by Mackintosh or Hoffmann. Unlike Horta's or Guimard's all-enveloping loops and tendrils, Behrens' curves were quiet and restrained, almost like after-thoughts. Many of his pieces of furniture assumed traditional rectilinear shapes.

Straight lines combined with subtle curves made up much of the furniture of Richard Riemerschmid, who was born in Munich and later allied with both the Vereinigte Werkstätten there and Dresden's Deutscher Werkbund. Also a talented painter, designer and architect, he designed a handsome music room for the 1899 German Art Exhibition in Dresden and a 'Room for an Art Lover' at the 1900 Paris Exposition. An outstanding design, c.1898, was for a simple oak chair used in both the Dresden and the Paris model-room settings.

It should be noted that in *fin de siècle* Germany, perhaps more than anywhere else in Europe, there were architects and designers who steadfastly clung to tradition, eschewing – indeed, castigating – any form of Modernism, notably Jugendstil. Historicized furniture, echoing both the Neoclassical and Baroque styles, was produced *en masse*, the former plain and severe, the latter heavily carved and solid.

OTHER COUNTRIES

Variations on and adaptions of – as well as reactions against and totally unrelated contemporaries of – French, German, Austrian and British turn-of-the-century Art Nouveau, Jugendstil, Secession and Arts and Crafts furniture appeared all over the European Continent.

In the Netherlands, where a tradition of sturdy well-made furniture for the *burgher* (bourgeois) reigned, the curves and decoration of French and Belgian Art Nouveau were on the whole scorned by furniture-makers, although not by painters and designers in other media. The Dutch Society of Arts and Crafts was established in 1904, in part to offset what was seen as the negative influence of Art Nouveau.

Throughout the Scandinavian countries, notable, although not especially innovative, furniture designers were working at the turn of the century. Most adhered to a historicizing idiom which combined elements of native peasant or folk art with traditional forms. Swedish furniture design was more

apt to reflect a Continental influence. An example is the White Drawing Room by Alf Wallander (1862–1914), with its white-painted cabinet and chairs (based on eighteenth-century Swedish models and decorated with carved leaf designs). Painted furniture was indeed highly popular in Sweden. This was exemplified by the charming illustrations of Carl Larsson.

As in Scandinavia, in eastern Europe native folk-art forms and decoration predominated. 'Historical nationalism', as it has been called, manifested itself in ethnic furniture and in the other decorative arts of Russia, Poland, Hungary and elsewhere. Moreover, Arts and Crafts communities – along the lines of Ashbee's Guild of Handicraft and other British artists' groups – were formed, and the principles of William Morris, John Ruskin and others were duly embraced. Three such communities were formed in Russia – Abramtsevo, Trocadero and Talashkino and all produced furniture and other works in the applied arts based on a strong folk tradition.

On the whole, the furniture that was being made in other eastern European countries at this time was likewise inspired by nationalistic folk art, although some Hungarian designers, drawing upon their Magyar roots, created more exotic, Byzantine confections.

Two of the most original and eccentric furniture designers at the turn of the century were Antonio Gaudí y Cornet (1852–1926), who worked in Barcelona, and Carlo Bugatti (1856–1940), who from 1904 resided in France, but whose furniture was made in his native Milan.

Antonio Gaudí, the son of a coppersmith, is best known as a visionary if idiosyncratic architect (notably of the church of the Sagrada Familia in Barcelona), but he also designed furniture, from gilded, neo-Rococo confections to simply carved forms. These latter pieces have often been described as bone-like, and indeed it is easy to see their dark-wood shapes, with their joints, curves and indentations, as resembling skeletal pieces conjoined to produce eerie benches, chairs and pews. Yet they have a lightness and a delicacy about them; they are wisps of wood that strangely are inviting to, yet at

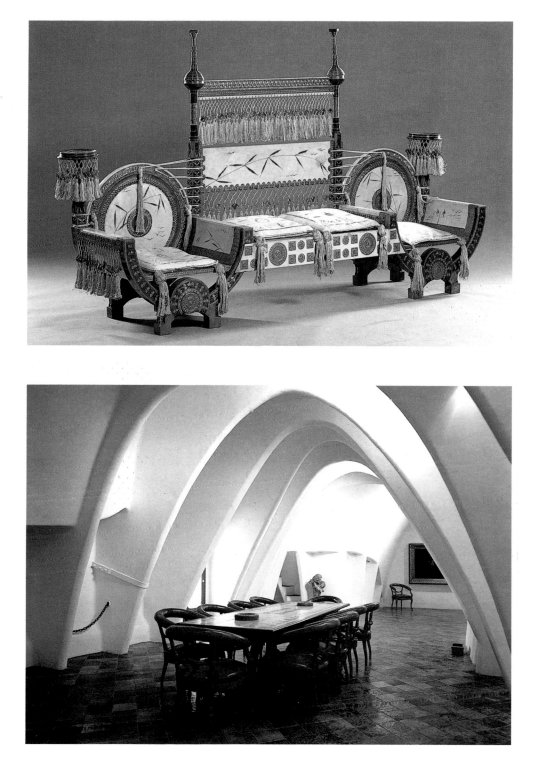

the same time reminiscent of, human forms.

Carlo Bugatti was born in Milan and educated at the Brera, though he later encouraged the myth that he was self-educated. In 1888 he set up his own atelier in the city of his birth. His designs could perhaps loosely be termed pseudo-Moorish-cum-Far-Eastern furniture fantasies: they were non-traditional, having no real antecedents, and were neither very functional nor very well constructed – but despite all this they somehow possess a somewhat magical, runic appeal.

Wholly hand-crafted concoctions that were put together in his workshop, Bugatti's desks, chairs, screens, settees, cabinets and so on were bizarre amalgams of (mostly) wood and metal, often with leather or, incredibly, vellum seats, backs and tops (these sometimes painted with Japanese-inspired plant, bird or ideogrammatic forms) and with inlaid bits of smooth or beaten metal (brass, pewter, rose metal or copper), ivory or mother-of-pearl. Tasselled fringes added decorative fillips and shield backs, crescent legs and sometimes even minaret-like upright sections completed the exotic look.

Bugatti's work was displayed at the 1900 Paris Exposition and then again in 1902 in Turin, where his four model rooms and a number of individual designs caused quite a sensation and won him a Diploma of Honour. Unlike his earlier, more rigid-formed, busily decorated pieces, these designs, with their sleek, serpentine curves and their light colours, showed the undeniable influence of the Parisian designers although still retaining certain elements of Bugatti's former phase.

Just as one of the Art Nouveau era's most fascinating and individualistic furniture designers, namely Carlo Bugatti, originated in Italy, so it was that in that same country – at the 1902 Esposizione Internationale in Turin – the style experienced its final triumph. Soon afterwards, more sleek, geometric styles – the straightforward, sharp Moderne and the opulent, sophisticated Art Deco – predominated. The curves, tendrils and blossoms of Art Nouveau became the outmoded design follies and excesses of the recent past.

ATTIC ROOM, CASA BATLLÓ, BARCELONA, ANTONIO GAUDÍ, 1904–6 *(above)*

Gaudí's distinctive form of Catalan Art Nouveau is seen here at its more controlled.

WOOD, METAL AND VELLUM BENCH SEAT, CARLO BUGATTI, c.1900 *(top)*

Bugatti's influences ranged from Japanese to Moorish, and most of them could be seen simultaneously.

THE MACHINE AGE

To call the period from around 1910 to 1945 the Machine Age is to emphasize only one of its features: the profoundest developments, in fact, were neither in technology nor in the arts, but in the pure sciences, with men such as Albert Einstein and Max Planck altering our conception of the universe. On a more mundane level, however, there was indeed the steady advance of the machine. The early twentieth century saw a new set of machine images added to the prolific collection left over from the late nineteenth century. The machine dominated not only factory production, but also transportation, with moving machines now on the road and in the air, not just on railroad tracks. In 1885 came the first internal combustion engine, and only three decades later, by 1915, Henry Ford was producing a million cars in a year. On the domestic front, by the 1930s and 1940s radios, refrigerators, vacuum cleaners and electric irons, among other appliances, had become fixtures in millions of American and European homes. Without a doubt, the machine had entered into every aspect of popular Western culture and had affected virtually every member of its populace.

The two world wars forced on industry the need for greater efficiency and at the same time by necessity upgraded the quality and accuracy of lathes and various machine tools. Of direct effect upon furniture designers were new developments in materials technology — for example, tubular steel, bent plywood and aluminium. Plastics, a novelty of the 1920s, did not make much of an impact on furniture design until after World War II.

Artists, too, were inventing new forms. In Paris a landmark exhibition of Cubist paintings by Pablo Picasso and Georges Braque opened in 1907. Two years later, an Italian artist, Filippo Marinetti, launched Futurism with a manifesto that proclaimed a 'new beauty, a roaring motor car, which runs like a machine gun'. Russian artists were especially

BIRCH STACKING STOOLS, ALVAR AALTO, FOR ARTEK, 1933

*Bold use of natural materials shows evidence of Aalto's architectural
training. He created functional pieces at a low unit
cost which were also aesthetically pleasing.*

excited by Futurism. Indeed the Russian contributions to modern art were considerable, most notably Constructivism, a movement of abstract art, spurred on in part by the 1917 Russian Revolution, which fused ideology with avant-garde art. In its sculptures and architecture the stress was on engineering and visible structures, not heavy mass or encased volumes. Some of the most important abstract paintings of the early twentieth century were those of Piet Mondrian and Theo van Doesburg in Holland. They led to the *De Stijl* movement, a more rigid art than Constructivism, but which had a notable effect on architecture and influenced Gerrit Rietveld, whose infamous 'Red and Blue Chair' (1918) is one of the icons of modern furniture design. Surrealism, which drew liberally on Freud's ideas, flourished in the 1920s and 1930s as well. Characterized by abundant juxtaposition of unlikely objects with mundane ones, dream-like scenes, and sexual metaphors and puns, its best-known practitioners were the Belgian René Magritte and the Spaniard Salvador Dali. The latter, in fact, produced a design for a plush shocking-pink sofa made in 1936–37: it took the sensuous form of the actress Mae West's lips, a design which could not be more antithetical to Rietveld's aforementioned geometric structure.

Even to try to make generalized statements about the years encompassing the Machine Age, however, is a mistake. Depending on a variety of factors – including background, training, working methods, clientele, critics, personal values, ideologies and intellectual beliefs (or lack of them) – furniture designers and makers in the productive period of 1910 to 1945 produced a range of forms in a wide variety of styles and materials, from the most hackneyed revivalist mahogany and upholstered sofa, to the most innovative chrome-and-leather rectilinear *chaise-longue*. Indeed, Machine Age furniture could be confrontational, angular and edgy (as it was with many Bauhaus creations) or it could be opulent, exotic and rounded, as fashioned by Parisian Art Deco designers. Or it could be sculptural, smooth and organic, such as the vessel-like chairs of American Charles Eames, which embraced the user, albeit giving him or her rather less in terms of soft comfort.

At the same time as designers were making their strong decorative, or anti-decorative, statements, there continued the undiminishing demand from consumers who were perfectly content to buy heavily upholstered furniture that was based on traditional forms. In Britain, France, Germany and the United States, the machine aesthetic never conquered the average domestic interior.

But even the more extreme of the Modernists needed their comfort. Fortunately, foam-rubber cushioning was invented: this could be cut into flat rectangles and, even when covered in leather, retained enough angularity to express modernity.

To be 'modern' during the first decades of this century the designer for the most part chose to work in metal rather than wood, this perhaps for symbolic reasons. Although bentwood furniture seemed to fit with Modernist guidelines – it was plain, light and easy to mass-manufacture – it had a major ideological drawback: it was *wood*. Moreover, it was a nineteenth-century material, going back to Michael Thonet and the classic Viennese café chair. Bent wood had too many bad connotations for most Modernists. Putting it the other way around, metal played the same role in furniture that concrete did in architecture, a point made by Le Corbusier's associate, Charlotte Perriand.

Indeed, the key to the attenuated, puritanical 'machine' expressionism in furniture can be found in architecture. Soon after Rietveld designed the 'Red and Blue Chair', he was working on his first major building, the Schröeder house. In 1914 Walter Gropius and

TUBULAR-STEEL *CHAISE-LONGUE*, LE CORBUSIER AND CHARLOTTE PERRIAND, 1928

Adolf Meyer saw the opening of the Fagus shoe-factory building which they had designed. In the same year Le Corbusier was developing schemes for mass-produced housing. In the 1930s, even Frank Lloyd Wright, one of the earliest prophets of the machine aesthetic, was designing Modernist metal office furniture (albeit with wooden elements) for his Johnson Building, Wisconsin. It was clear that the new architects wanted a new furniture, and during the 1920s and 1930s this was what they received.

The new furniture had to express the mysticism of the machine while also, it seems, articulating a radicalism and a break with the old (and even some contemporaneous) orders. As the 1920s progressed, the architecture and the furniture were, quite literally, tensed, or cantilevered. There was a great sense of energy caught up in the furniture which can be interpreted as either aggression or vitality.

French Art Deco and its various offshoots aside, the opposition to ornament was strong. This was nothing new, of course; throughout the history of architecture and the applied arts there have been periodic reactions to any excess in decoration. However, the Modernists did seek to give finesse to their designs: they attempted a richness in their plainness. This was seen most effectively later, in post-World War II reissues of designs such as the reproduction of the sumptuous and extremely comfortable 'Brno' chair (designed 1929–30) by Ludwig Mies van der Rohe, which was made from high-tensile flat steel with a polished chrome finish and a leather-cased foam-rubber seat and back.

HOLLAND

Despite technological developments in the treatment of materials the most startling chair of the Machine Age was made of wood. It was designed and built by Gerrit Rietveld (1888–1964), the

LACQUERED OAK 'RED AND BLUE CHAIR', GERRIT RIETVELD, 1918

An icon of Modernism, this chair parallels Piet Mondrian's abstract paintings and echoes Frank Lloyd Wright's earlier work.

Dutch architect and designer who began his Modernist career in 1916 by designing the furniture for a pioneering concrete house by the architect Robert van t'Hoff. In 1917 Rietveld designed a wooden chair which was made from fifteen lintels and a plank each for the back and seat. It displayed neither cabinet-making nor fine wood-working craftsmanship. By 1918 a version of the chair was lacquered: the lintels were black with yellow ends, the back was red and the seat was blue. Rietveld may have been influenced in part by Piet Mondrian's grid-like primary-coloured abstract paintings and in part by those of Theo van Doesburg, a painter and

writer with whom Rietveld collaborated. One of van Doesburg's paintings, *Russian Dance* (1918), could be said to resemble a flat-plan of a components kit for Rietveld's celebrated 'Red and Blue Chair'.

Rietveld was really a craftsman. He had worked on shop and interior conversions and it can be argued that it was because of his experience as a *maker* rather than as a draughtsman that he designed using cardboard models. The Russian artist and designer El Lissitzky, who visited the Rietveld-designed Schröeder house in Utrecht in 1926 commented: 'He does all with models, feeling things with his hands; and therefore his product is not abstract. One cannot judge such works by photographs, since by photographs we see only a view and not the life of the form.'

GERMANY

What we now call or instinctively think of as Modernist furniture — pieces with thin, tubular-metal arms and a minimum of decoration — developed from a number of sources, aside from Rietveld's pioneering work; indeed, its roots extend well back into the nineteenth century. However, the Modern style was given a considerable boost by the Bauhaus. This most famous of European art and design schools was established by the architect Walter Gropius (1883–1926) in Weimar, Germany, in 1919. His move to Dessau in 1925 marked the start of the development of industrial design as a separate area of study.

The Bauhaus was an extraordinarily argumentative, volatile place with people forming cliques and groups and falling in and out with one another. For example, Gropius himself and some other founder-members resigned in 1928 because they opposed the drive towards turning the school into a collective. Even after it had become more industrial in its orientation, comparatively few of the designs it generated were ever put into production — although under Hannes Meyer (1889–1954), who succeeded Gro-

pius, some cheap furniture and wallpaper designs were manufactured.

Nevertheless, the Bauhaus was a crucible of modern design. The design historian Reyner Banham noted that at the Bauhaus all the innovations — such as cantilevers and glass walling in buildings, metal-bending and fabrication techniques in furniture and so on — became coherent through being given a single style. This style was distilled through the making of models and prototypes — and through endless debates and rows. The Bauhaus experiments were fed by a rich mixture of ideas from the Futurists, the Constructivists and the *De Stijl* group.

In 1925 Marcel Breuer (1902–81), first a student then later a teacher at the Bauhaus, designed his famous 'Wassily' chair — a nickel-plated, steel-framed structure with leather arms, seat and back-rest. In 1926, Mart Stam (b.1899), a Dutch architect connected with the Bauhaus, developed designs for cantilevered chairs. These were followed by Breuer's versions in 1928.

The 'Wassily' chair, which has been copied and reproduced for over sixty years, was rooted in Rietveld's 'Red and Blue Chair'. Some of the wooden lintels have been replaced by strips of leather, but the angularity and tension created by having the seat and back set at sharp angles to the vertical and horizontal lines of the structure derive from Rietveld.

Mart Stam's cantilevered tubular-steel chair was produced in 1924 but, without access to pipe-bending techniques, he was unable to make it properly until 1926. Both Breuer and Ludwig Mies van der Rohe (1886–1969) brought out their own versions, and there were arguments about whose had priority. Despite being nearly seventy years old, this springy cantilevered chair embodies the popular idea of what a modern interior should contain.

Mies van der Rohe's chairs are still in production. In 1929 he designed what has since become the most favoured prestigious modern chair of them all, the 'Barcelona' chair. Not only does this look as comfortable as it is, but its combination of leather, bright chrome and curves makes it the acceptable (and luxurious) face of Modernism.

MAHOGANY CUPBOARD WITH INLAID BRASS, WALTER GROPIUS, 1913 *(above)*

This attractive work shows that Gropius was influenced by the Biedermeier revival which was popular in early-twentieth-century Germany.

TUBULAR-STEEL AND CANE CHAIR, LUDWIG MIES VAN DER ROHE, 1927 *(right)*

This was one of the earliest of the many cantilevered chairs. It is stable but, as has already been noted, the unwary sitter can be pitched forward.

TUBULAR-STEEL AND LEATHER 'WASSILY' CHAIR, MARCEL BREUER, 1925 *(above)*

Originally designed for the painter, Wassily Kandinsky, this chair has been in production since 1945. The lean 'slat and bar' construction is a more acceptable version of Rietveld's radical 'Red and Blue Chair'.

BEECH WOOD WALL UNIT, CHARLOTTE PERRIAND, 1929 (left)

Perriand had a profound influence on Le Corbusier's furniture designs; she, in turn, was influenced by his architectural detailing.

LACQUERED STEEL DRESSING-TABLE, RENÉ HERBST, 1932 (below)

This desk resembles furniture Frank Lloyd Wright designed for the Larkin Building in 1904.

STEEL AND LEATHER 'BARCELONA' CHAIR, LUDWIG MIES VAN DER ROHE, 1929 (above)

This chair is still made by Knoll.

STEEL AND WOOD *CHAISE-LONGUE*, MARCEL BREUER, 1932 (right)

The chaise-longue was popular among Modernist designers.

FRANCE

The influence of the French architect, Le Corbusier (Charles-Édouard Jeanneret, 1887–1965), was contemporary with and as great as that of the Bauhaus. However, although he has been called 'the architect of the century', he certainly cannot be described as the Machine Age's most important furniture designer. Apart from anything else, his colleague Charlotte Perriand (b.1903) was just as important in the conception of designs which until recently were airily attributed to Le Corbusier alone. His partnership in furniture design with her was an equal one. She had been a student of interior design and he saw

her drawings for a roof-top bar in 1927. This began a period of professional collaboration that was to last until 1937.

Le Corbusier's belief in man as a human mechanism perfected by the evolutionary process of natural selection is reflected in his furniture designs. They are imbued with a highly developed sense of rationality and aesthetic integrity. He replaced 'furniture' with what he called 'beautiful equipment', intending pieces to be used interchangeably in his settings in order to attain his architectonic ideal.

Le Corbusier gave expression to Modernism's emotions, particularly those associated with the interior, which he discovered or at the very least reinterpreted: in particular, he created interiors in which the need for

contemplation was an integral element. He swept away clutter in order to create tranquillity and grandeur, reaching his apotheosis in this regard in Notre-Dame du Haut at Ronchamp, France (1951).

This search for purity embraced the idea of mass-manufacturing, on the basis that manufacture by machine is (ideally) predictable, consistent and certain; moreover, it appears to be untouched by human hand. The irony was that, like so much of the furniture designed by the Modernists, the furniture conceived by Le Corbusier was not easy to mass-produce with the methods of manufacture available at that time.

Le Corbusier was continually searching for order and meaning. He began putting storage furniture on the walls and reduced

the other items of furniture to two categories – tables and chairs, designed either for work or for leisure. For Le Corbusier furniture had to earn its keep.

And yet he liked luxury: in his designs he demonstrated a relish for both good leather and chromed-steel tubing. His 'Grand Confort' armchair (said to derive from English leather armchairs of the sort used in clubs) is something to wallow in.

Le Corbusier first showed his chrome furniture, designed with Charlotte Perriand, in 1928. He was not, however, the leader in the field. Among the earlier designers of chrome furniture was Irish-born Eileen Gray (1878–1976). One of her most unusual chairs, the aptly titled 'Nonconformist' (1926–8), was made from continuous steel

tubing and upholstered in beige stitched canvas. It is asymmetrical, having only one elbow rest so as to 'allow more freedom to the body, which can lean to one side, bend, or turn the other way without any difficulty'. Unlike many male designers of the time, she was unwilling to sacrifice comfort to aesthetic ideology.

Art Deco

Along with Bauhaus Modern, the best-known style from the 1920s and 1930s is Art Deco. In the 1920s the prevailing Art Deco style was simple and elegant, using curved forms in the legs and arms. In the 1930s, however, Art Deco became less classical and, with its hexagons, octagons, wedges and

BLACK LACQUERED WOODEN SCREEN, EILEEN GRAY, 1924 (above)

An earlier white version of this screen was shown in Gray's seminal Monte Carlo room at the XIV Salon des Artistes Décorateurs in 1923.

TUBULAR-STEEL AND LEATHER 'GRAND CONFORT' CHAIR, LE CORBUSIER AND CHARLOTTE PERRIAND, 1928 (above left)

Le Corbusier and Perriand were not puritanical when it came to furniture and this chair with its rich black leather is supremely luxurious.

cylinders, much less 'human'. Wood, metal and glass were mixed with elaborate veneers, and frequently the results looked like something from a stage set, perhaps showing the influence of Hollywood. Art Deco sparkled with Noël Coward-like wit and the image of American cocktails, all framed in rich ebony, silver and gold; much of the furniture was varnished to a honey colour. Another ingredient was fragmented light: in bars, dance halls and cinemas, light was bounced off hard lacquer surfaces, chromium and bevel-edged, darkly lustred mirrors.

The style became debased as it went down-market during the later 1930s. Art Deco of this period is recognizable by its clumsiness: typical examples might be a hexagonal table-top on a pair of great bridge-like legs or a dressing-table which looks like the outside of a 1930s cinema.

Although we cannot point to any single event that marked the beginning of Art Deco, the 1925 Exposition Internationale des Arts Décoratifs et Industriels Modernes in Paris was certainly significant. Here Emile-Jacques Ruhlmann (1879–1933) showed a collection of his own works together with

designs by Pierre Legrain (1889–1929), Jean Dunand (1877–1942) and others. In the late 1920s Ruhlmann's pieces were of a modern classical style, presenting simple and elegant forms which often had tapering legs. Generally his furniture was a triumph of craftsmanship, expensively and quite ostentatiously finished using ebony, lacquer or even snakeskin. Ruhlmann knew his clients and what they wanted – they perceived value for money in terms of labour and materials. During the 1930s, as fashion inclined towards chromed metal, he adapted his designs accordingly. Pierre Legrain's work likewise used exotic materials, including sharkskin and ebony, but was bulkier and closely followed forms found in African furniture.

Jean Dunand, like Eileen Gray at the start of her career, became a skilled lacquerer in the 1920s. Both in fact studied with the Japanese master Sugawara in Paris, afterwards designing tables, chairs, cabinets and screens covered with lustrous Oriental lacquer in black, red, green and even unusual shades, such as blue and cream. Sometimes animal and figural subjects adorned their lacquered furniture; still other pieces were left starkly

but beautifully plain and simple.

Two significant Art Deco designers can be taken as representatives of the two extremes of the style, exoticism and angularity: Pierre Chareau (1883–1950) and Robert Mallet-Stevens (1886–1945). Chareau's work during the 1920s was simple, almost austere. Woods such as mahogany and oak were highly polished and set off against richly decorated upholstery. The textile and the hard bright surface together produced a combination of light effects: the hard surface reflected light while the fabric surface absorbed it; moreover, the absorbed light intensified the colour of the textile and so added to the richness. The richness was further heightened by the austerity of the wooden frame, which acted as a foil. Robert Mallet-Stevens was the first president of the Union des Artistes Modernes, founded in Paris in 1929. He opposed ornament and was committed to new materials: his furniture combined tubular steel with simply patterned fabrics. He believed in the functionalist visions of the Modernists, but his work of the 1930s was a lyrical rather than a brutalist expression of utilitarian ideals.

CARD-TABLE WITH BRASS *SABOTS*, EMILE-JACQUES RUHLMANN, 1922 *(left)*

One of the best-known designers of the 1920s in France, Ruhlmann exploited exotic materials coupled with fine workmanship.

MOTHER-OF-PEARL INLAID ARMCHAIR, EMILE-JACQUES RUHLMANN, 1925 *(above)*

This chair illustrates Ruhlmann's belief in 'pure form with directness of line'.

BRASS AND MARBLE DESK, FRENCH, 1932
(above)

This piece is decorated with reliefs symbolizing the triumphs of manufacturing.

INTERIOR FOR A BARGE MOORED ON THE
SEINE, PAUL POIRET, 1925 (above left)

Shown in the Paris Exposition of that year, this interior excited interest because of its obvious debt to Les Ballets Russes.

TAPESTRY FOUR-PIECE SUITE, MAURICE
DEFRÈNE, c.1925 (above)

The tapestry is by Jean Beaumont. The frames are carved, but have gesso and giltwood additions.

SIDEBOARD, ROBERT MALLET-STEVENS,
1931–2 (above centre)

This French architect was adept at combining functional simplicity with great finesse.

WALNUT AND
LEATHER CHAIR,
ERIK GUNNAR
ASPLUND, 1925
(left)

*The furniture designs of
Asplund were a great
influence on Aalto.*

PLYWOOD
ARMCHAIR, ALVAR
AALTO, 1935
(right)

*Aalto used compressed
plywood for many of
his furniture designs of
the 1930s.*

SCANDINAVIA

From 1917 through to the early 1930s, fashionable design seemed to be centred on Rietveld, the Bauhaus and Le Corbusier. But during this period important developments were also being made in Scandinavia.

The countries of Scandinavia share many values, but each retains its distinct culture and since World War I each has, in varying degrees, used design to make its products commercially attractive. Moreover, none of the Scandinavian nations had undergone an industrial revolution remotely equivalent to those of Britain, the United States or Germany. There was thus no impetus among Scandinavian designers (unlike, say, the Germans or Austrians) to express 'machine' imagery in their work. Also apparent is that, since the early part of this century, Scandinavian design has been consistent in wanting to express a range of social and humanistic values. Thus Rietveld's 'Red and Blue Chair' could not have been born in Sweden or Finland – it looks too harsh, too unsympathetic to the body.

The Danish designer Kaare Klint (1888–1954) incorporated the hand-made appearance as a feature of 'Scandinavian' design. His furniture designs were a celebration of skill, good joinery and an expression of Modernism appropriate for the intelligent and comfortably-off consumer.

He was one of the first designers to take the 'natural' in 'natural materials' literally. During World War I he began to experiment with unvarnished wood, preferring wax and polish because they enabled the grain of the wood to be revealed (and also allowed a softer handling of light). He used undyed leather, and fabrics coloured by using natural dyes. He studied the works of Chippendale, the nineteenth-century Shakers and Le Corbusier – and he was also well informed about recent tubular-metal furniture.

His use of textiles exemplified a peculiarly Scandinavian trait. Scandinavian designers favoured constructed textiles as opposed to printed fabrics – in part because they followed on from a strong crafts-based tradition of weaving but largely because of the Bauhaus notion that all structures, including woven ones, should be prized because of their connotations with engineering and the

honesty with which they reveal the fundamental logic of their design.

The most famous of the designers to come to prominence between the world wars was the Finnish architect Alvar Aalto (1898–1976). Like Klint he created furniture which was mass-produced yet nevertheless retained the idea of 'the individual hand'. Unlike Klint (who never used the material) Aalto developed and extended the possibilities of moulded plywood. His interest in wood was partly ideological – he believed the human body should come into contact only with organic materials – and partly practical: Finland has a lot of forest.

Plywood came into its own during World War I. Once regarded as nothing more than a cheap substitute for solid timber, it became a material respected in its own right because its structural properties were useful in the manufacture of boats and aircraft. By the late 1920s the chemicals industry had developed a new generation of glues, partly in response to the needs of the aircraft industry. These glues made it possible to create different kinds of laminated-wood structures, and Aalto began to experiment with the bending of wood laminates. In 1933 he patented a method of bending laminated wood (as used on his three-legged stacking stools, designed between 1930 and 1933, which were constructed from laminated birch). In 1935 he produced the all-plywood 'Spring-leaf Chair'. This had a seat and back made out of a single piece of moulded plywood and was supported on two 'springs' – a pair of continuous arms/legs, each made up from seven birch veneers.

Aalto also, consciously or not, initiated modern 'vessel' furniture, in that one of the possibilities of using a press-moulded material was the creation of forms that almost mould themselves around the body. (This possibility was to be fully realized in the United States during the late 1930s, when designers experimented with bending plywood in two planes rather than just one.) In 1934 the Swedish designer Bruno Mathsson (b.1907) developed one such chair: the beechwood frame is plain, although softened at the edges, and the seat and back are a latticework of strong cotton webbing.

VENEERED WARDROBE, HEAL & CO., 1926

This piece is obviously based on French designs, in particular those of Ruhlmann.

BRITAIN

Relatively speaking, it is tempting to suggest that little of real note was produced in British furniture design during the Machine Age. To go so far would be to mislead, but the harsh fact is that, with a few notable exceptions – such as the work of Wells Coates (1895–1958) and the PEL company – the British contribution to modern furniture design has been limited.

Coates was an engineer and a Modernist. He was a co-founder of the Isokon company, which was dedicated to applying functionalist design to houses and flats. In 1935 he also designed tubular furniture for PEL (Practical Equipment Ltd). PEL started life in 1931 when it produced such chairs as the 'RP6', which is a synthesis of the ideas of Breuer and Stam. Exported all over the world, the 'RP6' – with its tubular-metal frame and its canvas seat and back – is highly functional but a fairly elementary form of seating.

Britain continued its flirtation with hand-crafts – the 1920s saw yet another 'crafts revival'. As was the same in Sweden and Denmark, one or two individuals had feet in the camps of both 'craft' and 'design'. Among these was Gordon Russell (1892–1980). Russell began in the Arts and Crafts tradition – he was an enthusiastic amateur in a number of crafts, including cutting letters in stone and cabinet-making. After World War I he joined his father's firm at Broadway, in the Cotswolds. The workshops at that time relied heavily on hand-craftsmanship, but as the 1920s progressed Russell introduced more machines, arguing that hand and machine craftsmanship could coexist and that a synthesis of the two was not only possible but fruitful, assuming an emphasis on good carpentry and traditional joinery. One of the key contracts won by Gordon Russell Furniture Ltd was to design and make radio cabinets for Murphy Radio Ltd; the styling of these was done by Gordon's brother R.D. Russell (1903–81).

In 1943 Gordon Russell became chairman of the government-appointed committee in charge of Utility furniture. This was cheap, standardized but good-quality furnishing, intended for people who had lost their furniture in the bombing or who were setting up home. These items, however, did not coincide with popular taste and so, as soon as the 1950s gave them a choice, the public got rid of their Utility wares.

An Englishman whose approach was similar to Russell's was Ambrose Heal (1872–1959). He was educated at the Slade and then served an apprenticeship in cabinet-making. After entering the family firm of Heal's (furniture and bedding specialists) he designed furniture, initially in an Arts and Crafts English vernacular style. Later, during the 1930s, he became interested in the steel and laminated-wood designs of Continental Europe and these influenced his work.

During the same period there were other Englishmen who refused to enter into the spirit of the age. An especially good example – because he was a fine craftsman and, although he hated the word, a fine designer – was Edward Barnsley (1900–86), son of Sidney Barnsley, one of the leaders of the late-nineteenth-century Arts and Crafts Movement. Edward Barnsley produced simple furniture in wood, made largely by hand using the traditional carpentry techniques of the eighteenth and nineteenth centuries.

THE UNITED STATES

The period between the two world wars was, as has already been noted, dominated at first by European ideas. As the 1930s progressed, however, North America became increasingly important as a generator of innovative design.

In fact, the history of 'machine-style' furniture started in the United States with the architect Frank Lloyd Wright (1867–1959). Although Gerrit Rietveld's 'Red and Blue Chair' was a seminal object in modern furniture design, the severe, architectural designs for furniture which Wright produced during the early 1900s anticipated Rietveld's radicalism and may have influenced it. Certainly Wright's angular painted-metal furniture design in 1904 for the Larkin Building in Buffalo, New York, was far more adventurous than anything coming from Europe at the time. But the United States was not good at publicizing its indigenous talent during this period. For example, in the exhibitions of industrial design regularly staged during the 1920s and 1930s in New York, the work shown was predominantly from Europe, and American designers were not featured.

It is fair to say that in the 1920s American designers had little to add to the art coming out of the Bauhaus. However, in the 1930s it was American technology which enabled Bauhaus-inspired designs to be put into production. For example, the Chicago-based Howell Company imported samples of Breuer's work and adapted them for mass-production. By 1933 the company's range of tubular-steel furniture included items for the home, office and showroom.

WOOD AND BEATEN-METAL TABLE AND CHAIRS, FRANK LLOYD WRIGHT, MID 1920S

Designed for the Storer House, the furniture was considered as part of the whole architectural and decorative scheme.

Art Moderne

Art Deco made a great impact in the United States, where it was known as Art Moderne. Art Moderne began after World War I in Los Angeles and New York. Following the 1925 Paris Exposition des Arts Décoratifs, American designers turned to France for their inspiration. From the end of World War I through to the early 1930s the Metropolitan Museum of Art in New York presented a series of well-publicized industrial-design exhibitions, and designers such as the Viennese-born Joseph Urban (1872–1933), who settled in New York in 1911, became well known.

Some fine Art Deco furniture was produced in the United States. One of the country's strengths was a commitment to good manufacturing rooted in a strong crafts tradition. For example, in 1930 the Finnish-American architect Eliel Saarinen (1873–1950) produced some very elegant dining chairs with simple fluted backs. Made from holly and inlaid with strips of ebony, these chairs were designed for the president of the Cranbrook Academy of Art in Bloomfield Hills, Michigan, which Saarinen actually helped establish and of which he was made president in 1932.

The Viennese-born designer Paul T. Frank (1887–1958), who moved to New York in 1914, was renowned for his skyscraper-inspired furniture – stepped chests-of-drawers and cabinets of architectonic form – and also for lovely lacquered furniture pieces, which rivalled many French masterworks. Donald Deskey (b.1894), the designer responsible for the interior of Radio City Music Hall in New York, used bakelite, aluminium and other new materials to create furniture that mixed elements of both high-style Parisian Art Deco and functional, rectilinear Bauhaus.

On the West Coast, German-born industrial designer Karl Emmanuel Martin Weber (1889–1963) helped set the tone for a Californian version of Modernism. His furniture comprised mainly metal and glass, often featuring skyscraper-like elements.

Design historians have written up the period of 1930–45 in the United States as the

'Automobile Age'. The influence of car styles on other aspects of design became stronger as the 1930s progressed. One form of Art Deco furniture, since tagged as 'Streamlined Moderne', was prominent. Streamlining was a general style in which objects from writing-desks to railway locomotives were given slick torpedo-style curving.

However, there was opposition to the style. One of the dissenters was the architect Philip Johnson (b.1906). In 1934 he was the curator of a polemical exhibition, 'Machine Art', at the Museum of Modern Art, New York. In its catalogue he distanced himself and the exhibition from 'style' and streamlining and argued for a more basic vocabulary of the straight line and the circle.

Organic Design

Although the American kitchen might have been prepared to accept the tubular furniture of the 'new age', in American style generally there had always been a strong taste for the organic. The strength of the country's wood-craft traditions is in part based on a preference for softness. Even Marcel Breuer, when he settled in the United States in 1937, began designing softer forms.

Scandinavian furniture was by this time making an impact upon American designers. From the 1920s onwards there had been touring exhibitions of Scandinavian applied arts. A further contribution to the organic tendency in design was born from the practicalities of modern technology. For example, injection-moulded plastic forms had to be rounded, or 'organic', for purely practical reasons.

The rounded sculptural form became part of the classical mid-twentieth-century furni-ture-design vocabulary mainly through the work of Charles Eames (1907–78) and his wife Ray (née Kaiser). In 1940–41 the Museum of Modern Art, New York, orga-nized a competition and exhibition called 'Organic Design in Home Furnishings'. The competition was won by two colleagues who worked together at the Cranbrook Academy, Charles Eames and Eero Saarinen (1910–61), son of Eliel. Influenced by Alvar Aalto, who in 1939 had received a retrospec-

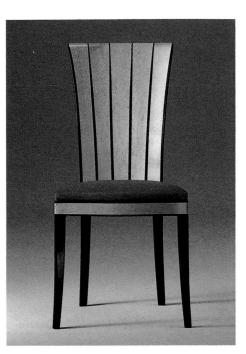

tive exhibition at the Museum of Modern Art, Saarinen and Eames began to experi-ment with bending plywood in two planes – as is necessary in order to create a 'vessel' effect from a flat sheet. Apparently Aalto himself did not approve of this sculptural effect; he thought the results were more akin to plastic moulding, and that pressing ply-wood into hollows 'violated the language of wood fibre'.

Between 1942 and 1946, while engaged also on work for the US Navy, Charles and Ray Eames developed a range of three-dimensionally moulded plywood chairs, some with bent-metal structures. The classic Eames chair is a broad, deep container, like a giant eggshell cut in half; it is furniture's answer to the womb. When the chairs went into production they became both commer-cially and intellectually successful.

As in Britain, some individuals went

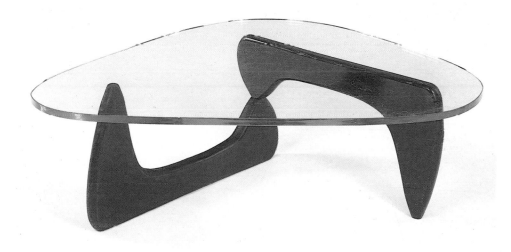

against the grain of design and production. The founder of the modern American wood-craft tradition, Wharton Esherick (1887–1970), was one such designer. His home and studio in Pennsylvania still stand and repre-sent a very odd mixture of styles. In the early 1930s Esherick produced chairs which show a family resemblance to Scandinavian Mod-ernism of the period, except that Esherick built his from the wheel-rims and shafts of an old horse-drawn cart.

GLASS-TOPPED LAMINATED-WOOD TABLE, ISAMU NOGUCHI, 1939 *(above)*

This piece was put into production by Herman Miller in 1945 and anticipated the amoebic shapes of the 1950s.

FIR AND EBONY DINING CHAIR, ELIEL SAARINEN, 1930 *(top)*

One of a set of eight, this chair was designed for the president's house at Cranbrook Academy, Michigan.

MODERN
TIMES

The development of furniture design during the twentieth century has been irregular. The Modernist ideals of the late 1920s and 1930s were not really practical. Originally conceived as products of an industrial age and intended for machine production on a large scale, the furniture of the Modernist architect-designers never accounted in fact for more than a small fraction of the market. Although the designs were simple in outline and often had few individual components, they were often very expensive to assemble, in terms of man-hours. For example, the *chaise-longue* designed by Le Corbusier and Perriand (see page 171) incorporated hand-finished welds and burnishing and hand-sewn leather upholstery. Although they claimed to be creating designs for industrial production, the Modernists had in fact produced furniture that was essentially elitist. Their concepts of simplicity and space were much applauded at the time, but it was not until the late 1980s that the leading Modernist designs became a fashionable and practical alternative. There are two main reasons for this irregularity in the development of the design of twentieth-century furniture. Firstly, there are the economics of production: young designers heralding 'a brave new world' tried to incorporate the newly developed man-made materials into their designs, but found that the costs were too high to enable manufacture in significant numbers. Secondly, the period has often been unstable. The two world wars created shortages of many materials and the money to produce and purchase the new designs was likewise in short supply. As is usual in times of hardship, the avant-garde was the first to suffer.

In the Western world, the period since 1945 has seen a general increase in the standard of living. The early post-war years witnessed limited demand and a concentration on functional necessities being gradually replaced by one of expanding affluence. The initial

LAMINATED 'CARLTON' SIDEBOARD AND ROOM DIVIDER, ETTORE SOTTSASS, 1981

*This piece was exhibited at the 1981 Milan Furniture Fair
where it caused a sensation.*

MACASSAR, EBONY
AND NICKEL-SILVER
CHAIR, JOHN
MAKEPEACE, 1978
(left)

*The curving Gothic
form of this chair
demonstrates a
highpoint of the
furniture-maker's art.*

WELDED-STEEL
'CHICKEN WIRE'
CHAIR, HARRY
BERTOIA, FOR
KNOLL, c.1952
(right)

*Bertoia was inspired by
Marcel Duchamp's
painting 'Nude
descending a staircase'
when making this piece,
saying that he wished
the chair to provide
interesting perspectives
as one moved around it.*

result was a demand for traditional if stilted furniture, prompting revivals of many earlier styles. However, the affluence of the 1960s encouraged development and experimentation, culminating in Pop culture. During the 1970s this breakdown of the barriers of conventional design promoted large-scale production of architect-designed furniture which had been conceived in conjunction with major manufacturers. This trend continued in the 1980s, but with an increasing awareness of classics from former eras and for beautifully hand-made craft furniture, as individual – rather than standard or universal – interior design came to the fore.

Consumers of the 1970s see-sawed in their demands, seeking both the latest and the best – a response to the conditioning of both the industrial age and the 'disposable society'. The consumers of the 1980s, by contrast, started to seek the quality products of former eras, first through buying antiques and more recently through the purchase of limited-edition or privately commissioned furniture. This development naturally led to an increase in the numbers of small groups of craftsmen and designers producing individual pieces of high-quality furniture using traditional techniques.

The greatest general change in the post-1945 period was the move away from the concept of designers or cabinet-makers producing one-off commissions and then designing pieces, in a modified and watered-down version, for mass-production at a lower price-level. By contrast, the post-war period has seen the architect-designer successfully collaborating with industrial production to create original furniture which can be manufactured cheaply and in large numbers.

TABLE AND CHAIRS,
CARLO MOLLINO,
c.1955 (left)

Sinuous moulded-wood forms reminiscent of French Art Nouveau were popular among Italian post-war designers, but few used them so successfully as Mollino to create furniture that was both lively and sculptural.

ITALY

The complete devastation of many Italian towns and cities at the end of World War II proved 'ironically' to be the nation's industrial life-line: with over three million houses and their contents destroyed, there was a large market demand. The ability to start anew (with substantial American aid) gave Italy the opportunity to build new factories utilizing state-of-the-art machines and technology. This development, combined with a healthy supply of cheap steel and Italian flair, produced a vibrant and expanding furniture industry. The designs generally blended the simple forms of the Modernist movement with a softness of line reminiscent of the organic curves of the late nineteenth century. This 'marriage' of utility and craft is clearly shown in the tables and chairs of Carlo Mollino (1905–73) and in the chair designed by Gastone Rinaldi (b.1920) for Rima, all charac-

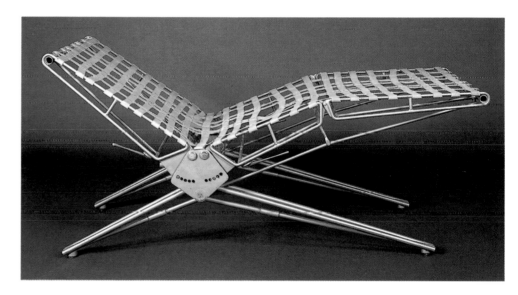

terized by their tapering, curved, tree-like legs and supports.

The new materials available enabled designers – many of whom were trained as architects in the Modernist tradition – to produce shapes and structures that had not previously been possible. In particular, moulded plywood and foam rubber could be used to provide sleek, strong, unjointed lines and soft, yet firm, silhouettes. The large Milanese firm of Cassina, bolstered by a substantial contract from the Italian Navy, employed several young designers – including Paolo Buffa, Franco Albini (1905–77) and Gio Ponti (1891–1979). The company's most successful design of the period was

STEEL RECLINING CHAIR, OSVALDO
BORSANI, FOR TECNO, c.1956 (above)

This perilous-looking chair demonstrates a relatively new phenomenon – furniture designed to be used either outside or indoors.

ASH 'SUPERLEGGERA' CHAIR, GIO PONTI,
FOR CASSINA, 1957 (above left)

Although this rush-seated chair embodies the spirit of 1950s Italian design, Ponti based it on fishermen's chairs he saw in Chiavari.

Ponti's 'Superleggera' chair, which combined Italy's traditional style with a strong dose of modern design. Other companies grew from the ashes of pre-war industry and often combined to form new entities; one such example was Tecno of Milan, for whom Osvaldo Borsani designed the foam-rubber-covered reclining chair 'P.40' in 1954.

At the end of the 1950s a new and affluent age arrived in Italy. Exports were high, unemployment had fallen and consequently there was a strong home demand as standards of living rose. The new age of prosperity prompted the use in furniture of other new materials – chrome-plated fittings,

adaptable environment whereby a single room might be used for eating, drinking, discussion, listening to music, watching television and sleeping. One result was the manufacture of multi-purpose modular furniture, which could be arranged as armchairs or combined into sofas or beds.

This period also produced the 'Anti-Design School', a typical product of the up-coming generation's rebellion against established concepts. Unfortunately, the essentially uncommercial nature of the school's designs meant that few ever entered manufacture. One which *was* made in large numbers was the 'Sacco' chair, designed by

COLLECTION OF SEATS AND TABLES, 1958–c.1967 *(below left)*

From left to right: inflatable polyvinyl armchair by Aubert Jungmann and Stinco; two laminated cylindrical chairs by Bernard Holdaway, 'Elephant' armchair in plastic by Rancillac; 'Armchair 300' in moulded polyester by Pierre Paulin; 'Tulip' chairs and table in fibreglass by Eero Saarinen.

PRINTED LAMINATE CABINET, PIERO FORNASETTI, c. 1950 *(below)*

Fornasetti's theatrical and Surrealist background provided him with rich resources for his designs.

smoked glass, marble, mirror glass, leather upholstery and, ever-more acceptable, plastic and Perspex. However, during this period it took some time for new designs to be put into production. Typical examples of designs from this period are the stacking children's chair, which was conceived by Marco Zanuso (b.1916) in 1961, yet not produced in large quantities until the late 1960s, and the plastic 'Tractor' seat designed by Achille Castiglioni (b.1918) in 1957 but not made in large numbers until, again, the late 1960s.

The designs of the latter half of the 1960s and the early 1970s responded also to the moral and psychological attitudes. The less formal social attitudes demanded more relaxed furniture, reflecting the desire for an

Gatti, Paolini & Teodoro of Turin for Zanotta in 1969. This forerunner of the bean-bag was filled with small polyurethane balls and it adapted to the posture of the user. The 'Blow' chair, designed by De Pas, D'Urbino & Lomazzi of Milan for Zanotta in 1967 was another classic of the Pop era. Made from inflatable polyvinyl, or PVC plastic, the chair was originally conceived for use in a swimming pool but soon became a cult object in the Pop interior.

The mid-1970s saw a period of decline in the Italian economy, and this was reflected in the furniture industry. The result was a consolidation of the industry, concentrating on the reproduction of successful traditional ideas and specialist pieces. Luxury or highly

ornate furniture, like the 'Maralunga' chair designed by Vico Magistretti (b.1920) and manufactured by Cassina in 1979, was generally displaced by cheaper mass-production lines aimed at the younger market and a hi-tech approach designed for the European market (hence the popularity at this time of the 'Tractor' seat). One of the exciting designers of this period was Joe Colombo (1930–71), whose 'rotoliving unit', shown in a 1972 exhibition of Italian design at the Museum of Modern Art in New York, presented the concept of multi-functional furniture units.

By the late 1970s the economic climate had improved and the furniture industry gradually began to respond. One example

FRENCH INTERIOR,
EARLY 1970S

*With its leather-
upholstered, rosewood
veneered '670' chairs
and '671' ottoman by
Charles Eames and its
Magistretti coffee
tables, the emphasis of
this room is on comfort.
It typifies the chic rather
than the cheap aspects of
modern design.*

from this period was the 'Spaghetti' chair, designed by Belotti and manufactured by Alias in 1979.

The 1980s provided a mixture of concepts from Italy including a return to the 'Anti-Design' theories of the mid-1960s. Although several individual pieces produced by this group were innovative, because of their sculptural nature they could be produced commercially on only a limited scale. Another group, called 'Memphis' and headed by the Austrian-born Ettore Sottsass (b.1917), emerged to lead contemporary Italian design. These designers of furniture, fabric and ceramics caused a sensation at the Milan Furniture Fair in 1981. The group drew on a wide range of references, from classical art to

1950s kitsch and modern pop music. They emphasized colour and texture, using surprising combinations of materials to create dramatic effects. Although the exuberant experimentalism of Memphis has offended more traditional designers, their furniture has enjoyed fashionable status since its bold inception in 1981.

Italy is today once again at the forefront of modern design. In recent years it has opened its doors to stimuli from other countries and more Italian designers are working abroad for a range of companies; for example, while the Frenchman Philippe Starck has been producing designs for Cassina and Tecno in Italy, Sottsass has been doing work for Knoll in the United States.

THE UNITED STATES

The United States was one of the few countries involved in World War II which did not suffer any extensive bombing or deprivation and consequently it was the main centre for growth and development of the furniture industry during the 1940s. In addition to the healthy state of the nation's economy and production capacity, the United States took in large numbers of European immigrants who provided both cheap skilled labour and new ideas. Two of the most famous of these 'new Americans'

were Walter Gropius and Ludwig Mies van der Rohe, both of whom came to the United States from Germany in the late 1930s. It was under their Modernist influence that the younger generation of American designers was to develop. The two leading designers in this new school were Charles Eames and Eero Saarinen, both architect-designers. Their first major success was the joint entry they submitted for the 'Organic Design in Home Furnishings' competition inaugurated by New York's Museum of Modern Art in 1940; they took first prize in the seat-furniture category. The design was revolutionary: the chair had a separate moulded monocoque shell (i.e., most of the load-bearing was done by the shell), padded for comfort with rubber and covered with fabric, all supported by a slender frame. Sadly, World War II stopped the immediate production of this design. When finally it did begin, the original aluminium legs were replaced by wooden ones, due to the post-war metal shortage. The Eames 'shell' concept is the distinguishing feature of his designs, which borrowed generously from nature to create their organic curved forms. These designs also incorporated the new materials of the era — moulded laminates, injection-moulded plastics, fibreglass and resins — all of which allowed the designer greater flexibility in the creation of fluid, unjointed lines.

Clearly, at this stage manufacturers were looking into the production costs associated with design and Eames came very close to the manufacturer's dream of a single-process production with his prize-winning entry in the International Competition for Low Cost Furniture (1948; sponsored by the Museum of Modern Art). The model was a single-mould fibreglass shell with a variety of different bases so that it could be adapted for different purposes. In the following years Eames turned his attention to cabinets, and in this field, too, he created an adaptable form based on a series of standard components which could be assembled in a variety of ways to produce different-shaped units for varying purposes.

Eero Saarinen produced a chair of similar concept known as the 'Womb' chair — so called because of its encompassing form and the way in which its interior was padded with soft foam rubber. By the late 1940s Saarinen was working for the innovative Knoll International, for whom he designed his classic 'Tulip' suite (produced in 1956). The seats — of moulded fibreglass with foam-rubber cushions — were set on slender stems of cast aluminium; the dining-table had a similar base and a white laminate top.

Also working at this time for Knoll was Harry Bertoia (1915–78). In the ultimate attempt to achieve a light yet strong and practical chair he designed his striking 'Chicken Wire' chair of 1950.

The most noted classics of the 1950s must, however, be the '670' chair and '671' ottoman designed in 1956 by Charles Eames and produced by Herman Miller, Inc. of Zeeland, Michigan. Once again there was the simple moulded shell on a spider-like base, but this time, in response to the demand of the period for greater comfort and perhaps even grandeur, the pieces were luxuriously upholstered in leather and had a fitted head-rest.

The 'laid-back' ideology from California meant that the United States was, arguably, the world leader in terms of the Pop culture, producing the largest number of contemporary designs on a significant scale. The 'conversation pit' and the inflatable chairs and tables made of brightly coloured Perspex were flirted with by the designers of the day in what was undoubtedly a period of experimentation.

Based on the ideals of the 1960s was the Craft Revival which took place in the late 1970s and early 1980s. This movement was a backlash against the synthetic materials used in the immediate post-war period and prompted a move towards a higher content of natural materials and an increased level of hand-craftsmanship. The leaders of the Craft Revival were Michael Coffey, Roy Superior and Peter Danko, all of whom worked in almost Art Nouveau forms, mainly in natural materials and using high-quality construction and craftsmanship. Wendell Castle (b. 1932), whose carved, laminated-wood furniture of the 1960s and 1970s was based on similar organic principles, has looked elsewhere for inspiration in the 1980s, in particular to French Art Deco. The result has been superbly crafted luxuriant pieces, often made of exotic woods and punctuated with post-modern decorative details.

Jacobsen, who had trained as an architect, was interested in the 'total environment'. He designed the 'Egg' and the 'Swan' chairs for the interior of the SAS hotel in Copenhagen.

'CHINESE' CHAIR, HANS WEGNER, 1968 (above)

LAMINATED CHERRYWOOD SETTEE, WENDELL CASTLE, c.1970 (top)

Castle led the American Craft Revival, using biomorphic forms in his designs. His furniture is defiantly hand-made, carved into intricate forms which even the most sophisticated machinery could not produce.

SCANDINAVIA

Scandinavian style has had its own distinctive 'feel' throughout the twentieth century. This has been based on a long tradition of combining craftsmanship and manufacture. Undoubtedly, the most widely used material has been natural wood. For example, although the work of Kaare Klint was true to the spirit of Modernism prevalent in Europe at the time, the clear-cut severity of the outline was softened through the use of pine in place of chromium-plated steel.

In Scandinavia there had not been a strong reaction for or against the Modernist principles of the Bauhaus. Rather, the post-war years saw a continuation of the Danish interpretation of the style, always highlighted by the exceptional standards of craftsmanship the Danes deployed. It was this quality – monitored by the guild of the Danish cabinet-makers and Den Permanente, a continuous exhibition of the best of Denmark's products – which so enamoured Scandinavian work to the export markets of the late 1950s and the 1960s.

Hans Wegner's (b.1914) 'The Chair' (1949) is a fine example of this period. It has a simple design and yet a sense of solidity – the wood, with its simple decoration, giving the chair a sense of softness, warmth and durability. Other outstanding designers of this period were Arne Jacobsen (1902–71) and Finn Juhl (b.1912). The former is noted

UPHOLSTERED FIBREGLASS 'GLOBE' CHAIR, EERO AARNIO FOR ASKO FINNTERNATIONAL, 1966 (above)

1960s' space exploration inspired a whole generation of designers who created fantasy furniture, like the 'Globe' chair by Aarnio, to reflect a new technological society.

for his 'Egg' chair and ottoman (designed in 1957 for Fritz Hansen) and his 'Swan' chair (1957, also made by Hansen), all three of which enjoyed a long production run. The latter is renowned for his more sculptural designs and extensive use of wood, particularly in a design of his for a desk, which won the prestigious Design Award at the American Institute in 1964.

Although the Pop movement was not greatly taken to heart by the top Scandinavian designers, the spirit of the New Modernism of the late 1960s and early 1970s was upheld by Arne Jacobsen and Poul Kjaerholm (1929–80). Verner Panton (b.1926) and Eero Aarnio (b.1932) were other exponents of the movement. The latter's design for the 'Globe' chair (1966), a further development of the womb/egg theme, is clearly a product of its era, in that it has a (then-fashionable) purple interior.

Scandinavian designers of the 1980s have placed a strong emphasis on ergonomics, and are perhaps unusual among their contemporaries in other countries because they still successfully combine craft and manufacture. The work of Alvar Aalto is now enjoying a tremendous revival. The young designers of the period, such as Terje Ekstrom and the Finnish Simo Heikkila, still work using predominantly natural materials; the fact that the latter's 'Experimental' chair (1982) was available only in a special limited edition is probably a reflection on the economics of production.

BRITAIN

World War II drained Britain of many of its manufacturing resources. The shortage of materials on the one hand and paying customers (due in part to high unemployment) on the other, combined with the Board of Trade's Domestic Furniture Act of 1942 to depress the market. The Act required all furniture production to be under licence to the Board of Trade, which in effect meant that it was restricted to Utility products.

Young British designers of this era looked to the United States as the leader in design and so (for example) Robin Day (b.1915) and Clive Latimer entered their designs into the Low Cost Furniture competition run by New York's Museum of Modern Art where they won a prize for their storage units. British work of this period may generally be considered as lacking in innovation, but a genuine commitment to the ideals of Modernism can be seen in the design of the 'Antelope' chair by Ernest Race (1913–63), produced especially for the Festival of Britain in 1951.

Many British designs of the period were clearly inspired by ideas from the United States, for example Day's 'Polyprop' injection-moulded stacking chairs. First manufactured in 1963 by Hille and still in production, the 'Polyprop' clearly owes its lines and form to the Eames and Saarinen chairs produced more than ten years earlier. Such interpretations of American ideas tended to dominate British design. However, although the British productions were not necessarily innovative, they were often well executed and frequently utilized state-of-the-art techniques in mass-

production. This was the age of the contract furnisher, whose designs were usually well conceived and beautifully executed, like those of Archie Shine, Ernest Race and Russell Furnishings.

The United Kingdom, like other countries, went through an experimental period during the 1960s, in accordance with the new feelings of the decade, but little of this furniture design has remained or been noted. In large part this is because a great deal of it was of limited durability – such as Peter Murdoch's (b.1940) cardboard chair for a throwaway society or the 1970 'Comfort Explosion' chair by Prepell Oliver, which was made from solid blocks of foam. Other designs of the period were, while practical, often unremarkable – such as the contract upholstered furniture of the 'Maxima' collection created by Max Glendinning for Race Furnishing Ltd. in 1966. Exceptions were more sculpture-based furniture-makers, whose work is today collected for its sculptural qualities more than its functional design; the fetishistic chairs and tables of Allen Jones (b.1937) are examples.

COATED-STEEL 'RIB' CHAIR, PAUL CHAMBERLAIN AND PETER
CHRISTIAN (FLUX), 1988 *(opposite left)*

POLYPROPYLENE STACKING CHAIR, ROBIN DAY, 1962
(opposite right)

FIBREBOARD CHAIR,
PETER MURDOCH
FOR INTERNATIONAL
PAPER, 1966 *(right)*

*The in-built obsolescence
of this chair reflects its
creation at the advent of
the throw-away society*

SHEET-STEEL
WARDROBE, RON
ARAD, 1988 *(far right)*

*In the 1980s industrial
materials were used to
make domestic furniture;
they were designed to
draw attention to their
substance rather than to
conceal it.*

British designers of the 1980s have tended towards limited-capacity manufacture, many of them being craft-based rather than architecture-based. As in some circles of the fine-arts world, there has been a desire to see the overt display of skill and talent. This has certainly been catered for by the traditional works of Craft Revival artist-craftsmen such as John Makepeace (b.1939), Rupert Williamson (b.1945) and Martin Grierson. Their pieces involve hours of highly skilled labour and materials that are often far from readily malleable.

In the late 1980s several different schools of design were developing, the strongest of which appear to be the Victorian Revivalists and the New (or Modern) Historicists. Both are characterized by a high degree of hand-finishing, much use of natural materials and a reworking with new emphasis on a mixture of different ideas from previous periods. Another field of design is typified by the output of Ron Arad. Working primarily with metal, he produces strikingly modern pieces that appear to have been made out of scrapmetal and are 'unfinished'.

FRANCE

For France the post-war period proved to be relatively uncreative as far as furniture design was concerned. There were two main schools of design, one based on Art Deco and the other on the New Modernism. The former catered for the demand for conservative reproductions of the Art Deco period, producing luxurious interpretations of the drawing- and dining-room suites and less stylized versions of the marquetry and cabinet-work of the late 1920s and 1930s. The latter was a revival of the Modernist ideal, the simple lines of functionalist furniture being adorned by luxurious supple suedes and leather.

During the 1960s and 1970s, designers such as Roger Tallon (b.1929) and Pierre Paulin (b.1927) moved with the spirit of the times and produced numerous designs using the new materials, but they rarely found that magic combination of style, strength and practicality. France's contribution to Surrealism and the Pop movement was marked

especially through the work of the artist César (César Baldacchini, b.1921), whose chair in the form of an open hand must be one of the classic designs of the period. François Lalanne has been another leading exponent of this genre. Primarily a sculptor, he has produced limited editions of furniture based on the forms of animals. His most famous design is his grazing-sheep stools; others have included a bar with a serving area supported by two ostriches.

French design of the 1980s has been predominantly Modernist in concept but with an emphasis on graceful – often extended – lines with definite sculptural overtones. Leaders of this school have been Philippe Starck, Pascal Mourgue, Martin Szekely and Marie Christine Dorner. All use metal as their most common manufacturing material, but have been experimenting with different finishes of metallic sprays and oxides in order to give subtle tone. Industry-based designs have been in evidence, exemplified by the work of Jean Nouvel, whose 'Coffre BAO' is a type of enlarged aluminium tool box. At the time of writing, there is also a crafts-influenced school, led by Garouste Bonetti, which on occasion exhibits strong ethnic influences.

In general, the furniture designs of the late 1980s, and hence presumably the early 1990s, appear to be going in the direction of the crafts movement. Furniture design for office or functional domestic use will no doubt retain its Modernist roots, albeit with an increasing emphasis on ergonomics. However, the design of domestic furniture – in a culture in which the possible range of interiors is frequently portrayed on television and in newspaper supplements and the plethora of specialist magazines – must surely turn towards the artist-craftsman for its inspiration.

ALUMINIUM 'COFFRE BAO' STORAGE CABINET, JEAN NOUVEL, 1986 *(left)*

ITALIAN INTERIOR, 1980s *(below)*

The grey and yellow linen chairs and sofa are by Paolo Deganello for Driade, the black lacquer chairs are by Philippe Starck for Aleph and the chrome and glass shelves are by Antonia Astoria.

EARLY FURNITURE

Carter, Howard: *The Tomb of Tut-Ankh-Amen*, Vol. 3, London and Toronto, 1923–33

Casson, Lionel: *Ancient Egypt*, Amsterdam, 1969

Eames, Penelope: *Furniture in England, France and the Netherlands from the Twelfth to the Fifteenth Century*, London, 1977

Liversidge, J.: *Furniture in Roman Britain*, London, 1955

Richter, G.M.A.: *Ancient Furniture: A history of Greek, Etruscan and Roman Furniture*, Oxford and New York, 1926; *Handbook of Greek Art*, London, 1959

THE RENAISSANCE

Burr, Grace H.: *Hispanic Furniture*, New York, 1964

Cescinsky, Herbert and Gribble, Ernest: *Early English Furniture and Woodwork*, 2 vols., London, 1922

Chinnery, Victor: *Oak Furniture – The British Tradition*, Woodbridge, 1979

Feulner, A.: *Kunstgeschichte des Möbels*, Berlin, 1980

Jervis, Simon (ed.): *Printed Furniture Designs before 1650*, London, 1974

Jourdain, Margaret: *English Decoration & Furniture of the Early Renaissance*, London, 1924

Morrazzoni, Guiseppe: *Il Mobilio Italiano*, Florence, 1940

Schade, G.: *Möbel der italienischen Renaissance*, Berlin, 1964

Viaux, Jacqueline: *Le Meuble en France*, Paris, 1962

THE BAROQUE

Evans Dee, Elaine and Walton, Guy: *Versailles: the view from Sweden*, exhibition catalogue Cooper-Hewitt Museum, New York, 1988

Fairbanks, Jonathan L. and Trent, Robert F. (eds.): *New England Begins*, 3 vols., exhibition catalogue, Museum of Fine Arts, Boston, 1982

Forman, Benno M.: *American Seating Furniture, 1630–1730*, New York, 1988

Jervis, Simon: 'A tortoiseshell cabinet and its precursors', *Victoria & Albert Museum Bulletin*, London, October 1968

Jobe, Brock and Myrna, Kaye: *New England Furniture: The Colonial Era, Selections from the Society for the Preservation of New England Antiquities*, Boston, 1984

Lunsingh Scheurleer, Th. H.,: 'Pierre Golle, ébéniste du roi Louis XIV' *Burlington Magazine*, London, June 1980

Sack, Albert: *Fine Points of Furniture: Early American*, New York, 1950

Symonds, R.W.: 'Furniture Making in Seventeenth & Eighteenth Century England', *The Connoisseur*, London, 1950

Thornton, Peter: *Seventeenth-Century Interior Decoration in England, France and Holland*, New Haven and London, 1978

Trent, Robert (ed.): *Pilgrim Century Furniture*, New York, 1980

Wolsey, S.W., and Luff, R.W.P.: *Furniture in England – The Age of the Joiner*, London, 1968

THE ROCOCO PERIOD

Bazin, Germain: *Baroque and Rococo*, London, 1964

Beard, Geoffrey, and Gilbert, Christopher (eds.): *Dictionary of English Furniture Makers*, London, 1968

Downs, Joseph: *American Furniture in the Henry Francis du Pont Winterthur Museum: Queen Anne and Chippendale Periods*, New York, 1952

Heckscher, Morrison H.: *American Furniture in the Metropolitan Museum of Art*, Metropolitan Museum of Art, New York, 1985

Wills, Geoffrey: *English Furniture, 1550–1760*, London, 1971; *English Furniture, 1760–1900*, London, 1971

THE CLASSICAL REVIVAL

Council of Europe Exhibition Catalogue: *The Age of Neo-classicism*, London, 1972

Eriksen, Svend: *Early Neoclassicism in France*, London, 1974

de Gröer, Léon: *Les Arts Décoratifs de 1790 à 1850*, Fribourg, 1985

Joy, Edward: *English Furniture 1800–1851*, London 1977

Montgomery, Charles F.: *American Furniture: The Federal Period in the Henry Francis du Pont Winterthur Museum*, New York, 1966

Ward, Gerald W.R: *American Case Furniture in the Mabel Brady Garvan and Other Collections at Yale University*, New Haven, 1988

ECLECTICISM

Agius, Pauline: *British Furniture, 1880–1915*, London, 1978

Art and Design in Europe and America at the Victoria and Albert Museum 1800–1900, London, 1987

Aslin, Elizabeth: *19th-Century English Furniture*, London, 1962

Cooper, Jeremy: *Victorian and Edwardian Furniture and Interiors*, London, 1987

Gloag, John: *Victorian Comfort: A Social History of Design from 1830 to 1900*, London, 1961

Joy, Edward: *A Pictorial Dictionary of Nineteenth Century Furniture Design*, Woodbridge, 1977

Ledoux-Lebard, Denise: *Les Ébénistes Parisiens (1795–1830)*, Paris, 1951

Mace, Rodney, Kirkham, Pat, and Porter, Julia: *Furnishing the World: The East London Furnishing Trade, 1830–1980*, London, 1987

Norbury, J.: *World of Victoriana*, 1972

Payne, Christopher: *19th Century European Furniture*, London, 1985

Sotheby's Catalogues: *Nineteenth- and Twentieth-Century Decorative Arts*, London, periodically from June 1982 to the present day.

CRAFT AND DESIGN

Buffet-Challie, Laurence: *The Art Nouveau Style*, London, 1982

Burke, Doreen Bolger, et al.: *In Pursuit of Beauty*, New York, 1986

Cathers, David M.: *Furniture of the American Arts and Crafts Movement*, New York, 1981

Comino, Mary: *Gimson and the Barnsleys*, London, 1980

Cooper, Jeremy: *Victorian and Edwardian Furniture and Interiors*, London, 1987

Kaplan, Wendy: 'The Art that is Life': The Arts and Crafts Movement in America, 1875–1920, Boston, 1987

Madsen, Stephan Tschudi: *Sources of Art Nouveau*, translated by R.I. Christopherson, New York, 1975

Schweiger, Werner J.: *Wiener Werkslütte: design in Vienna, 1903–1932*, New York, 1984

Selz, Peter, and Constantine, Mildred (eds.): *Art Nouveau: Art and Design at the Turn of the Century*, catalogue of exhibition, Museum of Modern Art, New York, 1959 (reprinted 1975)

Varnedoe, Kirk: *Vienna 1900: Art, Architecture and Design*, catalogue of exhibition, Museum of Modern Art, New York, 1986

Weisberg, Gabriel P.: *Art Nouveau Bing: Paris Style 1900*, New York, 1986

THE MACHINE AGE

Klein, D. and Bishop, M.: *Christie's Pictorial History of Decorative Art 1880–1980*, London, 1986

McFadden, D.R.: *Scandinavian Modern Design 1880–1980*, New York, Cooper-Hewitt Museum, 1982

Ostergard, D.E.: *Bentwood and Metal Furniture: 1850–1946*, Washington, 1987

Phillips, L. *High Styles: Twentieth-century American Design*, Whitney Museum of American Art, New York, 1985

Russell, F., Garner, P. and Read, J.: *A Century of Chair Design*, 1980

MODERN TIMES

Emilio Ambasz (ed.): *Italy: The New Domestic Landscape*, Museum of Modern Art, New York, 1972

Garner, Philippe: *Contemporary Decorative Arts from 1940 to the Present Day*, London, 1980; *Twentieth Century Furniture*, London, 1980

Hiesinger, K.B.. (ed.): *Design Since 1945*, London, 1983

Radice, Barbara, *Memphis*, London, 1985

Sparke, Penny: *Italian Design*, London, 1988

GLOSSARY

acanthus Ornament representing stylized form of thick, scallop-edged *Acanthus spinosus* leaf. Of classical origin, it has been used extensively as carved decoration on furniture.

acroterion Pedestal intended to support carved flowers, busts or urns on the centre or lower points of a pediment.

alto-relievo, see **relief**

amphora Classical two-handled storage jar later adopted as a Neoclassical decorative motif.

anthemion Decorative motif of Greek origin, the radiating pattern of which resembles the honeysuckle flower and leaves.

anthemion

applied decoration Decoration, normally carved, laid onto the surface of a piece of furniture.

apron Ornamental structure beneath the seat-rail of a chair or settee. Also used below the drawers or doors, or between the legs of **commodes**.

arabesque Literally 'Arabian', a scrolling and interlacing pattern of branches, leaves, flowers and scrollwork of Moorish origin. Found on sixteenth- and seventeenth-century Spanish and Portuguese furniture, it later spread to Northern Europe.

arcading Carved architectural ornament suggesting arches. Often used on chair-backs and applied on panels.

armoire Large cupboard with one or two doors, originating in late-sixteenth-century France.

astragal Small semicircular convex moulding commonly used as a glazing-bar on furniture. The reverse of **scotia**, and smaller than **torus**.

athénienne Basin on a tripod stand copied from an example found at Pompeii. Popular French Neoclassical and Empire form.

aumbry Late-medieval doored cupboard used to store food.

backstool Form of stool with a back developed in the late sixteenth century. By the mid-sixteenth century it had developed into a **single chair**.

baluster Turned, vase-shaped vertical post. A balustrade is a row of balusters with a joining rail at the top.

Bantam work Incised lacquer work named after Bantam, a province of Dutch Java, and commonly found on Dutch and English furniture. The design is cut into a black lacquer ground and is also known as cutwork.

bargueño, see *vargueño*

bas-relief, see **relief**

bergère Wing armchair with filled-in sides from French designs of *c.*1725. Early models were caned, later ones upholstered.

birdcage Hinged columnar mechanism used on tables which allows the top to revolve or tip vertically. Also known as a squirrel, this device was particularly popular on English and American eighteenth-century tripod tables. See **tip-top**.

blackamoor Negro figure often used as the carved central section of Louis XIV *guéridons*, whose name derives from Guéridon, a Moorish slave who was the subject of popular songs.

block-front Construction technique associated with American eighteenth-century **case furniture** made in Newport, Rhode Island. Usually consists of three vertical panels, the centre one concave, the outer two convex.

bombé Literally, 'blown-out', the front line of a piece of furniture which forms a convex, or belly-outward, curve. Popular in the mid-eighteenth century and enjoyed a nineteenth-century revival.

bonheur-du-jour This small, light lady's writing-desk was first made in France in the 1760s. It had a central drawer in front, tiered shelves and cupboards in the back and sometimes a shelf between the legs. Enjoyed a revival in mid-nineteenth-century France and England.

boss Small oval or circular projecting ornament often covering a join in mouldings.

Boulle work Type of **marquetry** using tortoiseshell and metal, usually brass. Brass on a shell ground is known as *première-partie* or first-part, work, shell on brass as *contre-partie*, or counterpart. Originally a tenth-century Italian process, this method was perfected by André-Charles Boulle in eighteenth-century France. Popular from the late seventeenth through to the nineteenth century, by which time the effect was simulated using a machine-based technique. Known as buhl work in nineteenth-century English furniture-making.

bracket Right-angled fitting acting as support to a horizontal member.

bracket foot A foot extending from each side of a corner to a centre point at the base. Often shaped or carved.

bronze doré, see **ormolu**

breakfront, or **broken front** Furniture in which the front line is interrupted. Usually, the central vertical section projects slightly in front of the side sections. Commonly found on eighteenth-century bookcases and cabinets.

buffet Side- or serving-table used from medieval times. In sixteenth- and seventeenth-century England, buffet was synonymous with court cupboard. Towards the end of the eighteenth century sideboards replaced buffets in the dining-room, although the buffet enjoyed renewed popularity during the nineteenth-century Gothic revival.

buhl work, see **Boulle work**

bun foot Round, turned and sometimes 'squashed' foot commonly used on William and Mary case furniture.

bureau Desk popular in late seventeenth-century England and France distinguished by its sloping fall-front. The flap is hinged at the base and rests on **lopers** when open, folds up at an angle when closed. Base often contains drawers. In America, used to describe a bedroom chest-of-drawers.

bureau à cylindre Popular late eighteenth-century desk with curved lid which slides beneath the underside of the top when opened. Also known as a roll-top desk. Occasionally the cylinder is of *tambour* form, i.e. made from slats of wood joined by a canvas backing.

bureau plat Flat writing-desk in the form of a large, elongated table, often with two or three drawers underneath. May have slides above the drawers to provide more writing space.

burled (American) or **burr** (British) wood **veneer** Popular from the seventeenth century. Made from the tumescent growth of certain trees (notably walnut). Valued for unusual but attractive grain.

butterfly hinge Hinge with two flared plates on either side of the join resembling butterfly wings. These replaced butt hinges on high-quality walnut furniture.

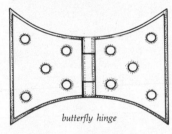
butterfly hinge

'C' and 'S' scrolls Based on the letters 'C' and 'S', these scrolls were popular Rococo motifs.

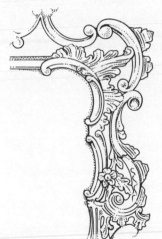
'C' and 'S' scrolls

cabochon Smooth round or oval raised decoration popular in sixteenth-century **strapwork** or, in the eighteenth century, surrounded by formalized **acanthus** leaves. Used with shellwork, it became a popular motif on Georgian **cabriole legs**.

cabochon

cabriole leg Stylized form of animal hind leg of elongated 'S' shape. Popular in late-eighteenth- and nineteenth-century Europe.

canapé Type of eighteenth-century French sofa.

canted A bevelled or **chamfered** surface; used to refer to furniture legs inclining outwards.

canterbury Mid-eighteenth-century low supper trolley more commonly known in its late-eighteenth- and nineteenth-century form: a stand with vertical compartments to hold sheet music.

capital Head or crowning feature of a column or **pilaster**.

caquetoire/euse Armchair of sixteenth-century French design, with a high narrow back and a trapezoidal seat.

carcase The main body or under-structure of a piece of furniture, over which a layer of **veneer** or other covering is applied.

cartonnier Eighteenth-century cabinet of French design.

cartouche Motif with curved or rolled edges suggesting a scroll shape or a piece of paper with curling edges. Often used as a surround for crests and inscriptions.

caryatid Decorative support in the form of a female figure. Derived from Greek architecture, the caryatid has been popular since the

cartouche

Renaissance and enjoyed particular favour in the Rococo and Neoclassical periods. Male caryatids are less common and are called telamones.

case furniture Furniture which provides storage space, as opposed to seat furniture.

cassone Italian dowry chests, often enhanced with carved, gilt, inlaid or painted decoration.

cavetto moulding Concave moulding, a quarter circle in cross-section, also known as hollow **chamfering**; opposite of **ovolo moulding**.

cellaret Deep, lockable box for dry storing wine bottles which dates from the eighteenth century. Free-standing or incorporated in a sideboard.

chamfer A **canted** surface produced by bevelling off an angle.

chest-on-chest, see **tallboy**

chevron Zigzag pattern of Anglo-Saxon derivation often used on

medieval, Gothic revival and Art Deco pieces.

chinoiserie General term for European adaptation of Oriental designs popular during late seventeenth century, Rococo and Regency periods. Motifs used include pagodas, **fretwork**,

Chinese-style **finials**, mandarins, coolies, birds, landscapes and rivers.

cinquefoil, see **trefoil**

claw-and-ball foot Foot of Oriental origin composed of talons holding a ball; dragon's claw replaced by eagle's claw in Europe.

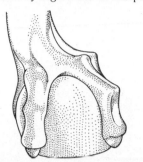
claw-and-ball foot

cock-beading Moulding dating from the early eighteenth century.

commode French form of low chest-of-drawers, originally intended for the drawing-room, dating from the mid-seventeenth century and very popular during the eighteenth century. Became a term for bedroom cupboards in the nineteenth century.

console table Form of side-table supported by wall bracket(s) with two front legs.

coquillage Form of decorative shell motif which became popular during the Baroque and Rococo periods.

corner cupboard Late seventeenth-century cupboard designed to fit into the corner of a room. Either hanging or free-standing.

cornice Highest part of three principal members of the entablature (architrave, frieze and cornice). Also horizontal moulding projecting from the top of **case** pieces such as bookcases and cabinets.

cornucopia Classical motif in the shape of a goat's horn out of which spill fruit, vegetables and flowers. A symbol of fertility and abundance popular during the Baroque/Rococo periods. Also called horn-of-plenty.

credenza Sideboard with doors often surmounted by drawers. Commonly used to describe Victorian side cabinets.

cresting Carved ornament on top of furniture, i.e. a mirror frame or the top-rail of a chair, headboard or footboard of a bed or along the back-rail of a day-bed.

crocket Popular Gothic motif often in the shape of a leaf or flower which projects from the surface of chairs and some case pieces.

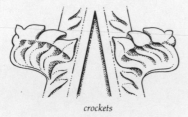

crockets

crossbanding Thin strips of decorative cross-grained **veneer**.

cross-member Horizontal, supporting **rail**.

curl mahogany Wood cut from the fork in branches of a mahogany tree. Prized for its mottled or feathery grain. Known as **crotch mahogany** in America.

curule chair, see **X-frame chair**

cutwork, see **Bantam work**

cyma curve, see **ogee**

davenport Chest-of-drawers with a sloping desk on top which became increasingly popular from 1830. Drawers open on one side, with sham-fronted ones on the other.

dentil motif Feature of classical architecture which became a popular furniture motif in the seventeenth century. Consists of a series of equally spaced square or rectangular tooth-like blocks.

diaper motif Trellis of repeated square or lozenge shapes sometimes enclosing carved decoration.

flower-head trellis

dovetail Right-angled joint held together by interlocking fan-shaped tenons. From the eighteenth century, lapped or secret dovetails were often used on high-quality furniture to conceal construction.

machine-made dovetail

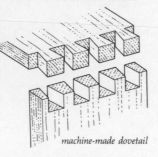

lapped dovetail

dowel Wooden pin used to secure **mortise-and-tenon** joints.

ébéniste Furniture-maker who specializes in the art of **veneering**.

egg-and-dart moulding A principal decorative motif of

classical origin consisting of **ovolo** or egg shapes alternating with leafy arrowheads.

encoignure A French form of standing **corner cupboard** often with a marble top.

escutcheon Metal plate fitted around a keyhole for protection and decoration.

Victorian escutcheon

étagère Set of free-standing or wall shelves used to display objects. Sometimes with doors or drawers.

fauteuil French form of open-armed chair with upholstered back and seat.

festoon, or **swag** Renaissance and Neoclassical motif in the shape of a suspended loop of drapery or a garland of fruit and flowers.

filigree Lace-like ornament made from delicately curled and twisted gold or silver wire.

finial Projecting ornament which can take many forms, including those of a ball, flame, flower, acorn, pineapple or vase.

fluting Decoration formed by making parallel, semicircular grooves; used on furniture since the sixteenth century.

fret pattern, see **key pattern**

fretwork Interlocking geometrical designs cut from thin wood and used ornamentally without contrasting backing in open fretwork and with backing in blind fretwork.

gadrooning Relief pattern developed from **reeding** consisting of a series of parallel, convex lobes, or inverted **fluting**. Popular in England in the late seventeenth

century and second half of the eighteenth century, its popularity spread to America during the eighteenth century. Also known as knurling or nulling.

fluting and gadrooning

garde du vin, see **cella et**

genre pittoresque, see *rocaille*

gesso Plaster-like compound of parchment size, whiting and linseed oil used as a base for gilding, incising or paint; can be carved when thick.

gilding Ornamental coating of goldleaf or gold dust, used alone or along with other forms of ornament, such as enamelling, to cover a piece of furniture.

gilt-bronze, see **ormolu**

girandole Elaborate candelabrum associated with Rococo and Neoclassical design. Also refers to heavily carved or gilded sconces or wall-brackets with mirrored backplates to reflect the candlelight.

Greek fret or **Greek key**, see **key pattern**

grisaille Painting in shades of black, grey and white which attempts to imitate marble relief ornament. Frequently applied to furniture during the Renaissance and Neoclassical periods.

grotesque Fanciful decoration comprising a combination of foliage, urns, animals, mythical creatures, etc. Term derived from Roman wall-paintings found in Nero's Golden House, the rooms of which became known as 'grottoes' when excavated in *c.*1500.

guéridon French candlestand or table for a candelabrum dating from the seventeenth and early-eighteenth centuries, usually in the shape of a footed column, pedestal or other central piece supporting a circular tray. Often took the form of Negro figures, or **blackamoors**.

guilloche Classical architectural motif forming a continuous figure-of-eight pattern. It became a popular furniture decoration from the sixteenth century onwards, especially during the Neoclassical period.

flower-head guilloche

Hadley chest Often elaborately carved rectangular dowry chest consisting of a set of drawers surmounted by a lidded chest. Made around Hadley, Massachusetts, c.1675–1740.

hairy-paw foot, see **paw foot**

halving joint Way of creating a flat join in crossing timbers by cutting out a half thickness from each piece.

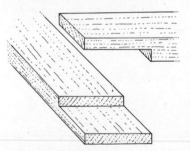

halving joint

highboy Tall chest made up of a chest-of-drawers set on a lowboy, sometimes standing on **cabriole legs**. The highboy, often made with a matching lowboy, enjoyed widespread popularity in eighteenth-century America.

hollow chamfering, see **cavetto moulding**

hunting board Sideboard or long table of the American South which, when first devised in the eighteenth century, was used for serving drinks to hunters.

inlay Form of decoration which involves cutting small pieces of ivory, precious metals, mother-of-pearl or wood which are then fitted into carved-out recesses of the same shape on a solid piece of furniture to create a picture or geometric design. This differs from **marquetry** which uses applied **veneers**, not whole pieces of wood.

intarsia Elaborate pictorial **marquetry** or inlaid panelling, used in Renaissance Italy and also sixteenth-century Germany.

japanning Term used for various Western methods which attempted to imitate Oriental **lacquer**. Coats of heat-hardened spirit varnishes and, later, cheap oil-based varnishes were types of japanning applied to furniture from the 1660s onwards.

key pattern Repeating motif of straight lines, usually at right angles, derived from classical Greek

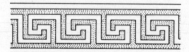

Greek key pattern

architecture; became a much-used border ornament. One example is the popular Greek key pattern.

klismos Classical Greek chair with **sabre legs**, the front ones curving forwards and the back ones backwards. The chair-back has a concave **top-rail** attached to verticals. Popular Neoclassical form in Europe and America.

knurling, see **gadrooning**

lacca Italian lacquer much used on the colourful, painted furniture of eighteenth-century Italy; can refer to true Oriental **lacquer** as well as **japanning**. Imitated more cheaply in *lacca contrafatta* or *arte povera*.

lacquer Oriental varnish made from tree gum. Its high-gloss finish became fashionable in Europe in the seventeenth century. Mother-of-pearl, coral and metals were often inlaid in the lacquer ground to create a decorative effect.

lambrequin Fringe-like motif imitating a fabric swag. The term originally referred to the scarf worn by a knight across his helmet.

lapped dovetail, see **dovetail**

linenfold Form of carving which imitated vertical folds of drapery. Probably Flemish in origin, it was widely used in the fifteenth and sixteenth centuries to decorate furniture and wall panelling.

lopers Poles, normally rectangular, which could be pulled out from the sides of a cabinet to support the flap-top of desks.

lunette Semicircular or half-moon shape making up a piece of furniture, often filled with carved decoration. Lunettes carved in this

way originated in the seventeenth century and enjoyed renewed popularity during the nineteenth-century Jacobean revival.

marquetry A type of ornamental **veneer** comprising shaped pieces of wood or other substances which form a mosaic, or kind of jigsaw-puzzle, in floral, landscape, **arabesque** or other patterns; if a geometric pattern, called parquetry. It differs from inlay, in which a cut-out recess on a solid piece of furniture is filled with decoration.

menuisier Furniture-maker specializing in carved pieces; usually applied to craftsmen in eighteenth- and nineteenth-century France.

mitre joint Corner joint used from the seventeenth century onwards. Pieces of wood are cut at an angle

so that when joined they form a right angle. They are then glued and/or nailed together.

monopodium Classical pedestal support composed of an animal head and a single leg; widely used in the early nineteenth century.

mortise-and-tenon Joint formed by cutting a hole, or mortise, in one piece of wood into which is fitted a projecting piece, or tenon, from another. Sometimes glued or held firm by a wooden dowel. Used since sixteenth century.

mortise-and-tenon

nulling, see **gadrooning**

ogee A continuous double curve in the shape of an 'S', referred to by Hogarth as 'the line of beauty'; used for mouldings. If concave above and convex below, called an ogee moulding, or *cyma recta*; if convex above and concave below, a reverse ogee moulding, or *cyma reversa*.

ormolu From the French *or moulu*, or ground gold; also known as gilt-bronze or *bronze doré*. Often used to refer to bronze furniture mounts enhanced by mercury-gilding.

ovolo moulding Classical convex moulding consisting of repeated oval shapes. Much used in the fourteenth and fifteenth centuries, it enjoyed a revival in Victorian England. The opposite of **cavetto moulding**.

oyster (or **oystershell**) **veneer** Late seventeenth- and early eighteenth-century **veneer**, made from symmetrically arranged cross-sections of small branches or roots from trees such as walnut, olive, laburnum and kingwood. The name comes from the resultant pattern of the grain, which resembles oyster shells. Primarily a Dutch decorative technique.

pad foot Club foot resting on an integral disc.

pad foot

paintbrush foot American term for **Spanish foot**.

palmette Fan-shaped pattern derived from the shape of a palm-tree frond. Neoclassical motif.

papier mâché Technique using sand, chalk, size and paper pulp which, when dry, forms a hard substance; later moulded to form furniture. Popular in nineteenth-century Europe and America.

parquetry, see **marquetry**

patera Round or oval medallion motif frequently incorporating fluting, leaves or flower petals in its design. Often carved, but also painted or inlaid into Neoclassical furniture.

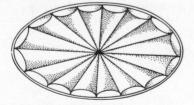

fan medallion

paw foot Leg terminal in the shape of an animal's paw. Originating in ancient Egypt, and used as well in classical Greece and Rome, this

form enjoyed a revival from the late seventeenth century to the end of the nineteenth century. A variation is the hairy-paw foot.

hairy-paw foot

pier-glass Tall, narrow mirror with a frame originally placed between windows to enhance light coming into a room. An accompaniment to a pier-table or **commode** in the seventeenth century.

pietre dure Form of decorative work using a variety of semiprecious stones perfected in Italy *c.*1600; if only a single type of stone is used, it is correctly called **pietra dura**. This method proved costly so a cheaper imitation, **scagliola**, was often used.

pilaster Architectural term for a flattened column attached to a façade for decoration rather than structural support.

prie-dieu A late-eighteenth-century, but commonly nineteenth-century low-seated armless chair with a high back and wide top-rail on which to rest a prayer book. Often upholstered with Berlin woolwork.

quatrefoil, see **trefoil**

rabbet joint, see **rebate joint**

rail A horizontal piece in the framework of a chair such as a seat-rail meant to support vertical members.

rebate joint Formed by cutting a groove, wedge or, most commonly, rectangular section along the edge of one piece of wood and fitting it

with another, matching piece of wood; can be glued or nailed. Used in cheaper furniture. Also known as a rabbet joint.

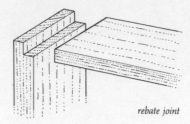

rebate joint

reeding Parallel, convex reed moulding derived from decoration used on classical columns. It is the opposite of **fluting**.

relief Forms of moulded, carved or stamped decoration raised from the surface of a piece of furniture forming a pattern in high (*alto-relievo*) or low relief (bas-relief).

rocaille Rococo form of decoration characteristic of the *genre pittoresque* using abstract shell- and rockwork in its design.

roll-top desk, see *bureau à cylindre*

'S' scroll, see **'C' and 'S' scrolls**

sabre leg Shaped like a sabre, either round- or square-sectioned, and gently tapering to the ground. Used on the Greek *klismos* and revived on eighteenth- and nineteenth-century seat furniture.

sarcophagus A rectangular, coffin-shaped box tapering to a smaller size at the bottom. Can be used as a cellaret or tea caddy etc.

scagliola, see *pietre dure*

sconce A bracketed wall-light comprising a decorative, often reflective, backplate and candleholders. Very fashionable from the late seventeenth century. Rococo versions are often called *girandoles*.

scotia Semicircular concave moulding. The reverse of an **astragal** moulding.

scroll foot Chair foot which terminates in a tight scrolled form; a popular eighteenth-century English foot.

scroll foot

secretaire Eighteenth-century desk with drawers hidden by the writing surface. In England and America, known as a secretary.

secrétaire à abattant Tall French writing-desk, the top part of which resembles an **armoire**, having a door at its base. The top is often flap-fronted to provide a larger writing surface when open.

secret dovetail, see **dovetail**

singerie Decoration depicting monkeys (*singes*) in human costumes and often comical situations. Associated with **chinoiserie**, it was popular during the Rococo period.

single chair or **side-chair** A chair without arms.

slipper foot Flat, elongated foot which differs from the snake foot in that its end is more pointed. Often found on Queen Anne furniture.

slipper foot

Spanish foot Formed from a scroll turning backwards in a curve at the bottom. Popular in the late seventeenth and first half of the eighteenth centuries. Also called a knurl foot, Braganza foot, and, in America, a paintbrush foot.

Spanish (or Braganza) foot

spice chest American form of **case furniture** taking the form of a chest mounted on a stand made during the eighteenth century to hold spices. The upper part has doors which open to reveal many drawers. These are often grand, lockable pieces reflecting the value of spices at the time.

spindle Slim, turned member which may be of constant width or decoratively turned.

splat Central flat support between a chair's seat and **top-rail**.

squirrel, see **birdcage**

stile Upright supporting post on a piece of furniture.

strapwork Originating in the sixteenth century in the Netherlands, this pattern of interlaced strap-like bands was extensively used in Northern European furniture in the sixteenth and seventeenth centuries; enjoyed a revival in the nineteenth century.

stretcher Strengthening or stabilizing **rail** which runs horizontally between furniture legs, often forming X, H or Y shapes.

style étrusque Neoclassical attempt to imitate the decoration on Etruscan vases. Much use of contrasting encaustic colour. Popular from 1760 and again in the 1840s.

swag, see **festoon**

tallboy Called a chest-on-chest until the eighteenth century, this high chest-of-drawers has more drawers below than on top.

tambour Thin strips of wood glued to canvas backing to form a flexible sheet used to conceal storage areas, for example in the lid of a *bureau à cylindre*.

term Statue or bust representing the upper part of the body, usually without arms, terminating below in a pedestal or pillar which tapers towards the base. Also known as terminus or herm. If load-bearing, also known as **caryatid** terminals.

tester Wooden canopy which projects over the top of the bed, known as a half-tester if supported only by headboard and footposts.

tip-top or **snap-top** Form of pedestal table in which the top is hinged to the base and tilts vertically when not in use. Became popular on both sides of the Atlantic in the eighteenth century. In America, known as a tilt-top.

tole Tinware which has been decorated by means of **japanning**; known in America as toleware.

tongue-and-groove Straight or right-angled joint made by cutting a groove into one piece of wood into which fits the projecting groove from another. Used from the nineteenth century onwards.

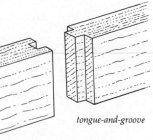

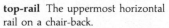

tongue-and-groove

top-rail The uppermost horizontal rail on a chair-back.

torchère A portable stand for a lamp or candle, often fashioned like a tall table with a small top.

torus Like an **astragal** moulding, only thicker, this form of moulding is often used at the end of columns, frequently entwined with foliage.

trefoil Form of Gothic ornament in the shape of three symmetrical leaves. A quatrefoil has four leaves, a cinquefoil five. Much used in the nineteenth-century Gothic revival.

trifid foot Foot with three toe-shaped sections. Popular on early Philadelphia chairs.

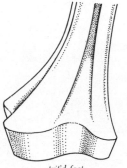

trifid foot

trompe l'oeil Painted decoration with natural shadows designed to 'deceive the eye' into believing they are real, i.e., three-dimensional.

turning Method of shaping wood by revolving it on a lathe. Different types of turning are created by altering the pressure of the lathe.

vargueño, or *bargueño* Spanish writing and storage desk dating from the sixteenth century, and consisting of a square or rectangular top, the flap-front of which conceals drawers. When opened, the flap-top is supported by **lopers** to form a writing-desk. The whole piece rests on an open or cupboard-like stand.

veneering Furniture-making technique which consists of affixing a thin layer or strips of fine wood to the surface of a piece of furniture, this usually of a coarser wood. Valuable woods such as mahogany, rosewood, walnut and satinwood were used to cover a cheaper *carcase*, often at the same time concealing construction detail. First used in ancient Egypt, and

then in Classical Greece and Rome, but not again until the seventeenth century in the Netherlands.

vernis Martin A sophisticated **japanning** technique developed by the Martin brothers in France *c.*1730. This form of reproducing the effect of Oriental **lacquer** reached the height of its popularity in mid-eighteenth-century France.

verre églomisé Technique widely used at the turn of the eighteenth century to produce highly decorative mirrors. Gold or silver foil was applied to the mirror back and engraved with a needle before placing black or another contrasting colour behind the foil. This was then enclosed with a second layer of glass or a coating of varnish.

vitrine Glass-fronted cabinet which stood independently or on a stand and was used to display china, silver and curios; normally nineteenth century.

Vitruvian scroll Repeating pattern resembling a series of 'C' **scrolls** or waves. Of classical origin, it was commonly used on eighteenth-century furniture.

volute An ornamental form of spiral scroll adopted from Ionic **capitals** in Greek architecture.

volute foot Outward-scrolling foot popular on Baroque furniture.

X-frame chair An X-shaped, often folding, structure was used to support this type of chair or stool, also called a curule. Known to have existed in ancient Egypt, Greece and Rome, this chair enjoyed a medieval revival as well as providing a popular prototype for the eighteenth- and nineteenth-century classical revivals.

yoke-rail, see **top-rail**

The drawings are for identification purposes only and are not necessarily drawn to scale.

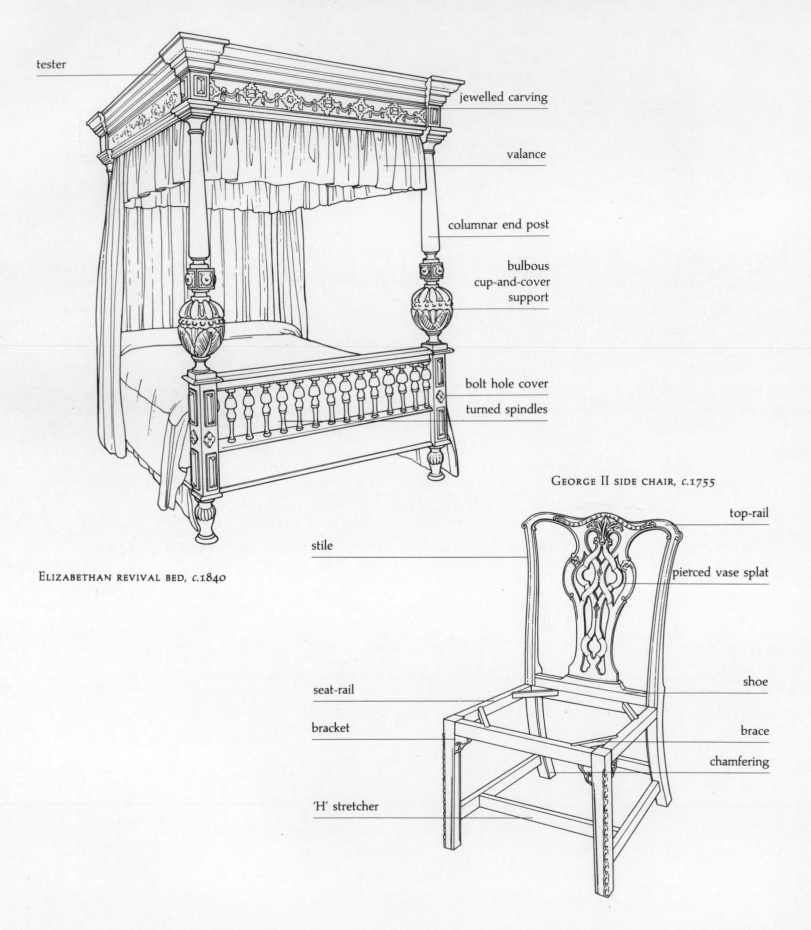

tester

jewelled carving

valance

columnar end post

bulbous
cup-and-cover
support

bolt hole cover

turned spindles

ELIZABETHAN REVIVAL BED, c.1840

GEORGE II SIDE CHAIR, c.1755

top-rail

stile

pierced vase splat

seat-rail

shoe

bracket

brace

chamfering

'H' stretcher

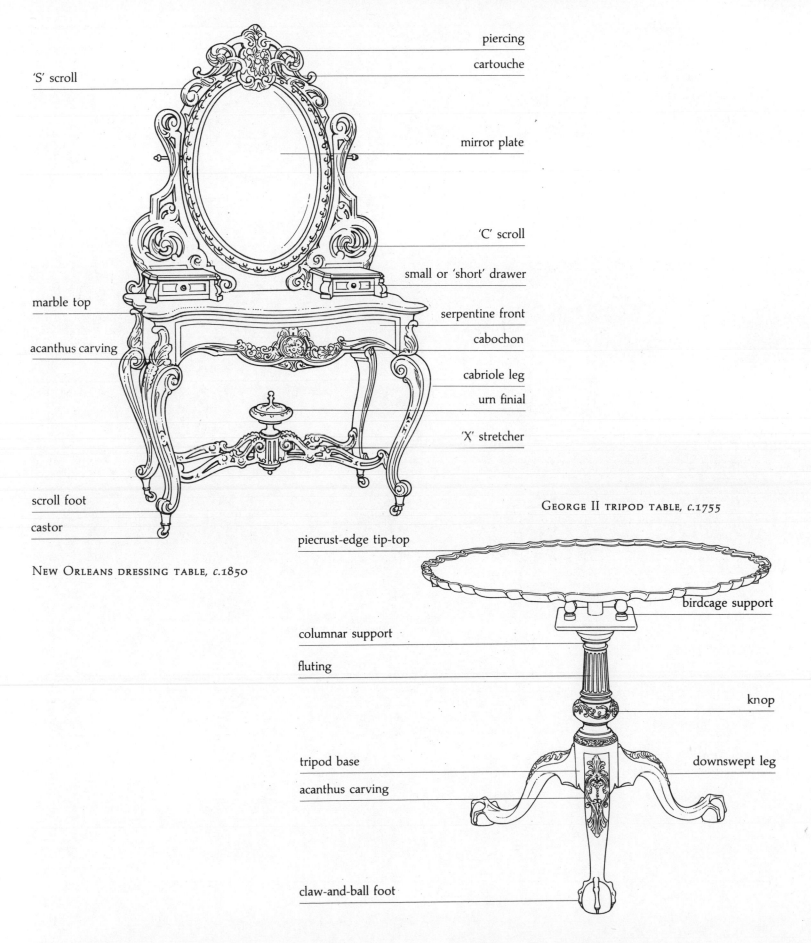

piercing

cartouche

'S' scroll

mirror plate

'C' scroll

small or 'short' drawer

marble top

serpentine front

cabochon

acanthus carving

cabriole leg

urn finial

'X' stretcher

scroll foot

castor

NEW ORLEANS DRESSING TABLE, c.1850

GEORGE II TRIPOD TABLE, c.1755

piecrust-edge tip-top

birdcage support

columnar support

fluting

knop

tripod base

downswept leg

acanthus carving

claw-and-ball foot

SUMMARY OF CHAIR STYLES

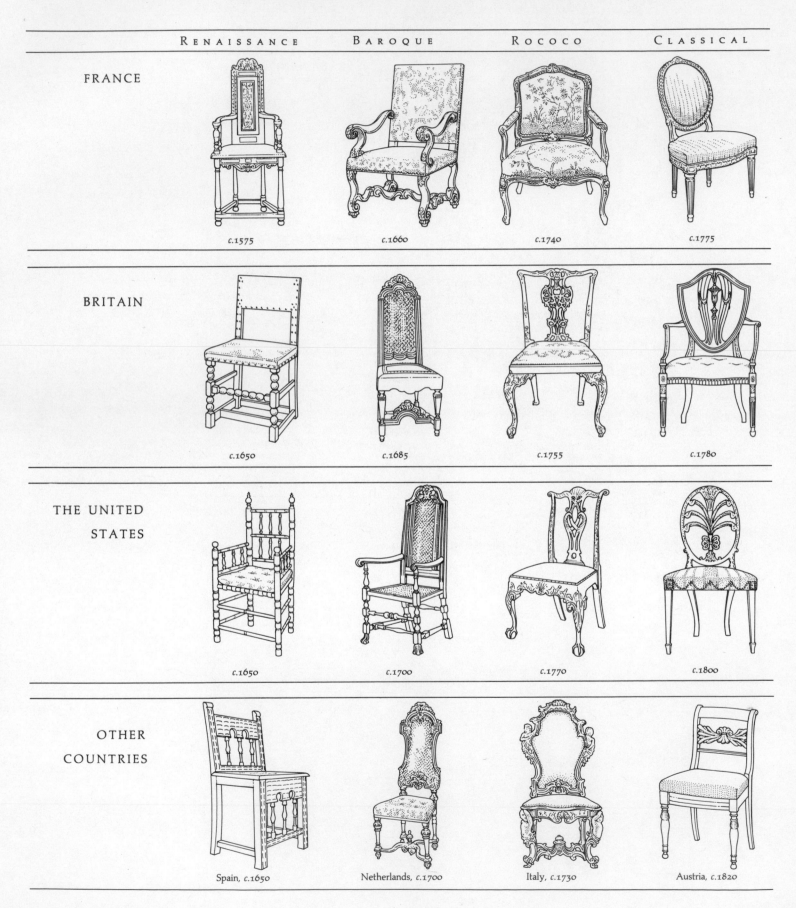

	RENAISSANCE	BAROQUE	ROCOCO	CLASSICAL
FRANCE	c.1575	c.1660	c.1740	c.1775
BRITAIN	c.1650	c.1685	c.1755	c.1780
THE UNITED STATES	c.1650	c.1700	c.1770	c.1800
OTHER COUNTRIES	Spain, c.1650	Netherlands, c.1700	Italy, c.1730	Austria, c.1820

ECLECTICISM	CRAFT & DESIGN	MACHINE AGE	MODERN TIMES	

FRANCE

c.1850 — c.1900 (L. Majorelle) — c.1925 (R. Mallet-Stevens) — 1965 (O. Morgue)

BRITAIN

1846 (A.W.N. Pugin) — c.1880 (W. Morris) — c.1930 (PEL) — 1951 (E. Race)

THE UNITED STATES

c.1860 — c.1903 (G. Stickley) — 1946 (C. Eames) — 1953 (E. Saarinen)

OTHER COUNTRIES

Germany, c.1830 (K.F. Schinkel) — Belgium, 1906 (H. van de Velde) — Germany, 1928 (M. Breuer) — Italy, 1968 (V. Magistretti)

INDEX

The publisher thanks the following photographers and organizations for their permission to reproduce the photographs in this book:

2 Balthazar Korab Ltd/Cranbrook Academy of Art Museum; 4–5 Angelo Hornak; 8 Ianthe Ruthven; 10 Bridgeman Art Library; 12 Robert Harding Picture Library; 14 centre Michael Holford/British Museum; 14 below, 15 Courtesy of the Trustees of the British Museum; 16, 17 above Michael Holford/British Museum; 17 below Bildarchiv Preussischer Kulturbesitz/Antikenmuseum; 18 left Scala, Florence/Museo Archivescovile, Ravenna; 18 right Robert Harding Picture Library/British Museum; 19 Museés Cantonaux, Sion/Photo H. Preisig; 20 above and centre By courtesy of the Board of Trustees of the Victoria & Albert Museum; 20 below Bayerisches National-museum, Munich; 21 By courtesy of the Board of Trustees of the Victoria & Albert Museum; 22 Germanisches Nationalmuseum, Nuremberg; 24 Angelo Hornak/Courtauld Institute Galleries, London (Lee Collection); 25 above right Scala, Florence/Palazzo Ducale, Urbino; 25 below Bridgeman Art Library/Galleria dell'Accademia, Venice; 26 above Giraudon/Louvre, Paris; 26 below By courtesy of the Board of Trustees of the Victoria & Albert Museum; 27 left Louvre/Réunion des Musées Nationaux; 27 right, 28 left Germanisches Nationalmuseum, Nuremberg; 28 right Bayerischer Verwaltung der Staatliche Schlosser, Garten und Seen/Residenz, Munich; 29 By courtesy of the Board of Trustees of the Victoria & Albert Museum; 30 left Swiss National Museum, Zurich; 31 below left National Trust Photo Library/John Bethell; 32 below Ashmolean Museum, Oxford; 33 Bridgeman Art Library/Victoria & Albert Museum; 34 Peter Baistow; 36 Megan Aldrich; 37 left By courtesy of the Board of Trustees of the Victoria & Albert Museum; 37 right Angelo Hornak; 39 below left By courtesy of the Board of Trustees of the Victoria & Albert Museum; 39 right Rijksmuseum, Amsterdam; 40 above Megan Aldrich; 40 below Bridgeman Art Library/Harold Samuel Collection, Corporation of London; 41 left Rijksmuseum, Amsterdam; 41 right By courtesy of the Board of Trustees of the Victoria & Albert Museum; 42 Bayerische Verwaltung der Staatliche Schlosser; 43 above left Schloss Charlottenburg/Photo JP Anders; 43 below right The Royal Collections, Stockholm; 44 Christie's, New York; 45 above left By courtesy of the Board of Trustees of the Victoria & Albert Museum; 45 below Scala, Florence; 46 Bridgeman Art Library; 47 above In the collection of the Duke of Buccleuch & Queensberry, KT; 47 Below left Bridgeman Art Library/Victoria & Albert Museum; 47 below right Courtesy of the Trustees of the British Museum; 48 above Louvre/Réunion des Musées Nationaux; 48 below Versailles/Réunion des Musées Nationaux; 49 below left Courtesy of 'Printed Furniture Designs before 1650' by Simon Jervis; 51 below left The National Trust Photo Library; 54 left Octopus Group Picture Library/Victoria & Albert Museum; 54 right Reproduced by Gracious Permission of Her Majesty The Queen; 56 left Bridgeman Art Library/Winterthur Museum, Delaware; 56 right The Carnegie Museum of Art. Museum Purchase: John Berdan Memorial Fund, Richard King Mellon Foundation Grant and Bequest of Myrtle Hoey Burns, by exchange, 1976; 58 Reproduced by courtesy of the Trustees, The National Gallery, London; 61 left British Library; 61 right Top Agence/Rosine Mazin; 63 above left Reproduced by permission of the Trustees, Wallace Collection, London; 63 above right By courtesy of the Board of Trustees of the Victoria & Albert Museum; 63 below right Bridgeman Art Library/Victoria & Albert Museum; 64 left Bridgeman Art Library; 65 (c) Christie's, London; 66 Scala, Florence/Palazzo Reale, Turin; 67 centre Bernheimer Fine Arts Ltd; 69 left Angelo Hornak/Victoria & Albert Museum; 69 above right By courtesy of the Board of Trustees of the

Victoria & Albert Museum; 69 below right (c) Christie's, London; 71 above Bridgeman Art Library; 72 Bridgeman Art Library/National Trust; 73 left and below right British Library; 74 left Leeds City Art Galleries; 74 above and below right Bridgeman Art Library; 75 above Bridgeman Art Library/Victoria & Albert Museum; 75 below Bridgeman Art Library; 76 right The Metropolitan Museum of Art, New York; 77 Macdonald/Aldus Archive/Winterthur Museum, Delaware; 78 The Metropolitan Museum of Art, New York; 79 above The Metropolitan Museum of Art, New York. Gift of Mrs Russell Square; 79 below right Dietrich American Foundation, Philadelphia, PA/Photo Will Brown, Philadelphia, PA; 80 Fritz von der Schulenburg; 82 left The British Architectural Library, RIBA, London; 82 right Top Agence/Catherine Bibollet; 85 left Bridgeman Art Library; 85 above right Top Agence/Rosine Mazin; 85 below right Windsor Castle Royal Library (c) 1989. Her Majesty The Queen; 86 Michael Holford; 88 Stylograph/JF Jaussard; 89 centre Collection du Musée des Arts Décoratifs, Paris/MAD/Sully-Jaulmes; 90 above Angelo Hornak/Victoria & Albert Museum; 91 Octopus Group Picture Library/Bibliothéque Nationale, Paris; 92 Bridgeman Art Library/Kenwood House; 93 left National Trust; 93 above right By courtesy of the Board of Trustees of the Victoria & Albert Museum; 93 below right Bridgeman Art Library/Harewood House; 94 top left Courtesy of 'The Cabinet Maker' by Thomas Sheraton; 95 British Library; 96 below Bridgeman Art Library; 97 below right Angelo Hornak; 98 left Bridgeman Art Library; 100 above Derry Moore; 101 above Angelo Hornak; 105 Fritz von der Schulenburg; 107 above left Maryland Historical Society, Baltimore; 107 above right Macdonald/Aldus Archive/Winterthur Museum, Delaware; 107 below Bridgeman Art Library/American Museum in Britain, Bath; 110 James Mortimer/World of Interiors; 113 left By courtesy of the Board of Trustees of the Victoria & Albert Museum; 113 Right (c) Christie's, London; 114 By courtesy of the Board of Trustees of the Victoria & Albert Museum; 118 Macdonald/Aldus Archive; 122 above and below left By courtesy of the Board of Trustees of the Victoria & Albert Museum; 122 below right Yu-Chee Chong; 123 By courtesy of the Board of Trustees of the Victoria & Albert Museum; 124 left Courtesy of Christopher Payne; 124 right Musée d'Orsay/Réunion des Musées Nationaux; 125 right By courtesy of the Board of Trustees of the Victoria & Albert Museum; 127 right Robert Harding Picture Library; 128 Macdonald/Aldus Archive; 129 above Bridgeman Art Library/Victoria & Albert Museum; 129 below Macdonald/Aldus Archive; 130 Angelo Hornak/National Trust; 131 above Mary Evans Picture Library; 132 right Bridgeman Art Library; 133 left Clive Corless/Octopus Group Picture Library; 135 above right Leeds City Art Galleries; 135 below left Bridgeman Art Library; 136 Macdonald/Aldus Archive; 137 left By courtesy of the Board of Trustees of the Victoria & Albert Museum; 137 right Bridgeman Art Library/Victoria & Albert Museum; 138 above RCHM, England; 138 below The Mansell Collection; 139 By courtesy of the Board of Trustees of the Victoria & Albert Museum; 141 above The Brooklyn Museum, 40.93CMN, Gift of Sarah Milligan Rand, Kate Milligan Brill & the Dick S. Ramsay Fund; 141 below The Brooklyn Museum, 39.30, Gift of Mrs Ernest Vietor; 142 right Collection of The Newark Museum, Gift of Miss Florence Sullivan, 1934; 143 centre Courtesy of 'Classic Wicker Furniture, 1898–1899, The Complete Illustrated Catalogue'; 143 right Macdonald/Aldus Archive; 144 Bastin & Evrard, Brussels; 147 left Bridgeman Art Library/Victoria & Albert Museum; 148 left Derry Moore; 148 right The Wiliam Morris Gallery, Walthamstow, London; 149 above By courtesy of the Board of Trustees of the Victoria & Albert Museum; 149 below Macdonald/Aldus Archive; 151 left Ianthe

Ruthven; 153 above The Metropolitan Museum of Art, New York; 153 below Octopus Group Picture Library/Chicago Architecture Foundation; 154 left (c) 1989 The Art Institute of Chicago, Gift of Mrs Philip Wrigley, 1973.772; 154 right Malden Public Library, Massachusetts; 155 right Elizabeth Whiting Associates/Tim Street-Porter; 156 above Cathers & Demrovsky, New York; 158 Collection du Musée des Arts Décoratifs, Paris/MAD/Sully-Jaulmes; 160 right Musée d'Orsay/Réunion des Musée Nationaux; 162 Bastin & Evrard, Brussels; 163 above Musée d'Orsay/Réunion des Musée Nationaux; 163 below Virginia Museum of Fine Arts, Richmond. Gift of Sydney & Frances Lewis. Photo by Katherine Wetzel; 164 left Musée d'Orsay/Réunion des Musées Nationaux; 165 Virginia Museum of Fine Arts, Richmond. Gift of Sydney & Frances Lewis. Photo by Katherine Wetzel; 166 Eileen Tweedy/Conran Octopus; 167 below AISA, Barcelona; 168 Fritz von der Schulenburg; 171 Simon Brown/Conran Octopus (c) DACS, 1989; 174 above and below right Connaissance des Arts/Edimedia/Roger Guillemot (c) DACS, 1989; 175 left Stylograph/S. Cossu (c) DACS, 1989; 175 right Virginia Museum of Fine Arts, Richmond. Gift of Sydney & Frances Lewis. Photo Ann Hutchison; 176 right Top Agence/Pascal Hinous; 177 above left Macdonald/Aldus Archive; 178 left 'Cassina the Masters' Collection; 178 right Fritz von der Schulenburg; 179 Angelo Hornak/Victoria & Albert Museum; 180 Arcaid/Richard Bryant; 181 above Balthazar Korab Ltd/Cranbrook Academy of Art Museum; 182 Aldo Ballo; 184 left John Makepeace, Parnham; 184 right Collection du Musée des Arts Décoratifs, Paris/MAD/Sully-Jaulmes; 185 left Cassina; 185 above right Stylograph/J.P. Godeaut; 186 left Top Agence/J.PH. Charbonnier; 187 Top Agence/G. Ehrmann; 188 Knoll International, New York; 189 above left Museum of Fine Arts, Boston. Funded by the National Endowment for the Arts and the Deborah M. Noonan Foundation; 189 centre By courtesy of the Board of Trustees of the Victoria & Albert Museum; 189 above right Octopus Group Picture Library/Victoria & Albert Museum; 189 below right Top Agence/J.PH. Charbonnier; 190 above left By courtesy of the Board of Trustees of the Victoria & Albert Museum; 190 above right Hille International Ltd; 191 left Clive Corless/Conran Octopus; 191 right One-Off, London; 192 above Jean Nouvel et Associés, Paris; 192 below Aldo Ballo;

Sotheby's London 1, 6, 25 above left, 38, left, 38 right, 39 above left, 43 above right, 45 above right, 49, above, 50 left, 50 right, 51 above left, 51 below right, 52 above, 52 below, 64 right, 67 below, 68, 70, 71 below, 73 above right, 83–84, 87 above, 87 below, 89 left, 89 right, 90 below, 94 right, 96 above, 97 above, 97 below left, 98 right, 99, 100 below, 101 below, 102–104, 115 above, 115 below, 116, 117 above, 117 below, 119, 120, 121, 125 left, 126, 127 left, 134, 135 above centre, 135 below right, 150, 151 right, 157, 159 left, 159 right, 160 left, 161 above, 167 above, ((c) DACS, 1989) 172, 174 below left, 177 centre.

Sotheby's Monaco 14 above, 49 below right, 161 below, 164 centre, 164 right, 176 left, 181 below, 186 right.

Sotheby's New York 55, 57 left, 57 right, 63 below left, 67 above, 76 left, 79 centre right, 108–9, 142 left, 155 left, 156 below, 173 above left, 177 above right, 177 below, 185 below right.

Special photography by Martin Trelawny for Conran Octopus as follows: 30 right, 31 above, 31 below right, 32 above, 51 above right, 53, 132 left, 147 above right (The Trustees, The Cecil Higgins Art Gallery, Bedford) 133 right, 143 left, 147 below right (Authentics, London) 173 above right, 173 below, 174 above left.